International HRM in an Uncertain World

This book explores international human resource management (IHRM) practices in the contexts of high uncertainties. It encompasses situations of financial crisis, political and civil uncertainty, environmental collapse and recession.

Research on unstable and unpredictable contexts on business and HRM remain relatively scarce and scattered across disciplines. This volume brings together recent thinking from a range of different perspectives and methodologies. MNEs are often distinguished by the supposedly superior ability to implement highly tactical, more robust talent management practices, including work-based, HRM-led and international systems, in line with the rest of their worldwide operations; however, they often fall short. The chapters in this book explore the how, why, and when. At a theoretical level, this collection brings together developments and extensions of a range of salient theories. They explore common methodological challenges and ways forward for future researchers on HRM in high contextual uncertainty.

The chapters in this book were originally published as a special issue of *The International Journal of Human Resource Management*.

Geoffrey Wood is DANCap Private Equity Chair and Professor, Western University, Canada, and Adjunct Professor, Trinity College, Dublin. He is editor of *Academy of Management Perspectives* and *Human Resource Management Journal*. He publishes widely in international business, HRM, and corporate finance.

Mehmet Demirbag is Professor at Essex Business School, University of Essex, United Kingdom. His current research interest focuses on multinational enterprises in and from emerging markets, offshore R&D activities of multinational enterprises, and the impact of institutional factors on multinational enterprises' operations, high performance work systems and talent management practices in emerging markets.

Caleb Kwong is Reader at Essex Business School, University of Essex, United Kingdom. His current research interest is in business and social organisations operating in uncertain and conflict environments.

Fang Lee Cooke is Professor at Monash Business School, Monash University, Australia. Her research interests are in the area of international HRM, gender studies, diversity management, strategic HRM, knowledge management and innovation, outsourcing, HRM in the care sector, digitalization and implications for employment and HRM.

International HRM in an Uncertain World

Edited by
Geoffrey Wood, Mehmet Demirbag,
Caleb Kwong and Fang Lee Cooke

Routledge
Taylor & Francis Group

LONDON AND NEW YORK

First published 2023
by Routledge
4 Park Square, Milton Park, Abingdon, Oxon OX14 4RN

and by Routledge
605 Third Avenue, New York, NY 10158

Routledge is an imprint of the Taylor & Francis Group, an informa business

British Library Cataloguing in Publication Data
A catalogue record for this book is available from the British Library

ISBN13: 978-1-032-32788-4 (hbk)
ISBN13: 978-1-032-32790-7 (pbk)
ISBN13: 978-1-003-31674-9 (ebk)

DOI: 10.4324/9781003316749

Typeset in Minion Pro
by Newgen Publishing UK

Publisher's Note
The publisher accepts responsibility for any inconsistencies that may have arisen during the conversion of this book from journal articles to book chapters, namely the inclusion of journal terminology.

Disclaimer
Every effort has been made to contact copyright holders for their permission to reprint material in this book. The publishers would be grateful to hear from any copyright holder who is not here acknowledged and will undertake to rectify any errors or omissions in future editions of this book.

Contents

Citation Information   vii

Notes on Contributors   ix

Preface   xi
Geoffrey Wood, Mehmet Demirbag, Caleb Kwong and Fang Lee Cooke

Introduction: Human resource management in the context of
high uncertainties   1
Caleb Kwong, Mehmet Demirbag, Geoffrey Wood and Fang Lee Cooke

1   Context-specific understandings of uncertainty: a focus on
    people management practices in Mongolia   32
    Marina Michalski, Martyna Śliwa and Saranzaya Manalsuren

2   Breaking away or holding on to the past? Exploring HRM
    systems of export-oriented SMEs in a highly uncertain context:
    insights from a transition economy in the periphery   59
    Dilshod Makhmadshoev and Knut Laaser

3   Variations and differences in the application of HR policies and
    practices by US hotel multinational firm's subsidiaries across
    coordinated and transitional periphery economies: a case approach   91
    Giovanni Oscar Serafini and Leslie Thomas Szamosi

4   Context, governance, associational trust and HRM: diversity
    and commonalities   128
    Marc Goergen, Salim Chahine, Chris Brewster and Geoffrey Wood

5   Human resource capabilities in uncertain environments   153
    Misagh Tasavori, Nayereh Eftekhar, Ghanbar Mohammadi Elyasi
    and Reza Zaefarian

6 Idiosyncratic deals in less competitive labor markets: testing career i-deals in the Greek context of high uncertainties 180
Anastasia A. Katou, Pawan S. Budhwar and Charmi Patel

Afterword
Researching IHRM in an uncertain world: methodological challenges and solutions 208
Geoffrey Wood, Mehmet Demirbag, Caleb Kwong and Fang Lee Cooke

Index 212

Citation Information

The following chapters were originally published in *The International Journal of Human Resource Management*, volume 32, issue 17 (2021). When citing this material, please use the original page numbering for each article, as follows:

Introduction

Human resource management in the context of high uncertainties
Caleb Kwong, Mehmet Demirbag, Geoffrey Wood and Fang Lee Cooke
The International Journal of Human Resource Management, volume 32, issue 17 (2021), pp. 3569–3599

Chapter 1

Context-specific understandings of uncertainty: a focus on people management practices in Mongolia
Marina Michalski, Martyna Śliwa and Saranzaya Manalsuren
The International Journal of Human Resource Management, volume 32, issue 17 (2021), pp. 3600–3626

Chapter 2

Breaking away or holding on to the past? Exploring HRM systems of export-oriented SMEs in a highly uncertain context: insights from a transition economy in the periphery
Dilshod Makhmadshoev and Knut Laaser
The International Journal of Human Resource Management, volume 32, issue 17 (2021), pp. 3627–3658

Chapter 3

Variations and differences in the application of HR policies and practices by US hotel multinational firm's subsidiaries across coordinated and transitional periphery economies: a case approach
Giovanni Oscar Serafini and Leslie Thomas Szamosi
The International Journal of Human Resource Management, volume 32, issue 17 (2021), pp. 3659–3695

Chapter 4

Context, governance, associational trust and HRM: diversity and commonalities
Marc Goergen, Salim Chahine, Chris Brewster and Geoffrey Wood
The International Journal of Human Resource Management, volume 32, issue 17 (2021), pp. 3696–3720

Chapter 5

Human resource capabilities in uncertain environments
Misagh Tasavori, Nayereh Eftekhar, Ghanbar Mohammadi Elyasi and Reza Zaefarian
The International Journal of Human Resource Management, volume 32, issue 17 (2021), pp. 3721–3747

Chapter 6

Idiosyncratic deals in less competitive labor markets: testing career i-deals in the Greek context of high uncertainties
Anastasia A. Katou, Pawan S. Budhwar and Charmi Patel
The International Journal of Human Resource Management, volume 32, issue 17 (2021), pp. 3748–3775

For any permission-related enquiries please visit:
www.tandfonline.com/page/help/permissions

Notes on Contributors

Chris Brewster, University of Reading – Henley Business School, Reading, UK.

Pawan S. Budhwar, International HRM, Aston Business School, Aston University, Birmingham, UK.

Salim Chahine, The Olayan School of Business, American University of Beirut, Beirut, Lebanon.

Fang Lee Cooke, Monash Business School, Monash University, Australia.

Mehmet Demirbag, Essex Business School, University of Essex, UK.

Nayereh Eftekhar, Faculty of Management, University of Tehran, Tehran, Iran.

Marc Goergen, IE University Business School, Madrid, Spain.

Anastasia A. Katou, Organizational Strategy, School of Business Administration, University of Macedonia, Thessaloniki, Greece.

Caleb Kwong, Essex Business School, University of Essex, UK.

Knut Laaser, Sociology, Brandenburg University of Technology Cottbus–Senftenberg, Germany.

Dilshod Makhmadshoev, Strathclyde Business School, University of Strathclyde, Glasgow, UK.

Saranzaya Manalsuren, Division of Urban, Environment and Leisure Studies, London Southbank University, UK.

Marina Michalski, Essex Business School, University of Essex, Colchester, UK.

Ghanbar Mohammadi Elyasi, Faculty of Entrepreneurship, University of Tehran, Tehran, Iran.

Charmi Patel, HRM, Henley Business School, University of Reading, Reading, UK.

Giovanni Oscar Serafini, Business Administration and Economics Department (BAED), University of Sheffield International Faculty, CITY College, Thessaloniki, Greece.

Martyna Śliwa, Essex Business School, University of Essex, Colchester, UK.

Leslie Thomas Szamosi, Business Administration and Economics Department (BAED), University of Sheffield International Faculty, CITY College, Thessaloniki, Greece.

Misagh Tasavori, Graduate School of Management and Economics, Sharif University of Technology, Tehran, Iran.

Geoffrey Wood, DAN Department of Management & Organizational Studies, Western University, Ontario, Canada.

Reza Zaefarian, Faculty of Entrepreneurship, University of Tehran, Tehran, Iran.

Preface

The world has become an increasingly uncertain place.

Just in the last couple of years alone, we have witnessed the destructive power of the pandemic, wars and political conflicts, economic crisis, and environmental blowback that wreaked havoc to the world of work. Uncertain contexts caused disruptions in the labour market, overwhelmed firm's human resource (HR) capacity, and brought about considerable human resource management (HRM) challenges to organisations and business owners (Ererdi et al., 2022). The validity of the established routines and HR practices is now being questioned (Psychogios and Prouska, 2019), with issues such as protecting workers, developing agile HR practices to retain and motivate talents, facilitating new ways of communications and collaborations, and supporting the development of employees' resilience, becoming more pressing than ever (Ab. Wahab et al., 2020; Roper et al., 2022). Nevertheless, organisations are not merely passive recipients of uncertainty outcomes; rather, they can proactively reshape their strategies to adapt to the changes in context. What is important is to understand how uncertainties create HRM challenges, and the HR responses that organisations and business owners came up with to mitigate their negative impacts.

Contextual uncertainty has for long been synonymous to the emerging economies with weaker institutions and economic infrastructure, even if more recently, institutional problems in the most developed countries, most notably the United States, have become more visible. Unsurprisingly, the pioneering studies of managing HR in uncertain contexts are being dominated by scholars specialised in these countries. Some of the notable work include Zheng and Lamond (2009), Becker and Smidt (2016), Horwitz, (2009), Wood et al., (2010), Cooke (2012), Bischoff and Wood (2012), Ketkar and Sett (2010), Walsh and Chu (2007), Fields et al., (2000; 2006), to name a few. Nevertheless, the contextual challenges highlighted above, coupled with the fact that the globalised world is becoming increasingly interconnected, resulted in the mainstreaming of the subject. A recent review by Ererdi et al. (2022) on human resource management in the contexts of uncertainty and crisis featured an increasing number of papers from the developed and the emerging world, confirming its worldwide relevance. Nevertheless, despite the fact that research on the role of HR in uncertain environment has increased, the field can still be considered in its early stages. The recent developments (i.e., Covid-19 pandemic around the world, conflicts, and disruptions to supply chains) increased the urgency to synthesise various dimensions of uncertainties and rethink of our current knowledge (Mithani et al., 2022). Undoubtedly the recent developments have highly significant impacts on global talent management, employee wellbeing, outsourcing of activities (including knowledge intensive parts of the value chain), re-locating, back-shoring work, and jobs.

It is in this backdrop that this book: *International Human Resource Management in an Uncertain World*, is developed. The chapters in this book were originally published as a special issue of *The International Journal of Human Resource Management* (2021, Volume 32, Issue 17). It intends to build on the previous work, by systematically drawing both from the existing theoretical framework of uncertainty management, but also, from empirical experiences across the world. It aims to supplement the increasing number of research highlighted in Ererdi et al. (2022), as well as a number of special issues in related topics, including the *Danger and Risk as Challenges for HRM* in *The International Journal of Human Resource Management* by Bader, Schuster and Dickman (2020, Volume 30, Issue 20) and *Strategic Human Resource Management in the Era of Environmental Disruptions* in the *Human Resource Management* by Kim, Vaiman and Sanders (2022; Volume 61).

It is hoped that the book will be of value to scholars, managers and policy makers interested in understanding the role of HRM in uncertain context, in particular:

- How HRM can help firms in coping with uncertain contexts?
- What are the HR practices that would enable workers to develop resilience in the contexts of high uncertainties?
- How do different communities cope with uncertainties through different HRM practices?
- How can we compare the types of uncertainty encountered in different parts of the world, and what does this mean for HRM?

Finally, we would like to thank the contributors, as well as the anonymous reviewers for their valuable support in improving the chapters and shaping this book.

Geoffrey Wood
Mehmet Demirbag
Caleb Kwong
Fang Lee Cooke

References

Ab. Wahab, M., Tatoglu, E., Glaister, A., and Demirbag, M. 2020. Countering uncertainty: High commitment work systems, performance, burnout, and well-being in Malaysia. *International Journal of Human Resource Management*, 32(1), pp. 24–48.

Becker, K. and Smidt, M., 2016. A risk perspective on human resource management: A review and directions for future research. *Human Resource Management Review*, 26(2), pp. 149–165.

Bischoff, C., and Wood, G. 2012. The practice of HRM in Africa in comparative perspective. In Brewster, C., Mayrhofer, W., & Farndale, E. (Eds.), *Handbook of Research on Comparative Human Resource Management* (pp. 494–512). Edward Elgar Publishing.

Cooke, F.L., 2012. The globalization of Chinese telecom corporations: Strategy, challenges and HR implications for the MNCs and host countries. *International Journal of Human Resource Management*, 23(9), pp. 1832–1852.

Ererdi, C., Nurgabdeshov, A., Kozhakhmet, S., Rofcanin, Y. and Demirbag, M., 2020. International HRM in the context of uncertainty and crisis: A systematic review of literature (2000–2018). *International Journal of Human Resource Management*, 33(12), 2503–2540.

Fields, D., Chan, A. and Akhtar, S., 2000. Organizational context and human resource management strategy: A structural equation analysis of Hong Kong firms. *International Journal of Human Resource Management*, 11(2), pp. 264–277.

Fields, D., Chan, A., Akhtar, S. and Blum, T.C., 2006. Human resource management strategies under uncertainty: How do US and Hong Kong Chinese companies differ? *Cross Cultural Management: An International Journal*, 13(2), pp. 171–186.

Horwitz, F. M. 2009. Managing human resources in Africa: Emergent market challenges. In John Storey, Patrick Wright, Dave Ulrich (Eds.), *The Routledge Companion to Strategic Human Resource Management* (pp. 462–475). Routledge Companions.

Ketkar, S. and Sett, P.K., 2010. Environmental dynamism, human resource flexibility, and firm performance: Analysis of a multi-level causal model. *International Journal of Human Resource Management*, 21(8), pp. 1173–1206.

Kim, S., Vaiman, V. and Sanders, K., 2022. Strategic human resource management in the era of environmental disruptions. *Human Resource Management*, 61(3), pp. 283–293.

Mithani, M.A., Narula, R., Surdu, I., and Verbeke, A. 2022. (Eds.) *Crisis and disruptions in international business: How multinationals respond the crisis.* Palgrave-McMillan.

Psychogios, A and Prouska, R. 2019. *Managing People in Small and Medium Enterprises in Turbulent Contexts* (Routledge Studies in Small Business). Oxon: Routledge.

Roper, I., Prouska, R. and Chatrakul Na Ayudhya, U., 2022. The rhetorics of 'agile' and the practices of 'agile working': Consequences for the worker experience and uncertain implications for HR practice. *International Journal of Human Resource Management*. Forthcoming.

Walsh, J. and Zhu, Y., 2007. Local complexities and global uncertainties: A study of foreign ownership and human resource management in China. *International Journal of Human Resource Management*, 18(2), pp. 249–267.

Wood, G., Dibben, P., Stride, C., and Webster, E. 2011. HRM in Mozambique: homogenization, path dependence or segmented business system? *Journal of World Business*, 46(1), pp. 31–41.

Zheng, C. and Lamond, D. 2009. A critical review of human resource management studies (1978–2007) in the People's Republic of China. *International Journal of Human Resource Management*, 20(11), pp. 2194–2227.

Human resource management in the context of high uncertainties

Caleb Kwong, Mehmet Demirbag ⓘ, Geoffrey Wood ⓘ and Fang Lee Cooke

ABSTRACT
This paper develops and extends the existing body of literature on human resource management (HRM) and contextual uncertainty. We identify and explore the consequences of present uncertainties of a broad scale and scope for the practice of HRM. We then review salient bodies of theorising, and map out relevant areas of application. This is followed by a presentation of some of the most recent work on uncertainty and HRM that is encompassed in this collection, which brings to bear evidence from around the world.

Introduction

Although business and management literature talks a great deal about unexpected events, the present condition is characterized by ones that transcend past human experience in terms of global scale and scope. This includes climate change, pandemics, and the unforeseen consequences of present technologies. In recent years, we have witnessed numerous political crises, wars and conflicts in many parts of the world. What is notable is that political instability is no longer confined to emerging economies. The boundaries between developed countries, with their seemingly mature institutions, and emerging ones seem less clear cut. Supranational organisations and political bodies, long credited for helping to bring peace, stability and economic progress, face unprecedented challenges, while the resurgence of the power of monopolies and oligopolies challenges the power of nation states. Such political tension is intertwined with the economic sphere. There has been a resurgence of protectionism. Economically, more than ten years on from the previous financial crisis, parts of the world are still reeling from its aftermath.

Within academic research, different definitions of uncertainty have been proposed and adopted, each of which has added to our understanding of uncertainties. Miller (1991) classifies uncertainties into three main categories based on their nature: general environmental, industry, and firm-specific, with the first being the main focus of the special issue. Environmental uncertainties, or state uncertainty, can be understood as the environmental factors that affect the business context across industries and firms (Miller, 1991; Milliken, 1987). Over time, scholars have proposed different typologies to aid our understanding. Some categorisations focus on the nature of the specific event or incident in question. Miller (1991), for example, highlights five aspects of uncertainties within the broad environmental spectrum, including political uncertainties, government policy uncertainties, macroeconomic uncertainties, social uncertainties, and natural uncertainties.

Others conceptualise uncertainties through their common characteristics, regardless of the specific event or incident in question. The first characteristic of environmental uncertainties is the lack of information available in relation to the changes in the environment (Milliken, 1987). While some of the direct consequences, such as the impact of the pandemic on medical professions, can be expected to be in alignment with the findings of studies on excessive demands and emotional exhaustion (e.g. Ererdi et al., 2021; Naveed & Rana, 2013), it is generally difficult to establish a cause-effect relationship (Duncan, 1972; Lawrence & Lorsch, 1967; van der Vorst & Beulens, 2002), including how the change in the external environment has resulted in changes in factors that are affecting firms and individuals, such as customers' preferences, and the purchasing power and supply chain (Bhatnagar & Sohal, 2005). The more volatility, complexity, and heterogeneity in the external environment, the harder it is for decision makers to predict the general nature of the changes. For example, the current pandemic has halted the global mobility of workers and the practice of expatriation; it has also triggered an acceleration in working from home, which was not anticipated.

While a firm may have a general sense of the number of people who will be working from home, they cannot predict how long such an arrangement will last, how that will affect performance within the context of family life, or the health, wellbeing and motivational impact that this can have on their employees, particularly for expatriates who are unable to return home (Ererdi et al., 2021). Although there is an extensive body of work on communication processes and the linkages to power relationships within and between organisations (Reunanen &

Kunelius, 2020), this literature assumes that communication encompasses a great deal of traditional face-to-face interactive activity within the workplace (Chriss, 1995). The consequences as to when this is wholly (or almost wholly) supplanted by virtual interactions such as *via* a meeting platform (e.g. zoom) remain uncertain. However, an emerging body of literature suggests that virtual interactions may lead to less empathy (Andrejevic & Volcic, 2020), more confrontational styles of interaction, and may cause a lengthening of the working day and work–life balance issues (Stich et al., 2018). In the case of MNEs, it may also lead to a reduction in cross-cultural awareness.

Much uncertainty surrounds what a return to normal will look like. Many organisations have realised that it is possible to make substantial rental savings through homeworking, while retaining or increasing productivity (Hensher, 2020). Again, at a time when there is growing public concern as to excessive air miles, and when many organisations have similarly realised that it is possible to get by without international face-to-face meetings, there may be a permanent reduction in business travel, especially as it remains unclear as to whether the budget airline model can be revived (Lew et al., 2020). However, historical evidence on past pandemics has suggested that societies were quick to revert to at least the trappings of the status quo before the event, and it may well be that this will be the case again, especially given the influence of powerful political lobbies (e.g. office property landlords) on politicians to find ways of encouraging such a return; a notorious if somewhat premature example is the UK Government's ill-advised August 2020 'get back to work or lose your job' campaign.

The second characteristic is that the effect of the uncertainties is hard to measure accurately (Milliken, 1987). It is very difficult to predict the future competitive situation, its possible effects, and/or the consequences of a firm's behaviours (Duncan, 1972; Pennings, 1981; Pennings & Tripathi, 1978; Pfeffer & Salancik, 1978). The difficulty in assigning probabilities as to the likelihood of future events is compounded by the fact that uncertainties not only create isolated, sector-specific challenges, but also create intertwined direct and indirect effects, with the latter particularly hard to measure. For example, a pandemic is not only a problem of public health; it can also affect other external factors such as the general state of the economy and policy making. Factors such as an unexpected decrease in purchasing power and the uncertain duration of a government's stimulus package can have a significant impact on firms through changes in the labour market, consumers' preferences and competitors' responses.

Unfortunately, a limitation of economic theory is that much more attention is devoted to accounting for present value than for accurately costing future value (Singer, 2011). This has meant that there is an inertia when it comes to dealing with global heating, as well as the threat of future pandemics and other high probability events. When it comes to HRM, this translates into a focus (if there is one) on the present rather than future well-being of employees, and the consequences in engagement, commitment and productivity of terms of the strategic choices made by managers today.

The third characteristic of uncertainty is the inability of firms to anticipate the impact of the different response options. The complexities highlighted above create challenges for organisations in formulating their responses to the uncertainties. While uncertain situations present both threats and opportunities to firms, and therefore widen the range of options at their disposal (Ererdi et al., 2021), the unpredictable and often unprecedented nature of most uncertain events means that there is little data and information for firms to analyse. The lack of processing capacity, therefore, means that firms are often unable to make accurate predictions about the impact of their subsequent business strategies and chosen control actions (Milliken, 1987; van der Vorst & Beulens, 2002). Yet, despite that, tremendous pressure has been put on managers to make swift managerial decisions in such a context, which intensifies the risk involved in the decision-making process.

There is a substantial body of work on human behaviour that confirms that the human brain reacts differently to bad and to good news (Coutts, 2019). In the case of the former, there is a tendency to denial and inaction, especially when threats are abstract and not immediately physically visible (Coutts, 2019). This means that managers may be a lot better at dealing with day-to-day business problems than either existential threats and/or fundamental challenges to existing ways of doing things (Coutts, 2019). An inability to even make decisions around practices (in the hope that inaction will somehow mean that old models and ways of doing things will somehow persist), is likely to add to uncertainties. Many so-called uncertainties or shocks were widely predicted in advance, but often those who had a chance to do something about them closed their eyes in the hope that they would not eventuate.

These uncertainties (whether genuinely unknown or not) are complex and can have a deep impact on how organisations, whether multinational corporations or domestic businesses, operate. While these uncertainty contexts are various in nature, the key common theme is the unexpected changes they have brought, creating considerable ambiguity for businesses, and having important human resource implications. Practically, every firm is exposed to some level of uncertainty at both micro and macro-levels (Miler, 1991). Lawrence and Losch (1969), for example, outline in their study that an organisation's internal structural arrangement is contingent upon the demands of the external environment (Lawrence & Losch, 1969). Macro-level uncertainties stem from contexts which often have far-reaching repercussions on market supplies and demands, forcing firms to make fundamental changes in their operations (Pfeffer & Salancik, 1978); this, in turn, can have an impact on the ways in which human resources are managed within firms (Boxall & Macky, 2009). The threat-rigidity model predicts that uncertainties may push firms to adopt risk-averse practices (Staw et al., 1981).

In the western, liberal economy where the reliance on shared ownership and external financing is great, the pressure of satisfying multiple stakeholders is likely to increase the need for short-term cost savings in various business functions, including human resource management (Hall & Soskice, 2001). The disconnected capitalism thesis (Thompson, 2003) suggests that, under such pressure, firms would typically forgo commitment-based and involvement-focused HR systems in pursuance of a 'low-road' strategy (Cook et al., 2016; Lahteenmaki et al., 1998); examples are redundancy, a retrenchment of the training and development budget, a reduction in compensation, incentive and other financial rewards, and a reversion of worker-level HR outcomes from commitment towards control and the erosion of mutual-gain HR practices (Charlton, 2008; Felstead, 2018; Hauff et al., 2014; Lallement, 2011; Thompson, 2003); these measures seek to improve operational efficiency and flexibility (Heyes, 2011; Mulholland, 2011) and potentially maximise the short-term benefits for the shareholders. Although many of these cost-cutting practices may be initiated in times of stability, the onset of uncertainty often speeds up and intensifies their implementation (Appelbaum et al., 2013). Undoubtedly, the above changes alter the dynamics between organisations and workers (Ramsay, 1977), with employee outcomes ranging from a demotivating effect causing job strain, to an increase in productivity due to the threat of job loss (Tsao et al., 2016; Van de Voorde & Beijer, 2015).

On the other hand, uncertain contexts present opportunities to entrepreneurial and visionary organisations (Ramsay, 1977). A crucial role of management involves devising mitigation strategies that could reduce the adverse impact of environmental uncertainties, which would enable an organisation to survive and even prosper (Pfeffer & Salancik, 1978). Therefore, organisations are not merely passive recipients of uncertainty outcomes; rather, they can proactively reshape their strategies in order to adapt to the changes in context. While retrenchment is a popular mitigation strategy that reduces HR functioning costs, it is arguably a short-term strategy. Organisations may pursue longer term strategic changes by adapting to changes in customer habits and labour market conditions arising from the uncertain situations (Cook et al., 2016). To do so requires considerable creativity and flexibility and openness to change (Heyes, 2011; Lallement, 2011). With studies long asserting connections between HR practices and the development of creativity, innovation and organisational flexibility (Jiang et al., 2012; Knox & Walsh, 2005; Kozica & Kaiser, 2012; Seeck & Diehl, 2017; Shipton et al., 2006), HR strategies may give competitive advantage in the face of uncertainties, which others can replicate or reverse engineer (Fields et al., 2006). For instance, while cutting training and development budgets is commonplace during uncertain situations such as a recession, training and development could stabilise the workforce, enhancing workers' innovation and flexibility (Roche et al., 2013). Moreover, as employee commitment may drive long term performance gain (Wall & Wood, 2005; Wood & de Menezes, 1998), visionary firms may choose job enlargement and job intensification to enhance their workforce flexibility, rather than exploiting the temporary heightened labour market power by dismissing workers and re-employing them on poor contractual terms (Cook et al., 2016). Nevertheless, these practices may have a demotivating effect in the longer term if they are used persistently (Cooke et al., 2015).

The above summary illustrates that the precise nature of the relationships between uncertainties and HRM remains contentious. A further layer of complexity is that the ways in which organisations deal with uncertainties are largely dependent on the environmental context that they are embedded in (Demirbag & Wood, 2018). These differences stem from various historical and cultural specificities as well as variations in political, economic and social systems (Hofstede, 1991; Holmes et al., 2013; Hofstede, 1980). Studies have found that people from different cultures perceive and interpret uncertainties in particular ways (Gunkel et al., 2014; Hofstede, 1991) which influence their choice of whether to embrace or to avoid what comes (Engelen et al., 2015). They have also suggested that people from different cultures develop different mitigation and learning strategies as coping mechanisms (Kim & McLean, 2014). Unsurprisingly, studies have found considerable variations, not only in terms of the nature of uncertainties faced by organisations in different countries, but also the ways in which organisations choose to deal with them (Grote, 2007).

Supporting ways of coping with and adapting to uncertainties

One stream of literature on uncertainties focuses on how employers can help the employees cope with an uncertain and changing environment. At the time of uncertainties, employees can play a strong role in helping organisations to steer away from troubled waters and develop a sustained performance despite the difficulties. However, while having a job in an uncertain context can provide income security, it may also bring stress, anxiety, and burnout (Ab Wahab et al., 2021; Ererdi et al., 2021), affecting employees' psychological and emotional wellbeing and relationship with the job (Ab Wahab et al., 2021; Reade, 2009). How employers handle employees' concerns during such difficult times affects employees' perceptions and attitudes towards the organisation. Poor handling potentially leads to anger, disconnection and other negative emotions (Mainiero & Gibson, 2003), and in turn, results in absenteeism, leave taking and job separation (Alexander, 2004; Howie, 2007). Studies have found that perceived organisational support is crucial for bringing about employee commitment and motivation (Reade, 2009). The question is how these valuable human resources can be best facilitated.

Organisational culture is being seen as a crucial enabler in supporting employees to cope with uncertainties (Cooke et al., 2019; Lewis et al., 2016). Studies have found that organisations can display adaptability in times of uncertainty that is contradictory to their expected dominant behaviours and responses (Meyer, 1982). Such an ability is supported by an organisational culture and ideologies that embrace openness and risk taking, a structure that is facilitative to change, and opportunities for employees to invest their energy in making changes happen (Meyer, 1982). Davies et al. (2019) study of Korean expatriates found that resilience is positively related to work adjustment and the effect is particularly strong when the expatriates perceive their organisational culture to be inclusive. Branicki et al. (2019) study focuses on uncertainties created by day-to-day stressors as opposed to those created by a one-off extreme event, and found that issues such as continually feeling stressed and anxious about impossible, unpleasant, unsupported and seemingly pointless work slowly chipped away the employees' self-efficacy, self-esteem and self-determination, and, in turn, demoralised them. Consistent with the view that resilience is a process (Kossek & Perrigino, 2016), their study points to the importance of a micro-process of managing resilience, and in particular, developing a resilient organisational culture through coherent HR practices. These foster healthy and supportive relationships between managers and workers, ensuring an emotional connection between them and establishing functions that can be effectively developed and maintained over time.

The second issue which arises from the management of uncertainties is the perspective that firms should plan to mitigate and manage risks (Gannon & Paraskevas, 2017; Morris & Calamai, 2009). van der Vegt et al. (2015) suggest that firms should take a pro-active approach in preventing and mitigating risk associated with uncertainties and ensure that employees are well-prepared for the potential challenges arising. These proactive practices can include information provision, communication, and clear policy and standards (Gannon & Paraskevas, 2017). Coutu (2002) explores how the development of a disaster preparedness programme prior to a disaster, involving repeated drills, rehearsals and preparation, as well as multiple contingency planning and alternative back-up plans that can be quickly materialised when the established plan is not working, would enable employees to feel confident to deal with changes when they eventually occur (Coutu, 2002). Such a view has important implications for HRM. For example, when an expatriate is entering an uncertain context, rigorous contingency training for the expatriate to prepare for unexpected events would enhance their self-efficacy and ability to deal with different eventualities (Gannon & Paraskevas, 2017). Empirically, it is found that firms are increasingly taking issues such as terrorism into the account in their HR planning (Ererdi et al., 2021; Reade, 2009).

A body of social theory has argued for some years that the modern condition (even prior to the irrefutable evidence of global heating) is fraught with greater risks brought about by societal and technological changes (Phan & Wood, 2020). Established social structures (e.g. the nuclear family, political orders built around broad social consensus) are under more pressure than ever, while ways of organizing work are much more dynamic with new applications of technology (Kalleberg & Vallas, 2018). Blowback from the natural world has heightened these risks, adding to underlying social and political tensions within and between nations (Phan & Wood, 2020). In turn, it could be argued that in many settings, HR is really about managing – and mediating – discontinuities in physical and social ecosystems.

The third issue that arises from the literature is how employers can support employees with their emotions and wellbeing in the process of change adaptation (Gannon & Paraskevas, 2017; Ramirez et al., 2016). Uncertainties bring about considerable anxiety and stress to employees (Coutu, 2002), affecting their physical and mental health and motivation (Hui & Lee, 2000; Pollard, 2001). Therefore, in uncertain circumstances, developing psychological capital to withstand challenges is crucial (Luthans, 2002; Youssef & Luthans, 2007). Resilience, or the ability to overcome and recover from severe adversities or setbacks, and to cope with implementing changes and performing under considerable pressure, is seen as crucial in the context of uncertainties (Carmeli & Markman, 2011; Linnenluecke, 2017; Walker et al., 2004; Williams & Shepherd, 2016). It has been suggested that resilience is 'arguably the most important positive resource for navigating a turbulent and stressful workplace' (Avey et al., 2009, p. 682).

At an individual level, resilience is perceived as both a crucial capability and a process that enables employees to adapt to the changes in job demands as the uncertain situation arises (Kossek & Perrigino, 2016). Studies have shown that people who are resilient are more able to make effective adaptations and to cope with major life events and traumatic experiences (Fredrickson et al., 2003; Waugh et al., 2008). Furthermore, resilient individuals are more able to learn proactively and attain personal growth through overcoming challenges, both at work and personally, and to recover from such an ordeal (Youssef & Luthans, 2007). This suggests that both work-related adjustments and social support enable employees to adapt to an uncertain context (Bader, 2015; Bader et al., 2015; Bader & Berg, 2014; Bader & Schuster, 2015; Gannon & Paraskevas, 2017; Suder et al., 2019).

Resilience was initially perceived as an innate trait, but as psychologists found that resilient people often possess higher levels of positive emotion and openness to new experiences (Carmeli et al., 2013; Tugade & Fredrickson, 2004), it has been suggested that employee resilience involves skills and attributes that can be developed through appropriate organisational interventions (Cooke et al., 2019; Wang et al., 2014). Therefore, research is beginning to look at how organisations could play a proactive role in enabling their employees to develop resilience in the workplace (Carmeli & Markman, 2011; Cooper et al., 2014; Ollier-Malaterre, 2010; Robertson et al., 2015; Robertson & Cooper, 2011; Stajkovic, 2006; Youssef & Luthans, 2007).

In particular, studies are beginning to explore the types of high-performance HR practices which may have greater impact on an individual's resilience and may lead to enhanced levels of employee engagement and in-role performance (Wang et al., 2014). Bardoel et al. (2014) highlight a set of HR practices that can reinforce social support for employees, including work-life balance practices, flexible work arrangements, employee development and assistance programmes, and occupational health and safety systems, which could improve employee resilience (Bardoel et al., 2014). Others highlight the provision of training such as situational awareness training, resilience coaching, humanistic counselling, and mindfulness techniques to help individuals create significance in their lives from adverse situations, to steer away from backward thinking about a hopeless situation to become forward looking, and to develop concrete goals in the long term that can be looked forward to when surviving, even though the short term is far from guaranteed (Contu, 2002; Frankl, 2017; Gannon & Paraskevas, 2017). This reflects back on earlier comments about negative human reactions to bad news; the brain may be wired in a certain way (survival mode: fight, flight or freeze), but social interactions and interventions may help make for better coping.

One key emphasis within the resilience literature is the need to ensure that a consistent, distinctive, and embodied HRM message across the

HR system has been cohesively implemented (Bardoel et a., 2014; Branicki et al., 2019; Cooke et al., 2019). Khan et al. (2019) study on the telecommunication sector of Pakistan found that the adoption of a bundle of mutually reinforcing HR practices, if implemented effectively, can support the development of employee resilience in a context of rapid sectoral liberation and diffusion of western practices that involve considerable changes and uncertainties. Cooke et al. (2019) study on the banking industry in China found that the adaptation of western high-performance work systems plays a role in increasing the level of resilience demonstrated by the employees amidst intensifying global competitive pressure, and improves their engagement with the organisation. Branicki et al. (2019) study recommends the provision of training to enable employees to develop positive cognitive attitudes towards challenges and problem-solving skills, as well as other resilience traits.

Finally, there has been increasing interest among academics in trying to understand the impact of HR practices on employee resilience as well as organisational performance (Bardoel et al., 2014; Cooke et al., 2019; Robertson et al., 2015). Studies found that organisations can support employees in developing their psychological capital such as self-efficacy to bolster their ability to handle change, and to develop learned optimism (Bakker & Demerouti, 2008; Seligman, 1998) by choosing to embrace positive rather than negative thoughts about the impact of uncertainties (Avery et al., 2009; Luthans, 2002). In turn, resilient employees are likely to be more engaged with the organisation, evidenced in their demonstrated sense of dedication, rigour, and absorption in their work (Cooke et al., 2019). However, resilience is often presented in non-material terms; that is, in the belief that problems with resilience can be sorted out with better communication, pep talks or top down initiatives to entice employees to interact better; but the employment contract is central to HRM (Hyman, 1997), and in the end, employees who are secure in their employment and incomes are likely to be much more resilient than those who are not; this obvious fact that it is too often denied or ignored in the literature.

Culture, institutions and HR practices

A key debate in international HRM is the extent to which national context influences the adoption of different HR policies and practices to suit specific needs (Cooke et al., 2017; Cooke et al., 2019; Demirbag et al., 2016). Studies have long found that formal and informal institutions in which individuals are based are underpinned by a broadly shared cognitive understanding and acceptance in relation to certain beliefs (Schooler, 1996), values (Hofstede, 1980), norms, priorities

(Sirmon & Lane, 2004), and assumptions (Huang & Harris, 1973) and over time, these become the governing codes of societies (Holmes et al., 2013; North, 1990; Redding, 2005; Williams & Vorley, 2015; Zucker, 1987). In turn, cultural and institutional differences determine ways in which people perceive and respond to changes in external environments, directing the types of responses that firms would come up with when facing uncertainties (Chattopadhyay et al., 2001; Hofstede, 2001).

In terms of cross-cultural approaches, numerous studies have found that firms from different countries exhibit different threat-rigidity responses when faced with situations beyond their control (Staw et al., 1981). For instance, the perception that the external environment is a challenge that needs to be controlled is far more prevalent in western societies with a more individualistic focus, compared to those from eastern cultures, such as China, which often taken a more passive, accommodative approach, focusing on harnessing the internal energy within the firm to come up with the most appropriate response (Fields et al., 2006; Hofstede, 2001). Other work suggests that cultural differences may determine differences in decision-making when uncertainties are faced. Davies (1997), for example, found that, while rules and procedures are relied on more by managers from collectivist cultures during times of uncertainties, managers from more individualistic cultures exercise discretion to ensure flexibility.

Fields et al. (2006) found that, in an uncertain economic situation, power distance between superiors affects preferences in performance assessment, a point that reinforced previous findings from Redding and Wong (1986) and Hofstede (2001). In the Chinese culture, employees see performance appraisal as a visual/physical reminder of the moral connection between workers and the firm, thereby binding them together, while in the US, employees may resent limitations on individuals' roles and scope to exercise their discretion at work, which affects their performance at times when changes and flexibility are required. Fields et al. (2006) highlight substantial differences in terms of training provision in times of uncertainties. In the western context, training and development may be considered non-essential and are dramatically reduced during times of uncertainty (Fields et al., 2006); but in a high power distance, collectivist culture, they are considered as a moral obligation to employees (Hui & Tan, 1996) and as a reward to bind workers to the company in the longer term (Drost et al., 2002). Therefore, organisations in such cultures would increase investment in training and development in times of uncertainty, to reinforce their moral connection with staff (Fields et al., 2006).

It has become quite fashionable to critique Hofstede, given the obvious clunkiness of the cultural taxonomies and apparently unscientific bases of their development (McSweeney, 2002). However, his work does raise a fundamental truth; cultures vary around the world and have important effects on behaviour within and between organisations. Yet, recent work on culture highlights that cultures are dynamic, and seemingly immutable cultural features are often reinterpreted or realigned to suit different purposes (Comaroff & Comaroff, 2019). Again, there is much cross-fertilization and hybridity between cultures (Comaroff & Comaroff, 2019). Further, cultures are likely to change by accident, or because it is in the interests of some or other societal grouping to redefine them to suit their economic and/or societal interests (Comaroff & Comaroff, 2019). This raises the question of how cultures relate to institutions. Traditional structuralist sociology would simply see culture as yet another institution (Parsons, 1972). However, while culture undeniably serves social and economic purposes, it is important to recognize that culture may also operate in other spheres of social life that are poorly aligned to any economic purpose.

In HRM and international business literature, comparative institutional analysis has increasingly been applied as the theoretical lens to describe and explain the adoption and diffusion of organisational forms and practices across institutional contexts (Demirbag et al., 2014; Hall & Soskice, 2001). From a very different starting point (Coasian economics and socio-economics vs traditional sociology), this supplements earlier work that looked at path dependence and the dissemination of practices at firm level (Schotter, Meyer, & Wood, 2021; see also Björkman et al., 2007; DiMaggio & Powell, 1983). In terms of comparative institutional analysis, the Varieties of Capitalism approach and the broadly compatible Business Systems theory suggest that both formal institutions, including laws, regulations, and the strength of collective bargaining, and informal institutions, such as norms, conventions and other informal practices, can significantly vary in the ways organisations and market operate (Whitley, 1994). Although early work focused on broad societal differences, in recent years, considerable attention has been paid to the impact of these formal and informal institutions on HRM and employment relations, applying a longer term historical framework from the institutionalist perspective to explain how different HR practices are formed and develop over time (Wilkinson et al., 2014; Wilkinson & Wood, 2012; Wood & Bischoff, 2020). The HR strategies adopted by firms within a country would typically reflect the dominant norms and values of the managers and employees, as well as formative historical developments, and institutionalisation of, inter alia, labour market practices (Bond, 1996; Boxall & Purcell, 2000; Fields et al., 2006; Gooderham et al., 1999; Tregaskis, 1997).

As people may interpret, react, and respond differently to uncertainties, organisations would typically deploy different HR strategies that are most aligned with the preferences and expectations of their employees (Fields et al., 2006). Fong and Wyer (2003) comparative study of managers in the US and China found that managers in the two countries adopted different approaches towards managing employee relations in the context of labour market uncertainties. While the former evaluates employee relations choices based on possible economic benefits, the latter, with a stronger emphasis on collectivism, tended to focus on group coherence, with minimisation of the risk of loss as a priority.

Once these institutions are shaped, they became stabilised over time (Beugelsdijk et al., 2015). Institutionalist thinking has highlighted the persistence of the influence of local cultural values in the workplace (Wood & Bischoff, 2020). Therefore, even when faced with rapid and often negative environmental change, pre-existing HRM practices and arrangements can often endure. In the Japanese context, a number of studies (Chuma, 2002; Grainger & Miyamoto, 2003) found that previous economic crises did very little to alter the adoption of the two main HRM pillars of long-term employment and seniority hierarchy, reflecting their cultural preferences for power distance and uncertainty avoidance. Instead, firms adapted by adopting alternative practices such as reducing overtime and the temporary reassignment of workers to its subsidiaries. Similarly, Morris et al. (2006) found that, although economic stagnation put considerable pressure on firms to minimise costs, long term employment systems, despite being altered, remained persistent and robust, as firms strove to ensure continuity and reduce the level of uncertainties created for the workers. Dibben et al. (2017) study in the economically unstable post-colonial context of Mozambique showed that, despite the country's economic transition towards a socialist model, established institutions from the pre-colonial era continued to govern firms' behaviours, including the ways human resources were managed. Their study points to the prevalence of institutional influences on HRMs; the uncertainties intensified the need for improvisation by continuing to utilise pre-existing structures and resources, leading to little or no change. The reduction of resources and knowhow within firms led to an emphasis on pragmatism, where organisations offered limited training to adapt to the new environment, and relied to a large extent on informal dissemination of skills, which favoured the status quo. On the other hand, Zoogah et al. (2018) study of five Northern African countries that share considerable historical and cultural commonalities, and where firms in these countries shared similar public sector-led economic development after independence from western powers in the aftermath of the Arab Spring, found that the divergence of HRM practices in firms in these countries began to accelerate, as the previously developed public sector-led HRM modules were no longer deemed relevant to the needs in an expanding private sector. Firms in some countries are found to be better adjusted to the challenges than others. Such differences can be explained both by the different ways they were affected by the local economic and political situation, and the long-standing differences in informal regulation and post-colonial political development.

Internationalisation of MNEs' uncertainties

The above differences create considerable challenges for multinational enterprises (MNEs) entering a new country. For MNEs that are spread out across multiple locations, country level variances in economic conditions and other factors create uncertainties, but when the destinations involve emerging economies with different cultural and institutional constraints, such uncertainties intensify (Cogin & Williamson, 2014; Horwitz, 2017; Mellahi et al., 2013). Protecting the enterprise's interests from a distance in a volatile but alien context can be difficult (Cantwell et al., 2010). The use and management of expatriates to complete strategically critical tasks becomes much more difficult when the countries of domicile are inherently less stable. However, uncertain situations often present golden opportunities for international businesses. Studies have found that the option value of MNEs on entering a country under uncertain conditions can be high (Miller, 1991). This is because government and international bodies often inject considerable investment into the affected countries in aiding the recovery and rebuilding process and, in turn, pump up the local aggregate demands, opening new opportunities for MNEs in relevant industries (Vigdor, 2008). At the same time, consumers' demand for products and services may change; demand may not necessarily decline, but what consumers want may be different. Furthermore, there are multinational organisations such as inter-governmental agencies and international relief organisations who purposefully send staff into countries experiencing crises. These considerations impact on MNE decisions to invest and reinvest in particular country settings (Oh & Oetzel, 2011), which, in turn, affects the demands placed on a firm's human resources in terms of expansion or contraction.

Research has been looking at how institutions can impact MNEs and ways in which HRM practices are being utilised to help them embed into the host's institutional environment (Sparrow, 2012). Studies have found that MNEs are under the heavy influence of the cultural and institutional context of the country in which their corporate headquarters are located, as well as the host country where their subsidiaries are established (Ferner & Quintanilla, 1998). The main debate in HRM evolves around the notion of global standardisation versus local responsiveness; in other words, whether MNEs merely transfer their HRM practices from their headquarters and adapt to the predominant ways of doing business in the host country, or whether they bring about a new, hybrid and transglobal model of HRM (Adams et al., 2017; Chang et al., 2009; Glover & Wilkinson, 2007; Tatoglu et al., 2016).

With regard to the first argument, studies have found that an uncertain context would encourage organisations to adopt a cautious approach towards HRM when entering into a host location. A desire for stability is often intensified by the fact that many of the MNEs are relatively new international firms from emerging economies with a low level of HR capabilities compared to the larger, more established MNEs from the west (Cooke et al., 2015; Wood et al., 2014). Adams et al. (2017) study on South African MNEs in Ghana found that most of these organisations initially transfer practices from the headquarters to avoid the initial labour market uncertainty associated with entering a new destination. They found that direct transfer of practices was more commonplace in recruitment and selection, performance appraisal, and talent management practices. This ensured that the organisation could effectively maintain control of labour quality in the context of uncertainty. The process of adjustment was incremental, involving small steps making minimal differences to adapt to the local cultural and institutional expectations, while at the same time, not diverging from the organisation's corporate culture and principles. However, although the study found direct transfer of practices was most prominent, they found the extent of reliance differed between different HRM components. Compensation and employee relations practices, for example, were more localised, depending on local legislation and labour market factors. In fact, many emerging MNEs in Africa are noted to plunge into the low wage economies, relying on unskilled labour, which can have considerable managerial implications (Wood et al., 2014).

Drawing heavily on the institutionalist perspective highlighted in the previous section, the second argument emphasises the understanding of how a host country's regulatory, normative, and cognitive institutional processes can influence the HR practices of subsidiaries (Hannon et al., 1995; Morgan, 2007). Studies have noted considerable institutional and cultural obstacles for HRMs to implement consistent HRM practices between MNE's operations (Chew & Horwitz, 2004; Wöcke et al., 2007), with considerable differences in the HR practices found across the subsidiaries of MNEs (Rosenzweig & Nohria, 1994). Cogin and Williamson (2014), for example, found that the human resource practices adopted by MNEs are contingent upon the social context of each particular subsidiary entered. This view highlights the importance of conforming in order to attain legitimacy, suggesting that MNEs are likely to mimic the local HR practices to suit the cultural and legislative environment (Kamoche et al., 2015). In the context of uncertainties, responsiveness and adaptation of HRM becomes particularly important (Cogin & Williamson, 2014; Horwitz, 2012). The context of uncertainties often alters customers' needs, demands, buying habits, buying frequency, brand orientation and price focus (Rust & Lemon, 2001; Sanzo & Vázquez, 2011). HR practices that are contingent on local consumers' preferences can help firms adapt to the changing needs of the customers (Cogin & Williamson, 2014; Peccei & Rosenthal, 2001), leading to higher customer satisfaction, retention and financial performance (Cogin & Williamson, 2014). Thus, while Cogin and Williamson (2014) found that standard-isation of HR practices across MNEs can be optimal in low uncertainty environments, managerial discretion involving the customisation of HRM is most important in settings involving high environmental uncertainties. The study suggests an emphasis on the hiring process in selecting inno-vative managerial applicants who are experienced in handling uncertain local contexts, as well as developing tailored training programmes to provide skills to adapt to fluctuation in demand and market expectations, would enable firms to meet customers' demands and remain competitive in highly uncertain environments. MNEs could also utilise performance appraisal practices that account for local customs and offer rewards that local staff value to guide them through the expected changes in behaviours that would meet with the new customers' needs and offset the stress and uncertainties associating with changes (Cogin & Williamson, 2014). Similarly, Akande et al. (2010) found that South African subor-dinates in US-South African joint ventures do not want the US partners to bring in wholesale changes; instead they prefer them to consider contextual differences and make local adaption according to needs. This raises important questions about training.

This raises two much bigger concerns. The first is that the HRM and international business literature do much to draw a comforting distinction between the developed and developing world, or even more comforting, mature vs emerging markets. However, not only have many emerging markets experienced rapid growth and development without showing much inclination or willingness to converge with mature ones, but some mature markets, most notably the US, have increasingly been bedevilled with what were historically depicted as 'third world' characteristics, includ-ing infrastructural decay, political instability, and stagnation or decline in the key indices of human development. In turn, this challenges what we might see as advanced or most functional HR practices, and whether models from the 'first world' are necessarily the best or most appropriate.

It also raises difficult questions as to whether choices in people management (e.g. curtailing wage, job and retirement security) might have something to do with the rise of right wing populism, and a host of other societal and economic ills (Cumming et al., 2020).

The second concern is that, as many firms in the US and the UK have come to centre their business model on what Lazonick and Shin (2019) call 'predatory value extraction', that is, *via* debt-funded share buy-backs and dividends, the liquidation of accumulated assets, and other mechanisms that do not generate real value, the traditional process of production of goods or services may become of incidental significance. This, in turn, may impart much uncertainty to the HR function; it, and a firm's people, may become of incidental importance or little more than a liability. The uneven diffusion of this model around the world imparts a further layer of uncertainty to the HR function.

Emerging issues

The aim of this special issue is to examine more closely the implementation of human resource management practices in the context of high uncertainties. The collection of articles in this special issue identifies gaps and explores new directions in this field, focusing on different natures of uncertainties, and how they impact on ways in which firms respond through their HRM practices.

Michalski et al.'s (2021) study from Mongolia examines how cultural factors affect the perception of uncertainties, in turn affecting firms' approaches towards human resource development. The study highlights the historical factors that led to the development of certain perceptions and mindsets towards uncertainties, which in turn influence the decision-making logic of managers as well as the receptiveness of certain HRD practices amongst employees. The economic context of Mongolia is one that is typical of many emerging economies, with generally weak institutions and fast-changing political situations since its transition towards a multi-party state, creating considerable economic uncertainties. However, the authors argue that uncertainty is more deeply rooted in Mongolian societies, and that the historical nomadic cultural context also played a prominent role in the shaping the notion of uncertainty, as well as people's responses towards it. The authors highlight a number of cognitive characteristics, including the perception of life as temporal, the normalisation of uncertainties, and the recognition of their positive aspects, as well as flexibility in handling them, that are unique in Mongolian culture. The authors argue that employers need to develop very specific human resource practices to help employees cope with the uncertainties associated with the economic, social and cultural contexts.

Makhmadshoev and Laaser's (2021) paper, set in the highly uncertain context of the post-socialist economy of Kyrgyzstan, highlights the challenges for small-and-medium-sized enterprises (SMEs) in supporting their workers through the uncertainties caused by the transition from a socialist to a capitalist economy. The study found that SMEs typically deployed one of the two, emergent, HR strategies that centre on the notion of path-dependence, with the aim of enabling workers to gain a sense of continuity while adapting to the new market-led system. On the one hand, some SMEs continued to deploy a command-and-control system, largely through establishing explicit sets of rules, procedures and expectations. This control system stems from the assumption of low trust, a mechanistic view of workers from the Soviet era. The explicit nature of this control approach has the advantage of being path-dependent, providing clear guidance to workers on how to understand the expected behaviours in a more individualised capitalist economic system. The downside of the system is that as market opportunities arise elsewhere, workers seek better pay and work conditions. Consequently, SMEs adopting this control approach suffered from high turnover, which was not a problem during the socialist era. This, in turn, discouraged SMEs from investing in workers' training and development, potentially making them less competitive in the long run. On the other hand, other SMEs implemented a commitment-based incentive system drawn from western ideologies, with the downside of being misaligned with the norms and workers' expectations developed during the Soviet era. To combat this, SMEs adopted a distinctive approach combining autonomy with a paternalistic management style, and deployed largely group rather than individual incentives, aligning with workers' expectations that were developed through the country's culture and history.

Serafini and Szamosi's (2021) qualitative study on American luxury hotel chains compares their HRM practices in both stable and uncertain contexts. Focusing on the transitional and peripheral economies of Central Asia and the Caucasus, the study found that the cultural and historical legacies resulted in a weakened institutional context. The development of the different forms of capitalism, which contributed to the unique blend of HR practices adapted by these multinational hotel chains, typically involved a mixture of professional practices adopted from the country of origin, as well as informal practices, such as in recruitment and performance management, that aligned with the local expectations. Fulfilling such expectations could enable firms to foster a more content and stable workforce, allowing them to take a long-term view of training and development, resulting in greater productivity.

As discussed in the literature review earlier, the underlying context of a country has a significant impact on how HRM is operated within organisations. Goergen et al. (2021) examine the issue of institutional trust in the implementation of communication practices by both MNEs and their domestic peers. Instead of focusing on personal attributes and behaviours of managers, their study utilises a cross-country dataset to examine how institutional trust at the societal level can impact on the nature of communication and depth of exchanges between employers and employees within firms. The study found that in countries where associated trust is high, firms are more likely to pay careful attention to their employer-employee communication, including the sharing of business information and financial matters, and more inclined to co-determine the employment contract with their employees. The study also found that MNEs are likely to implement consistent communication practices with their domestic peers, rather than adopt practices from their country of origin. This suggests that adapting to the local context is particularly common and crucial for MNEs.

Katou et al.'s (2021) paper, set in the uncertain contexts of Greek manufacturing, services, and trading sectors, examines the role of idio-syncratic deals (i-deals) negotiation on organisational citizen behaviour. These arrangements are 'special terms of employment negotiated between individual workers and their employers that satisfy both parties' needs' (Rousseau et al., 2006, p. 977). The study found that, in the context of high political and economic uncertainties, customised and flexible employee arrangements in relation to career development can positively influence employees' perceptions of whether their psychological contract is being fulfilled. In turn, a positive perception can increase organisa-tional engagement and commitment, as well as the display of altruistic and civic behaviours within the workplace. The findings suggest that managers have a strong role in fulfilling what was promised in the i-deal to ensure organisational commitment can be activated.

Tasavori et al.'s (2021) paper highlights how dynamic capabilities in HRM can help MNEs to adapt to chronic uncertainties. Set in the context of Iran, where the country has been experiencing recurring economic sanctions from the west, the study describes how MNEs adapt to such adverse environments by repeatedly deploying a range of dynamic capacities in their HR practices. The cases illustrated are interesting, in that they show that, rather than maximising short-term profit, MNEs placed emphasis on longer-term potential beyond the immediate sanction period. Such a long-term emphasis is reflected in their more flexible HR practices, with the aim of keeping their employees on side for potential future expansion post-sanctions. To do so, MNEs deploy highly fluid compensation practices, focusing on retaining the best managers and personnel over periods of retrenchment. As the economic cost of such a talent retention strategy is inevitably high, these MNCs also adopt flexible compensation packages, which are cut down to the bare basics. To keep employees on side, HR departments also shift their operational emphasis by diverting funds from costs such as training and development towards satisfying the basic needs of the employees, as well as on their health and wellbeing. More importantly, the MNEs deploy honest and open communication with the employees, but also, the regular and transparent sharing of information. These practices are found to be useful in gaining trust and reducing anxiety and stress amongst employees. As and when the sanctions are lifted, even when only intermittently, these MNCs would be in a good position and the human resources within the MNEs would provide them with a strong platform from which to grow.

Conclusions

It is a truism to state that the world has become a more uncertain place. Intensifying sources of uncertainty and risk include environmental blowback from human activities in the form of global warming, pandemics and the like (Phan & Wood, 2020), and endogenous changes in society and firms. What we can learn from a growing body of rigorous work on emerging economies is that, even in response to the greatest of challenges, organisations may contrive solutions that allow for coping, and, indeed, in some instances that may be superior to what has gone before them. At a time when many developed economies are facing internal and external challenges, much can be learned from HR experiments and solutions in the workplace within contexts of high uncertainty around the world. It is hoped that this collection may help encourage a greater sharing of examples of how and how not to cope with dynamic environments, where fundamental understandings and rules of the game are no longer as certain. Researchers might wish to deploy this emerging body of evidence as a basis for future theorising on how we understand organisational responses to risk, and genuine or perceived uncertainties.

Disclosure statement

No potential conflict of interest was reported by the authors.

ORCID

Mehmet Demirbag (iD) http://orcid.org/0000-0002-4417-5780
Geoffrey Wood (iD) http://orcid.org/0000-0001-9709-1823

References

Adams, K., Nyuur, R. B., Ellis, F. Y., & Debrah, Y. A. (2017). South African MNCs' HRM systems and practices at the subsidiary level: Insights from subsidiaries in Ghana. *Journal of International Management*, *23*(2), 180–193. https://doi.org/10.1016/j.intman.2016.07.001

Akande, W. A., Adetoun, B. E., Tserere, M. M., Adewuyi, M. F., & Akande, E. T. (2010). Should we put locals in charge? Managing relationships within prospective us – South African joint ventures. *Journal of Business Economics & Management*, *11*, 550–575. https://doi.org/doi: https://doi.org/10.3846/jbem. 2010.27

Alexander, D. C. (2004). *Business confronts terrorism: Risks and responses*. University of Wisconsin Press.

Andrejevic, M., & Volcic, Z. (2020). Virtual empathy. *Communication, Culture and Critique*, *13*(3), 295–310. https://doi.org/10.1093/ccc/tcz035

Appelbaum, E., Batt, R., & Clark, I. (2013). Implications for employment relations research: Evidence from breach of trust and implicit contracts in private equity buy outs. *British Journal of Industrial Relations*, *51*(3), 498–518. https://doi.org/10.1111/bjir.12009

Avery, D. R., Richeson, J. A., Hebl, M. R., & Ambady, N. (2009). It does not have to be uncomfortable: The role of behavioral scripts in Black–White interracial interactions. *Journal of Applied Psychology*, *94*(6), 1382–1393.

Avey, J. B., Luthans, F., & Jensen, S. M. (2009). Psychological capital: A positive resource for combating employee stress and turnover. *Human Resource Management*, *48*(5), 677–693. https://doi.org/10.1002/hrm.20294

Bader, B. (2015). The power of support in high-risk countries: Compensation and social support as antecedents of expatriate work attitudes. *The International Journal of Human Resource Management*, *26*(13), 1712–1736. https://doi.org/10.1080/09585192.2014.962071

Bader, B., & Berg, N. (2014). The influence of terrorism on expatriate performance: A conceptual approach. *The International Journal of Human Resource Management*, *25*(4), 539–557. https://doi.org/10.1080/09585192.2013.814702

Bader, B., & Schuster, T. (2015). Expatriate social networks in terrorism-endangered countries: An empirical analysis in Afghanistan, India, Pakistan, and Saudi Arabia. *Journal of International Management*, *21*(1), 63–77. https://doi.org/10.1016/j.intman.2014.09.004

Bader, B., Schuster, T., & Dickmann, M. (2015). Special issue of international journal of human resource management: Danger and risk as challenges for HRM: How to manage people in hostile environments. *The International Journal of Human Resource Management*, *26*(11), 1517–1519. https://doi.org/10.1080/09585192.2015.1019256

Bakker, A. B., & Demerouti, E. (2008). Towards a model of work engagement. Career development international. *Career Development International*, *13*(3), 209–223. https://doi.org/10.1108/13620430810870476

Bardoel, E. A., Pettit, T. M., De Cieri, H., & McMillan, L. (2014). Employee resilience: An emerging challenge for HRM. *Asia Pacific Journal of Human Resources*, *52*(3), 279–297. https://doi.org/10.1111/1744-7941.12033

Beugelsdijk, S., Maseland, R., & Van Hoorn, A. (2015). Are scores on Hofstede's dimensions of national culture stable over time? A cohort analysis. *Global Strategy Journal*, *5*(3), 223–240. https://doi.org/10.1002/gsj.1098

Bhatnagar, R. & Sohal, A.S. (2005). Supply chain competitiveness: Measuring the impact of location factors, uncertainty and manufacturing practices. *Technovation*, *25*(5), 443–456.

Björkman, I., Fey, C. F., & Park, H. J. (2007). Institutional theory and MNC subsidiary HRM practices: Evidence from a three-country study. *Journal of International Business Studies*, *38*(3), 430–446. https://doi.org/10.1057/palgrave.jibs.8400267

Bond, M. (1996). Chinese values. In M. H. Bond (Ed.), *The Handbook of Chinese psychology*. Oxford University Press.

Boxall, P., & Macky, K. (2009). Research and theory on high-performance work systems: Progressing the high-involvement stream. *Human Resource Management Journal*, *19*(1), 3–23. https://doi.org/10.1111/j.1748-8583.2008.00082.x

Boxall, P., & Purcell, J. (2000). Strategic human resource management: Where have we come from and where are we going?*International Journal of Management Reviews*, *2*(2), 183–203. https://doi.org/10.1111/1468-2370.00037

Branicki, L., Steyer, V., & Sullivan-Taylor, B. (2019). Why resilience managers aren't resilient, and what human resource management can do about it. *The International Journal of Human Resource Management*, *30*(8), 1261–1286. https://doi.org/10.1080/09585192.2016.1244104

Cantwell, J., Dunning, J. H., & Lundan, S. M. (2010). An evolutionary approach to understanding international business activity: The co-evolution of MNEs and the institutional environment. *Journal of International Business Studies*, *41*(4), 567–586. https://doi.org/10.1057/jibs.2009.95

Carmeli, A., Gelbard, R., & Reiter-Palmon, R. (2013). Leadership, creative problem-solving capacity, and creative performance: The importance of knowledge sharing. *Human Resource Management*, *52*(1), 95–121.

Carmeli, A., & Markman, G. D. (2011). Capture, governance, and resilience: Strategy implications from the history of Rome. *Strategic Management Journal*, *32*(3), 322–341. https://doi.org/10.1002/smj.880

Chang, Y. Y., Mellahi, K., & Wilkinson, A. (2009). Control of subsidiaries of MNCs from emerging economies in developed countries: The case of Taiwanese MNCs in the UK. *The International Journal of Human Resource Management*, *20*(1), 75–95. https://doi.org/10.1080/09585190802528383

Chattopadhyay, P., Glick, W. H., & Huber, G. P. (2001). Organizational actions in response to threats and opportunities. *Academy of Management Journal*, *44*(5), 937–955.

Chew, I. K., & Horwitz, F. M. (2004). Human resource management strategies in practice: Case-study findings in multinational firms. *Asia Pacific Journal of Human Resources*, *42*(1), 32–56. https://doi.org/10.1177/1038411104041536

Chriss, J. J. (1995). Habermas, Goffman, and communicative action: Implications for professional practice. *American Sociological Review*, *60*(4), 545–565. https://doi.org/10.2307/2096294

Chuma, A. H. (2002). Employment adjustments in Japanese firms during the current crisis. *Industrial Relations: A Journal of Economy and Society*, *41*(4), 653–682. https://doi.org/10.1111/1468-232X.00268

Cogin, J. A., & Williamson, I. O. (2014). Standardize or customize: The interactive effects of HRM and environment uncertainty on MNC subsidiary performance. *Human Resource Management*, *53*(5), 701–721. https://doi.org/10.1002/hrm.21602

Comaroff, J., & Comaroff, J. (2019). *Ethnography and the historical imagination*. Routledge.

Contu, D. (2002). Organizational structure: How resilience works. *Harvard Business Review*, (May)

Cook, H., MacKenzie, R., & Forde, C. (2016). HRM and performance: The vulnerability of soft HRM practices during recession and retrenchment. *Human Resource Management Journal*, *26*(4), 557–571. https://doi.org/10.1111/1748-8583.12122

Cooke, F. L., Cooper, B., Bartram, T., Wang, J., & Mei, H. (2019). Mapping the relationships between high-performance work systems, employee resilience and engagement: A study of the banking industry in China. *The International Journal of Human Resource Management*, *30*(8), 1239–1260. https://doi.org/10.1080/09585192.2015.1137618

Cooke, F. L., Liu, M., Liu, L. A., & Chen, C. C. (2019). Human resource management and industrial relations in multinational corporations in and from China: Challenges and new insights. *Human Resource Management*, *58*(5), 455–471. https://doi.org/10.1002/hrm.21986

Cooke, F. L., Veen, A., & Wood, G. (2017). What do we know about cross-country comparative studies in HRM? A critical review of literature in the period of 2000-2014. *The International Journal of Human Resource Management*, *28*(1), 196–233. https://doi.org/10.1080/09585192.2016.1245671

Cooke, F. L., Wood, G., & Horwitz, F. (2015). Multinational firms from emerging economies in Africa: Implications for research and practice in human resource management. *The International Journal of Human Resource Management*, *26*(21), 2653–2675. https://doi.org/10.1080/09585192.2015.1071546

Cooke, F. L., Wood, G., Wang, M., & Veen, A. (2019). How far has international HRM travelled? A systematic review of literature on multinational corporations (2000–2014). *Human Resource Management Review*, *29*(1), 59–75. https://doi.org/10.1016/j.hrmr.2018.05.001

Cooper, C. L., Liu, Y., & Tarba, S. Y. (2014).Resilience, HRM practices and impact on organizational performance and employee well-being. *International Journal of Human Resource Management*, *25*(17), 2466-2471.

Coutts, A. (2019). Good news and bad news are still news: Experimental evidence on belief updating. *Experimental Economics*, *22*(2), 369–395. https://doi.org/10.1007/s10683-018-9572-5

Coutu, D. L. (2002). How resilience works. *Harvard Business Review*, *80*(5), 46–56.

Cumming, D. J., Wood, G., & Zahra, S. A. (2020). Human resource management practices in the context of rising right-wing populism. *Human Resource Management Journal*, *30*(4), 525–536. https://doi.org/10.1111/1748-8583.12269

Davies, S. E., Stoermer, S., & Froese, F. J. (2019). When the going gets tough: The influence of expatriate resilience and perceived organizational inclusion climate on work adjustment and turnover intentions. *The International Journal of Human Resource Management*, *30*(8), 1393–1417. https://doi.org/10.1080/09585192.2018.1528558

Demirbag, M., & Wood, G. (2018). *Comparative Capitalism and the Transitional Periphery: Firm Centred Perspectives*, Edward Elgar. Cheltenham, UK.

Demirbag, M., Collings, D. G., Tatoglu, E., Mellahi, K., & Wood, G. (2014). High-performance work systems and organizational performance in emerging economies: Evidence from MNEs in Turkey. *Management International Review*, *54*(3), 325–359. https://doi.org/10.1007/s11575-014-0204-9

Demirbag, M., Tatoglu, E., & Wilkinson, A. (2016). Adoption of high-performance work systems by local subsidiaries of developed country and Turkish MNEs and indigenous firms in Turkey. *Human Resource Management*, *55* (6), 1001–1024. https://doi.org/10.1002/hrm.21706

Dibben, P., Brewster, C., Brookes, M., Cunha, R., Webster, E., & Wood, G. (2017). Institutional legacies and HRM: Similarities and differences in HRM practices in Portugal and Mozambique. *The International Journal of Human Resource Management*, *28*(18), 2519–2537. https://doi.org/10.1080/09585192.2016.1164225

DiMaggio, P. J., & Powell, W. W. (1983). The iron cage revisited: Institutional isomorphism and collective rationality in organizational fields. *American Sociological Review*, *48*(2), 147–160. [Database] https://doi.org/10.2307/2095101

Drost, H., Frayne, C., Lowe, K., & Geringer, J. M. (2002). Benchmarking training and development practices: A multi-country comparative analysis. *Human Resource Management*, *41*(1), 67–86. https://doi.org/10.1002/hrm.10020

Duncan, R. B. (1972). Characteristics of organizational environments and perceived environmental uncertainty. *Administrative Science Quarterly*, *17*(3), 313–327. https://doi.org/10.2307/2392145

Engelen, A., Schmidt, S., & Buchsteiner, M. (2015). The simultaneous influence of national culture and market turbulence on entrepreneurial orientation: A nine-country study. *Journal of International Management*, *21*(1), 18–30. https://doi.org/10.1016/j.intman.2014.12.002

Ererdi, C., Nurgabdeshov, A., Kozhakhmet, S., Rofcanin, Y., & Demirbag, M. (2021). International HRM in the context of uncertainty and crisis: A systematic review of literature (2000–2018). *The International Journal of Human Resource Management*. https://doi.org/10.1080/09585192.2020.1863247

Felstead, A. (2018). Tracing the connections: Short-termism, training and the recession. *The International Journal of Human Resource Management*, *29*(4), 664–682. https://doi.org/10.1080/09585192.2016.1184176

Ferner, A., & Quintanilla, J. (1998). Multinationals, national business systems and HRM: The enduring influence of national identity or a process of 'Anglo-Saxonization. *The International Journal of Human Resource Management*, *9*(4), 710–731. https://doi.org/10.1080/095851998340973

Fields, D., Chan, A., Akhtar, S., & Blum, T. C. (2006). Human resource management strategies under uncertainty. *Cross Cultural Management. An International Journal*, *13*(2), 167–189.

Fong, C. P., & Wyer, R. S.Jr, (2003). Cultural, social, and emotional determinants of decisions under uncertainty. *Organizational Behavior and Human Decision Processes*, *90*(2), 304–322. https://doi.org/10.1016/S0749-5978(02)00528-9

Frankl, V. E. (2017). *Man's Search for Meaning*. Beacon Press.

Fredrickson, B. L., Tugade, M. M., Waugh, C. E., & Larkin, G. R. (2003). What good are positive emotions in crisis? A prospective study of resilience and emotions following the terrorist attacks on the United States on September 11th, 2001. *Journal of Personality and Social Psychology*, *84*(2), 365–378. https://doi.org/10.1037/0022-3514.84.2.365

Gannon, J., & Paraskevas, A. (2017). In the line of fire: Managing expatriates in hostile environments. *The International Journal of Human Resource Management*, *30-11*, 1737–1768.

Glover, L., & Wilkinson, A. (2007). Worlds colliding: The translation of modern management practices within a UK based subsidiary of a Korean-owned MNC. *The International Journal of Human Resource Management*, *18*(8), 1437–1455.

Goergen, M., Chahine, S., Brewster, C., & Wood, G. (2021). Context, governance, associational trust and HRM: diversity and commonalities. *The International Journal of Human Resource Management*. https://doi.org/10.1080/09585192.2020.1841817

Gooderham, P., Nordhaug, O., & Ringdal, K. (1999). Institutional and rational determinants of organizational practices: Human resource management in European firms. *Administrative Science Quarterly*, *44*(3), 507–531. https://doi.org/10.2307/2666960

Grainger, R. J., & Miyamoto, T. (2003). Human values and HRM practice: The Japanese Shukko system. *Journal of Human Values*, *9*(2), 105–115. https://doi.org/10.1177/097168580300900202

Grote, G. (2007). Understanding and assessing safety culture through the lens of organizational management of uncertainty. *Safety Science*, *45*(6), 637–652. https://doi.org/10.1016/j.ssci.2007.04.002

Gunkel, M., Schlägel, C., & Engle, R. L. (2014). Culture's influence on emotional intelligence: An empirical study of nine countries. *Journal of International Management*, *20*(2), 256–274. https://doi.org/10.1016/j.intman.2013.10.002

Hall, P. A., & Soskice, D. (Eds.), (2001). *An introduction to varieties of capitalism*. Oxford University Press.

Hannon, J. M., Huang, I.-C., & Jaw, B.-S. (1995). International human resources strategy and its determinants: The case of subsidiaries in Taiwan. *Journal of International Business Studies*, *26*(3), 531–554. https://doi.org/10.1057/palgrave.jibs.8490185

Hauff, S., Alewell, D., & Hansen, N. K. (2014). HRM systems between control and commitment: Occurrence, characteristics and effects on HRM outcomes and firm performance. *Human Resource Management Journal*, *24*(4), 424–441. https://doi.org/10.1111/1748-8583.12054

Hensher, D. A. (2020). What might Covid-19 mean for mobility as a service (MaaS)?*Transport Reviews*, *40* (5), 551–556. https://doi.org/10.1080/01441647.2020.1770487

Heyes, J. (2011). Flexicurity, employment protection and the jobs crisis. *Work, Employment and Society*, *25*(4), 642–657. https://doi.org/10.1177/0950017011419723

Hofstede, G. (2001). *Culture's consequences: Comparing values, behaviors, institutions and organizations across nations*. Sage publications.

Hofstede, G. (1980). *Cultural Consequences*. Sage.

Hofstede, G. (1991). *Cultures and organizations: Software of the mind*. McGraw-Hill.

Holmes, R. M., Jr, Miller, T., Hitt, M. A., & Salmador, M. P. (2013). The interrelationships among informal institutions, formal institutions, and inward foreign direct investment. *Journal of Management*, *39*(2), 531–566. https://doi.org/10.1177/0149206310393503

Horwitz, F. (2017). International HRM in South African multinational companies. *Journal of International Management*, *23*(2), 208–222. https://doi.org/10.1016/j.intman.2017.01.005

Horwitz, F. M. (2012). Evolving human resource management in Southern African multinational firms: Towards an Afro-Asian nexus. *The International Journal of Human Resource Management*, *23*(14), 2938–2958. https://doi.org/10.1080/09585192.2012.671512

Howie, L. (2007). The terrorism threat and managing workplaces. *Disaster Prevention and Management: An International Journal*, *16*(1), 70–78. https://doi.org/10.1108/09653560710729820

Huang, L. C., & Harris, M. B. (1973). Conformity in Chinese and Americans: A field experiment. *Journal of Cross-Cultural Psychology*, *4*(4), 427–434. https://doi.org/10.1177/002202217300400404

Hui, C., & Lee, C. (2000). Moderating effects of organization-based self-esteem on organizational uncertainty: Employee response relationships. *Journal of Management*, *26*(2), 215–232. https://doi.org/10.1177/014920630002600203

Hui, C., & Tan, C. K. (1996). Employee motivation and attitudes in the Chinese workplace. In Bond, M. H. (Ed.), *The handbook of Chinese psychology.*, Oxford University Press.

Hyman, R. (1997). The future of employee representation. *British Journal of Industrial Relations*, *35*(3), 309–336. https://doi.org/10.1111/1467-8543.00057

Jiang, J., Wang, S., & Zhao, S. (2012). Does HRM facilitate employee creativity and organizational innovation? A study of Chinese firms. *The International Journal of Human Resource Management*, *23*(19), 4025–4047. https://doi.org/10.1080/09585192.2012.690567

Kalleberg, A. L., & Vallas, S. P. (2018). Probing precarious work: Theory, research, and politics. *Research in the Sociology of Work*, *31*(1), 1–30.

Kamoche, K., Siebers, L. Q., Mamman, A., & Newenham-Kahindi, A. (2015). The dynamics of managing people in the diverse cultural and institutional context of Africa. *Personnel Review*, *44*(3), 330–378. https://doi.org/10.1108/PR-01-2015-0002

Katou, A. A., Budhwar, P. S., & Patel, C. (2021). Idiosyncratic deals in less competitive labor markets: Testing career i-deals in the Greek context of high uncertainties. *The International Journal of Human Resource Management*. https://doi.org/10.1080/09585192.2020.1759672

Khan, Z., Rao-Nicholson, R., Akhtar, P., Tarba, S., Ahammad, M., & Vorley, T. (2019). The role of HR practices in developing employee resilience: A case study from the Pakistani telecommunications sector. *The International Journal of Human Resource Management*, *30*(8), 1342–1369. https://doi.org/10.1080/09585192.2017.1316759

Kim, S., & McLean, G. N. (2014). The impact of national culture on informal learning in the workplace. *Adult Education Quarterly*, *64*(1), 39–59. https://doi.org/10.1177/0741713613504125

Knox, A., & Walsh, J. (2005). Organisational flexibility and HRM in the hotel industry: Evidence from Australia. *Human Resource Management Journal*, *15*(1), 57–75. https://doi.org/10.1111/j.1748-8583.2005.tb00140.x

Kossek, E. E., & Perrigino, M. B. (2016). Resilience: A review using a grounded integrated occupational approach. *Academy of Management Annals*, *10*(1), 00–255. https://doi.org/10.5465/19416520.2016.1159878

Kozica, A., & Kaiser, S. (2012). A sustainability perspective on flexible HRM: How to cope with paradoxes of contingent work. *Management Revue*, *23*(3), 239–261. https://doi.org/10.5771/0935-9915-2012-3-239

Lahteenmaki, S., Storey, J., & Vanhala, S. (1998). HRM and company performance: The use of measurement and the influence of economic cycles. *Human Resource Management Journal*, *8*(2), 51–65. https://doi.org/10.1111/j.1748-8583.1998.tb00166.x

Lallement, M. (2011). Europe and the economic crisis: Forms of labour market adjustment and varieties of capitalism. *Work, Employment and Society*, *25*(4), 627–641. https://doi.org/10.1177/0950017011419717

Lawrence, P. R., & Lorsch, J. W. (1967). Organization and Environment. *Administrative Science Quarterly*, *12*(1), 1–47. https://doi.org/10.2307/2391211

Lazonick, W., & Shin, J. S. (2019). *Predatory value extraction: How the looting of the business enterprise became the US norm and how sustainable prosperity can be restored.* Oxford University Press.

Lew, A. A., Cheer, J. M., Haywood, M., Brouder, P., & Salazar, N. B. (2020). Visions of travel and tourism after the global COVID-19 transformation of 2020. *Tourism Geographies*, *22*(3), 455–466. https://doi.org/10.1080/14616688.2020.1770326

Lewis, S., Anderson, D., Lyonette, C., Payne, N., & Wood, S. (Eds.) (2016). *Work-life balance in times of recession, austerity and beyond: Meeting the needs of employees, organizations and social justice.* Taylor & Francis.

Linnenluecke, M. K. (2017). Resilience in business and management research: A review of influential publications and a research agenda. *International Journal of Management Reviews*, *19*(1), 4–30. https://doi.org/10.1111/ijmr.12076

Luthans, F. (2002). Positive organizational behavior: Developing and managing psychological strengths. *Academy of Management Perspectives*, *16*(1), 57–72. https://doi.org/10.5465/ame.2002.6640181

Mainiero, L. A., & Gibson, D. E. (2003). Managing employee trauma: Dealing with the emotional fallout from. *Academy of Management Perspectives*, *17*(3), 130–11. 130, –143. https://doi.org/10.5465/ame.2003.10954782

Makhmadshoev, D., & Laaser, K. (2021). Breaking away or holding on to the past? Exploring HRM systems of export-oriented SMEs in a highly uncertain context:

insights from a transition economy in the periphery. *The International Journal of Human Resource Management*. https://doi.org/10.1080/09585192.2020.1841816

McSweeney, B. (2002). Hofstede's model of national cultural differences and their consequences: A triumph of faith-a failure of analysis. *Human Relations*, *55*(1), 89–118. https://doi.org/10.1177/0018726702551004

Mellahi, K., Demirbag, M., Collings, D. G., Tatoglu, E., & Hughes, M. (2013). Similarly different: A comparison of HRM practices in MNE subsidiaries and local firms in Turkey. *The International Journal of Human Resource Management*, *24*(12), 2339–2368. https://doi.org/10.1080/09585192.2013.781434

Meyer, A. D. (1982). Adapting to environmental jolts. *Administrative Science Quarterly*, *27*(4), 515–537. https://doi.org/10.2307/2392528

Michalski, M., Śliwa, M., & Manalsuren, S. (2021). Context-specific understandings of uncertainty: a focus on people management practices in Mongolia. *The International Journal of Human Resource Management*. https://doi.org/10.1080/09585192.2020.1819856

Miller, D. (1991). Stale in the saddle: CEO tenure and the match between organization and environment. *Management Science*, *37*(1), 34–52. https://doi.org/10.1287/mnsc.37.1.34

Milliken, F. (1987). Three types of perceived uncertainty about the environment: State, effect, and response uncertainty. *Academy of Management Review*, *12*(1), 133–143. https://doi.org/10.5465/amr.1987.4306502

Morgan, G. (2007). National business systems research: Progress and prospects. *Scandinavian Journal of Management*, *23*(2), 127–145. https://doi.org/10.1016/j.scaman.2007.02.008

Morris, S. S. & Calamai, R. (2009). Dynamic HR: Global applications from IBM. *Human Resource Management*, *48*(4), 641–648.

Morris, J., Hassard, J., & McCann, L. (2006). New organizational forms, human resource management and structural convergence? A study of Japanese organizations. *Organization Studies*, *27*(10), 1485–1511. https://doi.org/10.1177/0170840606067513

Mulholland, K. (2011). In search of teamworking in a major supermarket: A fig-leaf for flexibility? In: Grugulis, I., & Bozkurt, O. (Eds.), *Critical Perspectives on Work and Employment: Retail Work*. Palgrave Macmillan. 213–233.

Naveed, S., & Rana, N. S. (2013).Job burnout process and its implications in HRM practices: A case study of trainee doctors in public health organization. *Asian Journal of Business Management*, *5*(1),113-123.

North, D. C. (1990). *Institutions, institutional change and economic performance*. Cambridge university press.

Oh, C. H., & Oetzel, J. (2011). Multinationals' response to major disasters: How does subsidiary investment vary in response to the type of disaster and the quality of country governance?*Strategic Management Journal*, *32*(6), 658–681. https://doi.org/10.1002/smj.904

Ollier-Malaterre, A. (2010). Contributions of work—Life and resilience initiatives to the individual/organization relationship. *Human Relations*, *63*(1), 41–62. https://doi.org/10.1177/0018726709342458

Parsons, T. (1972). Culture and social system revisited. *Social Science Quarterly*, *53*(2), 253–266.

Peccei, R., & Rosenthal, P. (2001). Delivering customer oriented behavior through empowerment: An empirical test of HRM assumptions. *Journal of Management Studies*, *38*(6), 831–857. https://doi.org/10.1111/1467-6486.00261

Pennings, J. M. (1981). Strategically interdependent organizations. In *Handbook of Organizational Design*, *1* (pp. 433–455). Oxford University Press.

Pennings, J. M., & Tripathi, R. C. (1978). The organization-environment relationship: Dimensional versus typological viewpoints. In Karpik, L. (Ed.), *Organizations and environments: Theory, issues and reality* (pp. 171–195). Sage Publications.

Pfeffer, J., & Salancik, G. (1978). *The external control of organizations: A resource dependence perspective.* Harper and Row.

Phan, P. H., & Wood, G. (2020). Doomsday scenarios (or the Black Swan excuse for unpreparedness. *Academy of Management Perspectives, 34*(4), 425–433. https://doi.org/10.5465/amp.2020.0133

Pollard, T. M. (2001). Changes in mental well-being, blood pressure and total cholesterol levels during workplace reorganization: The impact of uncertainty. *Work & Stress, 15*(1), 14–28. https://doi.org/10.1080/02678370110064609

Ramirez, J., Madero, S., & Muñiz, C. (2016). The impact of narcoterrorism on HRM systems. *The International Journal of Human Resource Management, 27*(19), 2202–2232. https://doi.org/10.1080/09585192.2015.1091371

Ramsay, H. (1977). Cycles of control: Worker participation in sociological and historical perspective. *Sociology, 11*(3), 481–506. https://doi.org/10.1177/003803857701100304

Reade, C. (2009). Human resource management implications of terrorist threats to firms in the supply chain. *International Journal of Physical Distribution & Logistics Management, 39*(6), 469–485. https://doi.org/10.1108/09600030910985820

Redding, G. (2005). The thick description and comparison of societal systems of capitalism. *Journal of International Business Studies, 36*(2), 123–155. https://doi.org/10.1057/palgrave.jibs.8400129

Redding, G., & Wong, G. Y. Y. (1986). Chinese organizational behaviour. In Bond, M. H. (Ed.), *The psychology of the Chinese people* (pp. 267–295). Oxford University Press.

Reunanen, E., & Kunelius, R. (2020). The transformation of communicative power into political power. *Communication Theory, 30*(1), 1–20.

Robertson, I. T., Cooper, C. L., Sarkar, M., & Curran, T. (2015). Resilience training in the workplace from 2003 to 2014: A systematic review. *Journal of Occupational and Organizational Psychology, 88*(3), 533–562. https://doi.org/10.1111/joop.12120

Robertson, I., & Cooper, C. (2011). *Well-being: Productivity and happiness at work.* Palgrave Macmillan.

Roche, B., Teague, P., Coughlan, A., & Fahy, M. (2013). *Recession at work: HRM in the Irish crisis.* Routledge.

Rosenzweig, P. M., & Nohria, N. (1994). Influences on human resource management practices in multinational corporations. *Journal of International Business Studies, 25*(2), 229–242. https://doi.org/10.1057/palgrave.jibs.8490199

Rousseau, D. M., Ho, V. T., & Greenberg, J. (2006). I-deals: Idiosyncratic terms in employment relationships. *Academy of Management Review, 31*(4), 977–994. https://doi.org/10.5465/amr.2006.22527470

Rust, R. T., & Lemon, K. N. (2001). E-service and the consumer. *International Journal of Electronic Commerce, 5*(3), 85–101. https://doi.org/10.1080/10864415.2001.11044216

Sanzo, M., & Vázquez, R. V. (2011). The influence of customer relationship marketing strategies on supply chain relationships: The moderating effects of environmental uncertainty and competitive rivalry. *Journal of Business-to-Business Marketing, 18*(1), 50–82. https://doi.org/10.1080/10517121003717799

Schooler, C. (1996). William Caudill and the reproduction of culture: Infant, child, and maternal behavior in Japan and the United States. In Schwalb, B., and Schwalb, D (Eds.), *Japanese childrearing: Two generations of scholarship.* Guilford Press. 139–176.

Schotter, A. P., Meyer, K., & Wood, G. (2021). Organizational and comparative institutionalism in international HRM: Toward an integrative research agenda. *Human Resource Management, 60*(1), 205–227. https://doi.org/10.1002/hrm.22053

Seeck, H., & Diehl, M. R. (2017). A literature review on HRM and innovation–taking stock and future directions. *The International Journal of Human Resource Management*, *28*(6), 913–944. https://doi.org/10.1080/09585192.2016.1143862

Seligman, M. E. (1998). President's column: Building human strength: Psychology's forgotten mission. *APA Monitor*, *29* (1), 1.

Serafini, G. O., & Szamosi, L. T. (2021). Variations and differences in the application of HR policies and practices by US hotel multinational firm's subsidiaries across coordinated and transitional periphery economies: a case approach. *The International Journal of Human Resource Management*. https://doi.org/10.1080/09585192.2020.182 8993

Shipton, H., West, M. A., Dawson, J., Birdi, K., & Patterson, M. (2006). HRM as a predictor of innovation. *Human Resource Management Journal*, *16*(1), 3–27. https://doi.org/10.1111/j.1748-8583.2006.00002.x

Singer, P. (2011). *Practical ethics*. Cambridge University Press.

Sirmon, D. G., & Lane, P. J. (2004). A model of cultural differences and international alliance performance. *Journal of International Business Studies*, *35*(4), 306–319. https://doi.org/10.1057/palgrave.jibs.8400089

Sparrow, P. (2012). Globalising the international mobility function: The role of emerging markets, flexibility and strategic delivery models. *The International Journal of Human Resource Management*, *23*(12), 2404–2427. https://doi.org/10.1080/09585192. 2012.668384

Stajkovic, A. D. (2006). Development of a core confidence-higher order construct. *The Journal of Applied Psychology*, *91*(6), 1208–1234. https://doi.org/10.1037/0021-9010.91.6.1208

Staw, B. M., Sandelands, L. E., & Dutton, J. E. (1981). Threat rigidity effects in organizational behavior: A multilevel analysis. *Administrative Science Quarterly*, *26*(4), 501–524. https://doi.org/10.2307/2392337

Stich, J. F., Tarafdar, M., & Cooper, C. L. (2018). Electronic communication in the workplace: Boon or bane?*Journal of Organizational Effectiveness: People and Performance*, *5*(1), 98–106. https://doi.org/10.1108/JOEPP-05-2017-0046

Suder, G., Reade, C., Riviere, M., Birnik, A., & Nielsen, N. (2019). Mind the gap: The role of HRM in creating, capturing and leveraging rare knowledge in hostile environments. *The International Journal of Human Resource Management*, *30*(11), 1794–1821.

Tasavori, M., Eftekhar, N., Elyasi, G. M., & Zaefarian, R. (2021). Human resource capabilities in uncertain environments. *The International Journal of Human Resource Management*. https://doi.org/10.1080/09585192.2020.1845776

Tatoglu, E., Glaister, A. J., & Demirbag, M. (2016). Talent management motives and practices in an emerging market: A comparison between MNEs and local firms. *Journal of World Business*, *51*(2), 278–293. https://doi.org/10.1016/j.jwb.2015.11.001

Thompson, P. (2003). Disconnected capitalism: Or why employers can't keep their side of the bargain. *Work, Employment and Society*, *17*(2), 359–378. https://doi.org/10.1177/0950017003017002007

Tregaskis, O. (1997). The role of national context and HR strategy in shaping training and development practice in French and UK organizations. *Organization Studies*, *18*(5), 839–856.

Tsao, C. W., Newman, A., Chen, S. J., & Wang, M. J. (2016). HRM retrenchment practices and firm performance in times of economic downturn: Exploring the moderating effects of family involvement in management. *The International Journal*

of Human Resource Management, *27*(9), 954–973. https://doi.org/10.1080/09585192.2
015.1072098

Tugade, M. M., & Fredrickson, B. L. (2004). Resilient individuals use positive emotions
to bounce back from negative emotional experiences. *Journal of Personality and
Social Psychology*, *86*(2), 320–335.

van der Vegt, G. S., Essens, P., Wahlström, M., & George, G. (2015). Managing risk
and resilience. *Academy of Management Journal*, *50*(4), 971–980.

van der Vorst, J. G., & Beulens, A. J. (2002). Identifying sources of uncertainty to
generate supply chain redesign strategies. *International Journal of Physical Distribution
& Logistics Management*, *32*(6), 409–430. https://doi.org/10.1108/09600030210437951

Vigdor, J. (2008). The economic aftermath of Hurricane Katrina. *Journal of Economic
Perspectives*, *22*(4), 135–154. https://doi.org/10.1257/jep.22.4.135

Van De Voorde, K., & Beijer, S.(2015). The role of employee HR attributions in the
relationship between high-performance work systems and employee outcomes. *Human
Resource Management Journal*, *25*(1), 62-78.

Walker, B., Holling, C. S., Carpenter, S. R., & Kinzig, A. (2004). Resilience, adaptability and transformability in social–ecological systems. *Ecology and Society*, *9*(2), 5–8.
[Database] https://doi.org/10.5751/ES-00650-090205

Wall, T., & Wood, S. (2005). The romance of human resource management and business performance, and the case for big science. *Human Relations*, *58*(4), 429–462.
https://doi.org/10.1177/0018726705055032

Wang, J., Cooke, F. L., & Huang, W. (2014). How resilient is the (future) workforce in
C hina? A study of the banking sector and implications for human resource development. *Asia Pacific Journal of Human Resources*, *52*(2), 132–154. https://doi.
org/10.1111/1744-7941.12026

Waugh, C. E., Fredrickson, B. L., & Taylor, S. F. (2008). Adapting to life's slings and
arrows: Individual differences in resilience when recovering from an anticipated
threat. *Journal of Research in Personality*, *42*(4), 1031–1046. https://doi.org/10.1016/j.
jrp.2008.02.005

Whitley, R. (1994). *Business systems*. Manchester Business School.

Wilkinson, A., & Wood, G. (2012). Institutions and employment relations: The state
of the art. *Industrial Relations: A Journal of Economy and Society*, *51*(3), 373–388.

Wilkinson, A., Wood, G., & Deeg, R. (eds.) (2014). *The Oxford handbook of employment
relations: Comparative employment systems*. Oxford University Press.

Williams, T. A., & Shepherd, D. A. (2016). Building resilience or providing sustenance:
Different paths of emergent ventures in the aftermath of Haiti earthquake. *Academy
of Management Journal*, *59*(6), 2069–2102.

Williams, N., & Vorley, T. (2015). Institutional asymmetry: How formal and informal
institutions affect entrepreneurship in Bulgaria. *International Small Business Journal:
Researching Entrepreneurship*, *33*(8), 840–861. https://doi.org/10.1177/0266242614534280

Wöcke, A., Bendixen, M., & Rijamampianina, R. (2007). Building flexibility into
multi-national human resource strategy: A study of four South African multi-national
enterprises. *The International Journal of Human Resource Management*, *18*(5), 829–844.
https://doi.org/10.1080/09585190701249115

Wood, G., & Bischoff, C. (2020). Human resource management in Africa: Current
research and future directions–evidence from South Africa and across the continent.
The International Journal of Human Resource Management, 1–28. https://doi.org/10.
1080/09585192.2019.1711443

Wood, G., Mazouz, K., Yin, Y., & Cheah, J. (2014). Foreign direct investment from emerging markets to Africa: The HRM context. *Human Resource Management, 53*(1), 179–201. https://doi.org/10.1002/hrm.21550

Wood, S., & de Menezes, L. (1998). High commitment management in the UK: Evidence from the Workplace Industrial Relations Survey and the Employer's Manpower Skills Practices Survey. *Human Relations, 51*(4), 485–515. https://doi.org/10.1177/001872679805100403

Youssef, C. M., & Luthans, F. (2007). Positive organizational behavior in the workplace: The impact of hope, optimism, and resilience. *Journal of Management, 33*(5), 774–800. https://doi.org/10.1177/0149206307305562

Zoogah, D. B., Metwally, E. K., & Tantoush, T. (2018). HRM in Northern Africa. In Brewster, C., Mayrhofer, W., & Farndale, E. (Eds.). *Handbook of research on comparative human resource management* (2nd ed.,500–517). Edward Elgar Publishing.

Zucker, L. G. (1987). Institutional theories of organization. *Annual Review of Sociology, 13*(1), 443–464. https://doi.org/10.1146/annurev.so.13.080187.002303

Context-specific understandings of uncertainty: a focus on people management practices in Mongolia

Marina Michalski, Martyna Śliwa and Saranzaya Manalsuren

ABSTRACT

This paper addresses the link between local understandings of uncertainty and people management practices in the under-researched and uncertain context of Mongolia. It draws on a qualitative, interpretive study of 34 top and middle managers with people management responsibilities in Mongolian organisations. We put forward the concept of a 'mindset *about* uncertainty' for examining Mongolian practitioners' understandings of and responses to the uncertainty inherent in the country's institutional environment. We identify four elements of the Mongolian mindset about uncertainty: (1) belief that impermanence is natural; (2) consideration of uncertainty as normal; (3) framing of uncertainty as positive; and (4) emphasis on flexibility in adapting to changing circumstances. We discuss this approach to dealing with uncertainty as a potentially valuable source of learning for Multinational Enterprises (MNEs) and International Human Resource Development (IHRD) practitioners in unstable environments.

Introduction

There is much to be learned about how organisations can remain resilient in unstable environments (Cunha & Clegg, 2019; Jordaan, 2019; Williams et al., 2017). Attempts to measure uncertainty can help in this regard; however, a different, yet potentially insightful approach to this learning involves clarifying how uncertainty is understood, and what skills are deemed relevant for managers and employees (Buchanan & Hällgren, 2019; Dibben et al., 2017; Williams et al., 2017). This is particularly important in relation to people management, as developing human resources supports organisational survival and resilience in crisis-fostering environments (Dibben et al., 2017; Hutchins & Wang, 2009; Williams et al., 2017).

Assessing which human resource management (HRM) approaches are appropriate is a context-dependent task (Budhwar et al., 2016; Pudelko et al., 2015). HRM is embedded in country level institutions, be they regulative systems or culturally shaped norms and cognitions (Björkman et al., 2008; Björkman & Welch, 2015; Edwards et al., 2019). Reciprocal interactions between institutional and cultural contexts shape values, behaviours and opinions about acceptable conduct and people management approaches (Reiche et al., 2018). Nevertheless, making sense of the interactions between regulative, normative and cultural-cognitive institutional dimensions (Scott, 2014) is crucial to multinational enterprises' (MNEs') ability to devise appropriate HRM policies (Brewster, Wood & Brookes, 2008; Edwards et al., 2019).

This paper contributes to international human resource management (IHRM) research by addressing the link between local understandings of uncertainty and people management in the Mongolian context, through mobilising the concept of mindsets (see Stokes et al., 2016) as an analytical device. Rather than aiming to theorise about mindsets *per se*, we extend the discussion of mindsets *about* multiple phenomena and specific management issues (Caniëls, Semeijn & Renders, 2018; Keating & Heslin, 2015; Wicks et al., 2012) by putting forward the concept of *mindsets about uncertainty* within the target research context. Following Murphy and Dweck (2010), we see individual and collective levels of mindsets as interacting with each other, and embrace a working definition of mindsets as composed of particularly relevant context-specific beliefs, assumptions and cognitive framings. We also articulate *mindsets about uncertainty* as incorporating behavioural rationales, predispositions, coping resources and repertoires (Andresen & Bergdolt, 2017; Stokes et al., 2016; Swidler, 1986).

Throughout the paper, uncertainty is conceptualised with reference to subjective meaning-making (e.g. Edwards et al., 2008; Magnani & Zhucchella, 2018; Rathbun, 2007). In line with Magnani and Zhucchella (2018), we consider organisations' ability to deal with uncertainty – or even leverage its positive aspects (De Villa & Rajwani, 2013) – as linked to managerial cognitive limits and perceptions of risk, and as framed by complex socio-cultural and institutional contexts (Edwards et al., 2008). Therefore, rather than focusing on categorisations and measurement of uncertainty and associated responses, our main motivation is to generate knowledge of the more abstract underpinnings of people's responses to uncertainty within our research context (Lowe et al., 2015). Drawing on an indigenous perspective (Lowe et al., 2015) on uncertainty allows us to complement extant body of research, and to draw conclusions for contextually-sensitive (I)HRM practice.

Although as yet an under-researched context (Demirbag & Wood, 2018), Mongolia provides a useful site for enriching the debate on coping with a highly uncertain institutional environment. Uncertainty in Mongolia is not rooted in extreme conditions – such as terrorism, violent disorder, crime or other physical risks. Rather, the country is characterised by 'initially seemingly peaceful forms of uncertainty', which, nevertheless, create 'considerable ambiguity for businesses and how they manage their people' (Wood et al., 2018, p. 1365). Notwithstanding the economic growth since 2000, businesses in Mongolia have been exposed to political, economic and legal unpredictability (Authors; World Bank, 2020). Uncertainty in the country is reinforced by socio-economic disparities, an over-reliance on unexpected resource booms, a high risk of climate shocks, fluctuating foreign direct investment, and limited progress with banking sector and anti-money laundering reforms (Best's Country Risk Report, 2019; World Bank, 2020).

The above challenges render Mongolia's business context highly unpredictable. They also present a research opportunity for generating insights about how complexities of an uncertain context shape people's mindsets about uncertainly. Focusing on Mongolia contributes to building knowledge that is potentially applicable to MNEs' practices, especially with respect to developing a context-sensitive approach to international HRM. Moreover, conducting a study in an under-researched periphery country serves to address the issue of biased conclusions and generalisations that are often associated with studies based in Western and developed contexts (Garavan et al., 2019).

We draw on qualitative material gathered from managers in Mongolian organisations, to create insights into local understandings of uncertainty and their influence on practices associated with people management. There is value in identifying locally generated people management practices (Kutaula et al., 2019). The companies in our sample, many of which are SMEs with weakly structured HRM systems, can be considered key 'learning sites' for MNEs interested in implementing contextually appropriate, sustainable and effective HRM policies and practices. The paper addresses the following questions: 1) How is uncertainty understood and approached by people management practitioners in Mongolian organisations? 2) What lessons for IHRM emerge from our analysis of the Mongolian mindset about uncertainty?

The paper contributes to IHRM research and practice by showing how behavioural rationales and predispositions with respect to uncertainty in Mongolia influence prevalent people management practices. It also contributes to existing literature through putting forward the concept of a 'mindset about uncertainty' as a tool for analysing context-specific understandings and responses to uncertainty. It demonstrates the importance of understanding local mindsets about uncertainty, with a view to designing and implementing effective HRM practices in a particular institutional context.

The following section situates uncertainty as subject to context-specific understandings and responses. We then discuss the concept of mindset, and consider its implications for people management and HRM practice at an international level. Next, we introduce the Mongolian context and explain our research methods. Subsequently, we discuss our findings and their implications with respect to IHRM research and practice, and conclude with outlining directions for further research.

A context-specific understanding of uncertainty

We focus on exploring understandings of uncertainty at the level of individual managers, and how their interpretations of uncertainty are framed by their complex socio-cultural context (Edwards et al., 2008). Following other scholars (e.g. Keating & Heslin, 2015; Murphy & Dweck, 2010), we consider individual and collective mindsets as connected. Consistently with this, our analysis is informed by the understanding that explanatory accounts of general contexts depend on researchers' ability to make sense of the particular (Welch et al., 2011).

This approach requires engagement with interpretations of unpredictability and associated subjective meaning-making (e.g. Edwards et al., 2008; Magnani & Zhucchella, 2018; Rathbun, 2007). For instance, individuals with a higher tolerance for ambiguity may perceive situations as less uncertain, or unpredictable situations as opportunities rather than threats (De Villa & Rajwani, 2013). Extending this logic over organisations, researchers have referred to productive affordances of unpredictable environments, such as enabling creativity and development of valuable competences (Edwards et al., 2019; McGaughey et al., 2016). There is also a growing emphasis on developing skills and competencies to increase organisational resilience under uncertainty (Cunha & Clegg, 2019; Jordaan, 2019; Teece et al., 2016; Williams et al., 2017). Importantly, improvisational capabilities originating within subsidiaries at the periphery may well be the source of MNEs' strategic renewal and innovation (Cunha et al., 2020). Therefore, multinational corporations from emerging markets (EMNCs), which previously were assumed to suffer from the 'liabilities of emergingness', are now also seen to potentially have 'adversity advantages' which they can use when expanding into various unstable contexts (Edwards et al., 2019; Ramamurti, 2009).

Although emerging economies can generally be described as highly uncertain and rapidly evolving, each of these contexts will necessarily have unique social institutions and configurations (Edwards et al., 2019; Kaynak et al., 2007; Serafini & Szamosi, 2015). Arguably, this will pose different sets of challenges for international HRM practitioners. For instance, there may be specific implications of uncertainty for particular HRM practices, such as recruitment or training. There may also be more far-reaching consequences for HRM governance, including the degree of decision-making centralisation, as well as value-laden evaluations of who the legitimate stakeholders are and what the firm's social responsibility should be (Edwards et al., 2019).

Generating insights into understandings and responses to uncertainty also involves a departure from simplistic categorisations of cultural distance attributed to non-Western settings (Kaynak et al., 2007), and from the often binary assumptions embedded in Western frames of reference (Chen & Miller, 2011; Herdin, 2012; Lowe et al., 2015). In the HRM sphere, for instance, Ulrich's (1997) well-known framework conceptualises HRM roles as separated into *either* 'strategic' *or* 'operational', and *either* 'people' *or* 'process' oriented. However, such dichotomous rationales may be of limited value for developing appropriate mechanisms for people management in uncertain environments (see also Mamman & Al Kulaiby, 2014).

Context-appropriate approaches do not only require an understanding of historically developed social and political institutions (Edwards et al. 2019; Kaynak et al., 2007; Scott 2014). They also call for an awareness of the more abstract, fundamental dimensions of contexts and people's reactions to them (Lowe et al., 2015). For example, understandings of and responses to uncertainty may reflect the extent of uncertainty to which country-specific contexts are exposed (Schneider & De Meyer, 1991; Williams et al., 2017). Depending on the context they live and work in, people develop habitual and proficient responses to familiar stimuli and recurring situations (Gronow, 2008). This perspective also resounds with Swidler's (1986, p. 277) view of culture as a toolkit of habits, skills and styles which become increasingly persistent, as people start to 'value ends for which their cultural equipment is well suited'.

In building context-specific knowledge about how uncertainty is understood and responded to, it is necessary to avoid gross generalisations and remain cautious towards frames of reference which represent cultural systems as unified, homogeneous, enduring and deterministic (Kaynak et al., 2007; McSweeney, 2012). However, it can also be productive to identify regularities within specific contexts (Pudelko et al., 2015). To accomplish this task, original insights can be generated through leveraging creative conceptual devices as tools for analysis. We consider one such tool to be the concept of 'mindset', which has already been used within organisation and international management studies (e.g. Meyer & Xin, 2018; Yari et al., 2020). Below we explain how it can be helpful in capturing managers' understandings of and responses to uncertainty, with an emphasis on people management practices in organisations operating in unstable environments.

Mindsets and their impact on people management under conditions of uncertainty

The concept of mindset was introduced to the academic literature in educational psychology, through Dweck's (1986, 2006) conceptualisation of 'fixed' and 'growth' mindsets. 'Mindset' has been defined as a mental framework composed of what people believe in and how they think, feel and act, with direct implications for the quality of their more instrumental achievements and ongoing personal development (Keating & Heslin, 2015). Mindsets are understood to incorporate personal attributes, cognitive knowledge and skills, motivation, and resources for adapting behaviour (Andresen & Bergdolt, 2017), which help shape behavioural rationales and predispositions (Stokes et al., 2016).

In Dweck's original conceptualisation (1986), a 'fixed' mindset was manifested in a person's belief that their skills and competences in a given sphere are pre-determined and unchanging. People with a 'growth' mindset, on the other hand, would believe in their ability to develop and grow, and act accordingly. Research into mindsets has addressed 'growth mindsets' and the feasibility of changing original mindsets (Clapp-Smith & Lester, 2014). Additionally, it has explored the necessary conditions for the cultivation of talent and intelligence (Keating & Heslin, 2015; Murphy & Dweck, 2010). Research has also highlighted that growth mindsets have positive implications for performance at the individual, relational and organisational levels (Han & Stieha, 2020).

In contrast to Dweck's original view of mindset as a characteristic of an individual, the concept of mindset has been further developed to consider the link between the individual and the collective levels, in that certain individual mindsets are endorsed collectively (Keating & Heslin, 2015; Murphy & Dweck, 2010), for example at a nation's level (Sparrow & Hiltrop, 1997). Underpinning this collective-based understanding of mindset is the idea that specific environmental conditions – such as, in a nation's case, exposure to the same sociocultural, economic and political circumstances – will result in similar mindsets amongst members of the collective (Yari et al., 2020). The type of mindset dominant in a certain geographical and cultural context will affect organisational practices, including HRM and HRD (Han & Stieha, 2020; Sparrow & Hiltrop, 1997; Stokes et al., 2016).

In management-related sub-fields such as international management and international HRM, the concept of mindset has most often been applied with reference to the 'global mindset' (e.g. Andresen & Bergdolt, 2017; Storgaard et al., 2020; Yari et al., 2020). A cultural complexity interpretation of this notion argues against an ethnocentric and dichotomous mindset in the practice of international HRM (Andresen & Bergdolt, 2017), and with regard to differences between the East and the West (Herdin, 2012; Lowe et al., 2015; Vu & Gill, 2019).

Another helpful concept for addressing managerial understandings of uncertainty and how they influence people management practices in a specific country is that of 'mindsets *about*' (Caniëls et al., 2018; Keating & Heslin, 2015; Wicks et al., 2012). In this respect, researchers have begun to discuss how individuals may have multiple mindsets, each one relating to specific phenomena, managerial issues (Wicks et al., 2012) or skills and abilities (Caniëls et al., 2018; Keating & Heslin, 2015; Williams et al., 2017). Acknowledging the existence of a multiplicity of mindsets about a variety of phenomena reinforces the need for more detailed and differentiated explanations of particular national context features in relation to the object of study. For our analysis, we put forward the concept of *mindset about uncertainty* and draw on it in studying, with a focus on people management, Mongolian managers' understandings and responses to uncertainty. This enables us to address the specificities of uncertainty-associated mindset features.

A further idea that contributes to the moderation of the characterisation of mindsets as ideal types emerges in Andresen and Bergdolt (2017) discussion of dimensions of mindsets. In their view, the dimensions comprising a mindset may carry different weighting. Such conceptualisation can allow for drawing conclusions regarding the degree to which there are regularities and context-specific beliefs, emotions, proclivities, personal attributes, cognitive knowledge and skills, motivation, and resources for adapting behaviour in response to uncertainty. Through our methodological approach, we did not aim at measuring mindsets and attributing weightings to their dimensions. Rather, we sought to identify different elements that comprise the Mongolian mindset about uncertainty in order to develop a fine-grained understanding of how this mindset impacts people management practices in Mongolian companies. Below, we provide background to the Mongolian context, highlighting the key factors that contribute to it being an uncertain and unstable business environment, before discussing the methods applied in the empirical research.

The Mongolian business environment

The Mongolian business environment is characterised by political, legal and economic uncertainty, with fluctuating foreign direct investment (Bumochir, 2020; CEIC Data, 2020), and marked disparities in health, education, social welfare and income distribution (Best's Country Risk Report, 2019; World Bank, 2020). Political party-motivated decision-making, corruption in the public sector and money laundering activities within the country have led to decreased trust in formal institutions and sparked civil society protests (authors; World Bank, 2020).

Despite being underpinned by democratic principles, Mongolia's political system has been lacking stability throughout the transition period, ever since the country's first democratic elections in 1990. Whilst the Mongolian People's party recorded a solid victory in the June 2020 elections, between 1992 and 2017, Mongolia had 15 different government cabinets, each lasting an average of 1,5 years (Edwards, 2017). Mongolians exhibit a high level of interest in getting involved in formal political institutions: at the time of writing, over 20% of the population are members of one of the 32 political parties registered in Mongolia (DeFacto, 2019). Ongoing tensions and shifts in the political arena are fuelled by the co-existence of competing ideologies: ideals of modernisation and neo-liberal reforms contrast with the embedded nationalism and pastoralism which shape relationships in the country (Bumochir, 2020).

Notwithstanding the uncertainty characterising Mongolia's business environment, there is scope for MNEs wishing to operate there. Most local companies are family-run SMEs, but there is a drive to attract MNEs with a view to boosting economic growth and diversification, the development of more complex products and services, access of local production to external markets, and new employment opportunities (ILO, 2019). Furthermore, MNEs can recruit talent from the new generation of well-educated employees for whom professional growth is a priority (Authors).

Research methods

There have been repeated calls for more qualitative studies investigating emerging market contexts and employees' reactions to critical events, towards a more holistic understanding of how HRM practices are developed (Kutaula et al., 2019; Serafini & Szamosi, 2015), and towards achieving non-essentialist, more complex and 'differentiated culture-specific' explanations (Pudelko et al., 2015, p. 86). Within qualitative methods, interpretive analysis is particularly well suited to the exploration of unique circumstances, and to the development of theoretical abstractions, analytical generalisations, implications and theory building that are different from and complement the type of knowledge obtained through statistical generalisation (Halkier, 2011).

In responding to these calls, this study was guided by a critical realist frame of reference (Bogna et al., 2020; Johnson & Duberley, 2000). Our approach embraces the view that knowledge about a context requires an understanding of the interactions between a relatively stable and independent reality, the embedded discourses and mechanisms that may contribute to stability, and human action that – intentionally or not – continuously reproduces or changes such reality in line with evolving interpretive frames, facilitators and, conversely, constraints (Johnson & Duberley, 2000).

To achieve this kind of understanding about the Mongolian context, we collected data through semi-structured interviews with Mongolian managers. Interviews offer an opportunity to explore, through face-to-face conversation, participants' lived reality of institutions and turbulent environments (Psychogios et al., 2020), as well as the interaction of structures, events, human actions and contexts (Tsang, 2014), along with context-specific understandings and responses (Punch, 2014).

Sampling

We applied purposive sampling as it allowed us to reflect the study aims and questions to guide the research design, internal consistency and coherent logic (e.g. Punch, 2014). The interviews used for this paper were originally part of a broader study into understandings of management in Mongolia, which also addressed uncertainty. Since we wished to focus on local understandings of uncertainty, we reconfigured our original sample of 45 to a modest extent. We selected 29 interviews – including three interviews completed during the pilot phase – with Mongolian managers, and also included five with non-Mongolian managers established in the country, given their valuable comments on the Mongolian context and approaches to uncertainty. Participants were chosen from companies operating in a broad range of sectors and organisational types. This approach is consistent with Garavan et al.'s (2019) suggestion that researchers use more diverse samples in terms of types of firms being represented. In total, 34 senior managers, including 12

CEOs/Founders and 22 mid- to upper-level managers shared with us their work experiences of managing within the Mongolian environment. We interviewed 20 managers from private SMEs, 10 from the public sector, and four from foreign-owned MNEs (see Table 1).

Within qualitative methods, it is accepted that data saturation mostly occurs after 12 semi-structured interviews, when examining common behaviour and views in groups of people who share the same culture (Guest et al., 2006). However, reviews of sample sizes in qualitative research practice have revealed a tendency towards somewhat larger samples, with an overall median of study participants found to be 32.5 (Marshall et al., 2013; Saunders & Townsend, 2016). Marshall et al. (2013) consider a range of 15-20 participants as an empirically justified size in cases of single group studies, while Saunders and Townsend's (2016) review quotes a median of 29.5 for the same type of study. Our sample size reflects current practice across qualitative projects, and has secured a solid amount of relevant and suitably rich data.

We saw local Mongolian companies as valuable 'learning sites' for MNEs wishing to develop context-appropriate practices of people management in Mongolia. Although Mongolian companies engage in people management practices such as hiring, training and promoting employees, they do not have a tradition of formalised, Western-style HRM systems employing professional HRM practitioners. To build knowledge about what Mongolian approaches to managing people involve – especially in response to uncertainty – it was therefore crucial to include SMEs and governmental organisations in our sample, with a view to understand how employees are managed in Mongolia. This sample enabled us to investigate the impact of local cultural-cognitive and normative institutional processes on people management practices in the context of uncertainty. At the same time, ours was a single group study, as participants belonged to the same profession (Marshall et al., 2013; Saunders & Townsend, 2016). Not only were they all managers, but, regardless of their official title, all participants also had roles and responsibilities that included overseeing the HR function in their organisation. That, in itself, illustrates how people management is organised in Mongolia.

Data collection

One of the authors is a native Mongolian, who has well-established connections with local business communities and foreign investors. We identified potential interviewees through 'logging time', an approach to building rapport and trust with potential research participants *via* social and business events (Glesne, 2011). Interviews were conducted in

Table 1. Participants' profile.

P. no.	Current sector	Current role	HR duties	No. of employees
P1	Telecommunication, private SME	Head of Department	Yes	200+
P2	Manufacturing, family-owned SME	Founder & Director	Yes	20-30
P3	Healthcare, family-owned SME	Founder & Director	Yes	20-30
P4	Trade, private SME	Marketing Director	Yes	50+
P5	Hospitality, private SME	HR Manager	Yes	100+
P6	Constructions, private SME	Head of HR	Yes	200+
P7	Logistics, family-run SME	Founder & CEO	Yes	20-30
P8	Hospitality, private SME	Head of HR	Yes	100+
P9	Manufacturing and trade, private SME	Head of Digital Innovation	Yes	500+
P10	Investment, SME	Founder & CEO	Yes	20-30
P11	Construction and banking, private SME	Head of Communication	Yes	200+
P12	Property development, private consultancy firm	Founder & CEO	Yes	15-20
P13	Insurance, private enterprise	Founder & CEO	Yes	100+
P14	Media and entertainment, private enterprise	Head of Division	Yes	100+
P15	Trading and property, family-run SME	Founder, Director	Yes	20-30
P16	Construction, family-run SME	Founder, Director	Yes	40-50
P17	Trading and property, family-run SME	Founder, Director	Yes	20-30
P18	Accounting consultancy, private SME	Founder & CEO	Yes	15-20
P19	Education, private	Head of HR	Yes	100+
P20	Hospitality, private SME	Founder & CEO	Yes	40-50
P21	Auditing, public sector	HR manager	Yes	30-40
P22	Finance, public sector	Head of Department	Yes	30-40
P23	Education, public enterprise	Head of School	Yes	100+
P24	Tax authority, public sector	Head of Department	Yes	100+
P25	Government Agency, Energy	HR Director	Yes	50-60
P26	Government organisation	Project Manager	Yes	20-30
P27	Finance and banking, public	Head of HR	Yes	20-30
P28	Post services, public entity	Head of PR	Yes	50-60
P29	Mining, public entity	HR Consultant	Yes	100+
P30	Banking and finance, MNE	Regional Director	Yes	30-40
P31	Automobile, MNE	Marketing Director	Yes	50+
P32	Mining, MNE	Head of HR	Yes	200+
P33	Mining, MNE	CFO	Yes	50-60
P34	Recruitment consultancy, private SME	Founder & Director	Yes	10-15

English and Mongolian. Initially, participants completed a short questionnaire about their age, educational and career background, and their role with regard to people management. As mentioned above, Table 1 illustrates the profile of study participants including their current role, sector, involvement in HR practices and number of employees. Interviewees were asked: 1) to comment on their experiences of managing people and organisations; 2) to give examples of uncertainty and explain what it means to them; 3) to elaborate on how they handle uncertainty in their daily tasks, especially in relation to their own approach to people management practices; and 4) to discuss how, in their experience, uncertainty influences their employees. They were also asked to share views about the challenges and opportunities for doing business in Mongolia. Participants were given space to elaborate on topics they found particularly relevant to the issue of uncertainty and people management in their practice. The questions asked during the interviews allowed for answering RQ1: How is uncertainty understood and approached by people management practitioners in Mongolian organisations? Each interview lasted between one and two hours, was recorded, transcribed and – in the case of interviews conducted in Mongolian – translated by the native speaking researcher.

Data analysis

Our analytical approach followed interpretive and emic rationales for exploring non-Western settings. An interpretive frame of analysis was helpful in fleshing out the more abstract, fundamental dimensions of the context at hand, with insights gained into managers' understandings of uncertainty, resilience and the way in which these influence their approaches to people management (Williams et al., 2017). To support this, an emic rationale connects the analysis to the local, historical, geographical and social context, and sensitises the researcher to look for particular ways in which familiar concepts are given novel, locally-bound meanings (Polsa, 2013). The inclusion of a native researcher in framing the research questions, collecting and translating data, interpreting the results, and deriving theoretical and practical conclusions has been crucial to our ability to develop a deeply contextualised set of conclusions (Holtbrügge, 2013).

All interviews were initially open-coded with the use of NVivo software to identify emergent and major themes. Data display, drawing and verifying conclusions followed analytical techniques for qualitative analysis (Glesne, 2011). A further step in the analysis focused more specifically on identifying a distinct Mongolian mindset about uncertainty. The identification and analysis of the empirical themes provided a solid basis for our exploration of the Mongolian context and mindset about uncertainty and its implications for HRM within a differentiated context-specific rationale. The next section analyses the findings of our empirical investigation.

The Mongolian mindset about uncertainty

Elements of the Mongolian mindset about uncertainty

The findings provide evidence of widely shared understandings, across the sample, of uncertainty and expectations regarding people management across our sample. Four elements of the Mongolian mindset about uncertainty were identified. The first was a belief that impermanence is *natural*, that it is in the nature of things to change constantly. This element was exemplified in both general statements such as '*the only certainty is uncertainty*' (P26, Government organisation: Head of Organisation), with implications for what Mongolians consider normal, how they frame the notion of uncertainty, and how everyday routines and people management practices evolve. For instance, uncertainty meant less stress in business-related contexts, since *'people have very relaxed attitudes towards last minute changes and often see* [change] *as a very normal thing to happen'* (P30, Banking and finance, MNE: Head of Region).

The second element was an understanding of uncertainty as *normal*, as something that Mongolians are 'used to'. This normalisation of uncertainty was explained with reference to both the contemporary circumstances of socioeconomic transition and the traditional nomadic Mongolian way of life:

> You never know what happens tomorrow and have to be ready for any challenge. Some of the uncertainties are to do with the country being in a transitional period but I think that Mongolians are used to living with unexpected situations like herders. (P34, Recruitment consultancy, private SME: Founder and Director)

The third element highlighted a *positive* framing of uncertainty, whereby uncertainty was considered a source of opportunities, rather than chaos and undesired instability:

> You'd never have a same [sic] day in UB. There are lots of changes happening here, and yes it brings much uncertainties, but it also brings many opportunities, too. (P18, Accounting consultancy, private SME: Founder and CEO)

This echoes Gronow's (2008, p. 368) view that a regular exposure to the same type of stimuli leads to a 'proficiency of habituated action'. Having been exposed to the uncertainty of change as a community – across the centuries as a nomadic population, and throughout phases of economic and political upheaval – Mongolians value uncertainty and challenging situations, and have developed relatively well institutionalised competencies and orientations to deal with it (Swidler, 1986).

The fourth element of the Mongolian mindset about uncertainty was an outcome of the combination of the first three elements: a shared emphasis on the importance of flexibility in adapting to changing circumstances. Flexibility emerged as a typically Mongolian response in the face of uncertainty, as illustrated in the comment about Mongolians being *'very good at dealing with uncertain situations and able to think on their feet'* (P18, Accounting consultancy, private SME: Founder and CEO). As such, uncertainty came hand-in-hand with flexibility: the way Mongolians react to unexpected change and make decisions is supported by a repertoire of resources (Swidler, 1986) that make them well adapted to uncertain environments.

The acknowledgement of the ability to respond to changes and crises was coupled with the recognition that Mongolian solutions tended to be temporary, with a 'fluid' approach to time: plans are only made for '*a short-term period rather than the longer future*' (P26, Government organisation, Project Manager), and '*nothing happens on scheduled time*' (P30, Banking and finance, MNE, Head of Region). As observed by Whitley (2005), this fits well with an institutional environment characterised by low levels of trust in formal regulatory, legal and political institutions.

Influence of the Mongolian mindset about uncertainty on people management

It emerged that the Mongolian mindset about uncertainty influences a range of people management practices. We divide these into: *staff recruitment, training and development*, and a *paternalistic leadership style interwoven with extra-organisational network management*. As previously mentioned, the Mongolian business context lacks a strong, systemic approach to managing human resources. This is underpinned by the traditional understanding of leader as the key decision-maker (see Badarch, 2013) who operates in the absence of formal HRM procedures and processes, and is also a consequence of a weak employment framework:

> Implementing Western HR techniques into [firms'] daily approaches is becoming a popular practice among local companies but it has proven ineffective [...] People, including HR managers themselves, do not understand why it is important to have structured systems and control in place as management is still a new subject in Mongolia. Secondly, there is a huge gap between today's HR technique implementation and the supporting legal framework [...] Much of employment law is still exactly the same as 50 years ago. (P32, Mining, MNE: Head of HR)

Obviously, even if not officially carried out by HR departments and defined in terms of formal processes, a range of 'conventional' HRM practices can be identified. One of these is recruitment and selection of new staff. Approaches to *staff recruitment based on existing relationships and networks* emerge as a specific response to uncertainty. Hiring staff through networks – for example on the basis of reputation or origin from the same county as the manager – provides a way of reducing risk associated with the new hires. The excerpt below demonstrates that this approach to staff recruitment is also seen as 'normal' and is generally positively assessed:

> Hiring people from the same locality is not just doing a favour to someone who I know. The nomadic tradition of hot ail [living and moving as a group of nomadic families] gives us the much-needed basis of reliability and trust in business. Because [Mongolians] have known people from the same county for generations it is hard to fail to do the personality checks. (P26, Government organisation, Project Manager)

The home county functions as a 'buffer' to counteract nomadic life-style's uncertainties and to provide individuals with a sense of belonging and stability across generations. In addition, the practice of hiring *nutgiin hun* (people from the same county) – with its implicit assumptions about the reliability of personal networks, mutual trust and the obligation on the part of the hired employees to act 'appropriately' – mitigates uncertainty associated with the lack of effective formalised recruitment processes and services.

Staff development and training is also influenced by the Mongolian mindset about uncertainty. The interviewees' accounts stress the need for a non-formalised, flexible approach to learning and updating one's own knowledge, due to dynamically changing circumstances – a behavioural response which fits well with the Mongolian understanding of change and impermanence as natural and normal:

> Learning and improving your personal and professional skills is the only way to stay balanced during changes, which occur daily [in Mongolia]. (P2, Manufacturing, family-owned SME: Founder and Director)

As explained above, these frequent changes are typically responded to flexibly, and Mongolian employees feel competent to go on learning what is required of them:

> Mongolians are fast learners (…) They are quick to adapt to any situation and able to think on their feet. Perhaps, it is again back to their nomadic way of life. (P31, Automobile industry, MNE: Head of Region)

The relationship between leaders and staff was another aspect affected by the Mongolian mindset about uncertainty. This manifested in several ways. First, since uncertainty is seen as natural and normal, a leader's flexibility towards uncertainty is accepted and valued by the employees. Generally, participants saw that flexibility as the managers' ability to change their mind comfortably in the face of circumstances beyond their control:

> To be a good leader is about recognising what you can and cannot control, and being able to steer things in the right direction. Being able to change your mind is seen as a strength. (P22, Finance, public sector: Head of Department)

This view of self-limitation in the face of uncertainty as a managerial virtue comes in stark contrast with a traditional Western management emphasis on managing risk and controlling uncertainty through data collection and analysis, thorough planning, and a decisive stance (Teece & Leih, 2016). In the Mongolian context, the leader's ability to change their mind is framed as a traditional societal value, part of 'the nomadic attitude' that is 'accepted by the whole community' (P33, Mining, MNE: CFO).

An understanding that it is the leader's responsibility to deal with uncertainty, and to take care of employees and the company, was also central to the Mongolian mindset's influence on people management. References to a 'parental' style of leadership, with expressions such as 'being a parent', 'mother-like nurturing' or 'father-like directiveness' were often used. This parental leadership style was discussed with positive connotations, as an approach to managing people aimed at creating conditions for subordinates to feel protected, equitably treated and assured of what needed to be done to survive in an often unpredictable environment:

> It takes a lot of work to make an employee. The manager has to do everything required including coaching, partying and telling them off. As a Head of the company you are expected to do what a father does to his kids, and in return, they trust and respect you. (P13, Insurance, private enterprise: Founder and CEO)

From the perspective of present-day Western HRM practice, such an infantilising view of employees is likely to appear problematic. However, the Mongolian managers repeatedly praised the virtues of an approach that involves 'treat(ing) my staff like my own children', and seeing as beneficial a situation where 'work colleagues become an extended family' (P17, Trading and property, Family-run SME: Founder and Director). It was considered to provide a reliable basis for building trust as a foundation of management under conditions of uncertainty.

The emphasis on a paternalistic model of managing employees (see also Aycan, 2006) was coupled with a belief in the superiority of a top-down approach to decision making, both as an effective, pragmatic enabler of 'getting the job done' and an approach that, in the participants' view, staff preferred (see also Authors). A directive style of management was seen to align with local expectations:

> Mongolians prefer having a strong leader, who knows the direction and provides guidance. Our plan of setting up a Google-type company (…) confused the team. As soon as we changed our approach to become stricter and blunter, they were much happier. (P34, Recruitment consultancy, SME: Founder and Director)

Associated with the (self-)understanding of Mongolian leaders as 'parents' to their employees was an emphasis on the manager's role in building a broader 'family' and looking after a range of people that did not only include colleagues but also relatives, nutgiin humuus (people from the same county) and former classmates.

The cultivation of a broad network that, in the Mongolian context, extends beyond blood relatives, involves exchanges of favours. Here, just as uncertainty is seen as natural and normal, so is the ability to 'get things done' using modes of operating outside the official systems – which, in any case, are often non-existent or do not function well. Order and legitimacy, therefore, are maintained through binding expectations over the leader's ability to fulfil social obligations rather than through regulative institutions (Scott, 2014). Being able to rely on favours from others, be it staff members or people outside the organisation, can alleviate potential adverse consequences of uncertainty, such as the lack of 'transparent and reliable information' (P31, Automobile industry, MNE: Marketing Director) and inefficient administrative processes. In this sense, people management practices inside Mongolian companies are interwoven with wider network management outside them, and is something that non-Mongolian managers have learned to appreciate:

> I learn a lot from my staff. They know the local attitudes and preferences, which can be the total opposite of a Western mindset at times. (P14, Head of Division, Private Enterprise: Media and entertainment)

Below, we discuss the implications of our study for IHRM research and practice.

Discussion

Through putting forward the concept of mindset about uncertainty, our research extends the literature on mindsets in management-related disciplines (e.g. Han & Stieha, 2020; Meyer & Xin, 2018; Yari et al., 2020). The empirical analysis has allowed us to identify four elements of the Mongolian mindset about uncertainty: (1) belief that impermanence is natural; (2) consideration of uncertainty as normal; (3) framing of uncertainty as positive; (4) emphasis on flexibility in adapting to changing circumstances. In response to the inherently uncertain conditions, Mongolian managers deploy a range of context-specific and often institutionalised repertoires of managerial practices (Swidler, 1986) and coping resources. These include the support, information and social sanctioning deriving from *nutgiin hummus* (people from the same county) and extended relationship networks. Specifically, with regard to people management practices, the Mongolian mindset about uncertainty manifests in: (1) network-based recruitment practices; (2) a lack of reliance on planning and a reactive approach to staff learning and development, characterised by an emphasis on individual and ad-hoc 'learning what needs to be learned' to address immediate problems, and (3) a focus on managing staff in paternalistic and relational, but not systemic, terms.

The findings shed light on Mongolia's institutional context. On a more superficial level, understandings and responses to uncertainty seem specifically associated with a cultural-cognitive institutional dimension. At the same time, the analysis has also provided explanations of how regulative, normative and cultural-cognitive systems and effects have shaped each other recursively (Scott, 2014). This study has provided additional evidence that informal institutions can prove more influential than formal ones (Yan et al., 2018). There was a clear overall engagement with a normative expectation that managers should honour a moral responsibility towards their *nutgiin hun* (people from the same county). Simultaneously, there was an underlying shared understanding that behavioural patterns also constitute a culturally-supported means to provide people in Mongolia with a necessary degree of certainty in their lives. Tight networks – between employer and employee, across and beyond organisations, and between specific leaders and political figures – were seen to provide organisations with the information, human resources and committed relationships they needed to maintain a healthy balance and survival on a day-to-day basis.

Our study also supports Andresen and Bergdolt (2017) view that certain mindset elements are more impactful than others: an unwavering belief that impermanence is natural and an expectation of a parent-like people-management style, along with associated behaviours, came across as central to Mongolia's highly relational ethos. Where systems and regulative frameworks not only fail but also prove inept in conditioning behaviour and enabling flexibility and fast responses to rapidly changing environments, line managers are deemed responsible for finding and implementing effective solutions. This role, rooted in the historical times of Mongols' nomadic way of life, continued to be re-interpreted and re-invented in light of the challenges of political and economic systemic changes over the years.

The idea of 'failing' regulative systems needs to be problematised with respect to the development of competencies for dealing with uncertain environments in Mongolia, and indeed to MNEs' opportunities for integrating into their repertoires a new 'cultural kit' (Swidler, 1986) for ensuring greater resilience in unstable environments (Williams et al., 2017). The fact that the regulative pillar in Mongolia has been weak throughout the nation's history has led to the development of flexibility of approaches, quick ad-hoc responses to crises, and a positive view of change and uncertainty. This recursive interaction between unreliable regulative systems, the dominance of pre-established social obligations and a well-institutionalised mindset about uncertainty have, in fact, generated adversity *advantages* (Edwards et al., 2019).

Implications for IHRM

Our analysis has granted further evidence to Björkman et al.'s (2008) argument that cultural-cognitive and normative institutional processes may play a central role in conditioning views of what constitutes appropriate HRM. Provided that MNEs' HRM strategies respect deeply embedded values of local cultures (Reiche et al., 2018), the resources and dispositions associated with the Mongolian mindset about uncertainty may potentially be leveraged. Assuming a growth perspective on mindsets (Keating & Heslin, 2015; Murphy & Dweck, 2010), the cultivation of competencies to deal with uncertainty, framed in positive terms, emerges as a promising avenue for MNEs open to engage in a reversal of learning flows. Consequentially, it makes possible the creation of new dynamics in centre/periphery relationships, which can support the production of new mindsets and reference points for HRM decisions, towards leveraging the positive aspects of uncertainty (De Villa & Rajwani, 2013) across the corporation and its various sites.

Following from our study, we highlight five implications for IHRM scholars and practitioners. First, instead of imposing a conventional Western conception of HRM onto the Mongolian context, it is necessary for MNEs to understand how people management practices are linked to the Mongolian mindset about uncertainty. This will enable (I)HRM professionals to fulfil a valuable role in the Mongolian context. As Hutchins and Wang (2009) have argued, HRM professionals can play important future-oriented roles in crisis management, as an organisational problem solver, organisational change agent, organisational designer, organisational empowerer, and a developer of human capital. In Mongolia, HRD professionals could support the development of expatriate managers' skills in dealing with crisis and instability, and ensure that they adopt the locally required kind of mentality to effectively approach uncertainty and risks. Dealing with adversity, preparing leaders to do so and being able to unite employees with a view to surviving and prospering in periods of crisis, therefore, potentially provides HRD professionals with a strong, value-based platform for bringing about positive change.

Second, prior to introducing formal HRM systems and procedures in Mongolia, it is important for MNE leadership to develop an in-depth understanding of how the relational dynamics between managers and employees in Mongolian companies operates. Whilst our study concurs with previous analyses that have highlighted the prevalence of a relational ethos in Asian cultures (Barkema et al., 2015; Chen & Miller, 2011), it also points to the specificities of the Mongolian approach to people management under the unstable business conditions found in this context. One such feature of the Mongolian approach to people management is that although leaders are expected to practise top-down decision-making, this does not equate with the subordinates' unconditional commitment or a lack of critical evaluation of those in power (see also

Badarch, 2013). Local employees actively scrutinise whether their leaders' efforts are duly used in reinforcing resilience through a relational ethos in people management.

Third, in designing an HRM system that is going to be effective in the Mongolian context, it is important for IHRM practitioners to be aware that Mongolian leaders are expected to perform a protective role towards the employees. This aspect of people management needs to be under-stood in non-binary terms: it is simultaneously of strategic and oper-ational importance. Mongolian leaders are expected to succeed in unifying people's efforts towards overcoming adversity (Badarch, 2013). Their flexibility in the face of uncertainty combined with relational skills and their role as an 'employee champion' come across as pivotal and value-creating (Ulrich & Brockbank, 2005) in securing organisa-tional resilience.

Fourth, any effort at implementing a system-oriented approach to HRM in Mongolia must acknowledge an understanding of 'people man-agement' that transcends organisational boundaries. Beyond recruiting and managing the company staff, it includes a key role in managing and relying on wider networks, which comprise leaders' own social connec-tions with their *nutgiin humuus* and former classmates, and at times also the networks of other non-managerial personnel. As one aspect of uncer-tainty in Mongolia is the lack of professional recruitment and selection services, extra-organisational networks serve as a source of trustworthy staff and valuable information about potential employees.

The final implication for IHRM drawn from our study refers to the recognition of the skills and competencies which enable effective responses to uncertainty, and which Mongolian managers seem to pos-sess. For example, uncertainty should ideally be approached with the help of improvisation capabilities (Cunha & Clegg, 2019), while organisa-tional agility depends on the development of a mindset that allows for the use of imagination, strong intuition, improvisation and flexibility to transform approaches (Jordaan, 2019; Teece et al., 2016; Williams et al., 2017). Our study has shown that Mongolian managers already exhibit the desirable people management competencies and an ad-hoc approach to decision-making that many Western authors and practitioners have been highlighting as important to acquire. Instead of aiming to curb uncertainty through intensive data collection and thorough planning, Mongolian managers follow a more equivocal approach to decision-making, and show fortitude to change their minds when and as deemed necessary. This adds to the growing recognition of the value of local Asian solutions as relevant not only in the context of their development, but also with respect to Western and global contexts (see also Lowe et al., 2015). As McGaughey et al. (2016) argue, context-specific institutional effects potentially enable the development of strategic competences that are appropriate both at a local and global level.

Conclusion

Managing people to accomplish greater resilience under conditions of uncertainty requires not only *respecting* local practices and values but also *recognising their value* and *leveraging* them for the benefit of the MNE globally. This means that the traditional flow of HR knowledge base, systems and best practices from the Western 'parent' to the rest of the organisation might not be the most effective or value-creating approach. It also means that IHRM professionals need to develop their own reflexive and analytical competencies, in order to challenge ethnocentric frames of reference, and be open to learning from local mindsets. This approach will grant MNEs and their HR practitioners the opportunity to learn from a multitude of different stakeholders and environments, and to develop their competencies in responding to uncertainty prone environments.

We close our paper with highlighting avenues for future research. Although we have identified relatively institutionalised features of the Mongolian mindset about uncertainty, we have not had the scope to explore the implications of differentiating features within our sample, such as the extent of management experience, educational background or gender. Neither have we had the opportunity to address employment relations in Mongolia through our study, or to compare people management practices between different types and sizes of companies. In future studies, through a more stratified approach to sampling which includes a broader range of stakeholders, additional insights into the impacts of uncertainty on local HRM practice could be obtained. This would potentially enable the generation of further contextual knowledge through a comparative analysis, with the application of quantitative or further qualitative research.

Through deepening our understanding of mindsets about uncertainty in different contexts, future research could also build on our work in bringing to the fore the complex ways in which risk is perceived in modern societies (Edwards et al., 2008). This would continue to inform IHRM researchers and practitioners in their effort to support the development of growth-generating competencies in an undeniably uncertain global sphere (Clapp-Smith & Lester, 2014; Edwards et al., 2019; McGaughey, et al., 2016).

Data availability statement

The data that support the findings of this study are available on request from the corresponding author [Author's initials]. The data are not publicly available due to their containing information that could compromise the anonymity and privacy of research participants.

Disclosure statement

No potential conflict of interest was reported by the authors.

References

Andresen, M., & Bergdolt, F. (2017). A systematic literature review on the definitions of global mindset and cultural intelligence–merging two different research streams. *The International Journal of Human Resource Management*, *28*(1), 170–195. https://doi.org/10.1080/09585192.2016.1243568

Aycan, Z. (2006). Paternalism - Towards conceptual refinement and operationalization. In U. Kim, K-S Yang & K-K Hwang (Eds.), *Indigenous and cultural psychology understanding people in context* (pp. 445–466). SpringerLink.

Badarch, K. (2013). *Integrating new values into Mongolian Public Management* [PhD thesis]. University of Potsdam.

Barkema, H. G., Chen, X. P., George, G., Luo, Y., & Tsui, A. S. (2015). West meets East: New concepts and theories. *Academy of Management Journal*, *58*(2), 460–479. https://doi.org/10.5465/amj.2015.4021

Best's Country Risk Report. (2019). *Mongolia – CRT 5*. http://www3.ambest.com/ratings/cr/reports/mongolia.pdf

Björkman, I., Budhwar, P., Smale, A., & Sumelius, J. (2008). Human resource management in foreign-owned subsidiaries: China versus India. *The International Journal of Human Resource Management*, *19*(5), 964–978. https://doi.org/10.1080/09585190801994180

Björkman, I., & Welch, D. (2015). Framing the field of international human resource management research. *The International Journal of Human Resource Management*, *26*(2), 136–150. https://doi.org/10.1080/09585192.2014.922361

Bogna, F., Raineri, A., & Dell, G. (2020). Critical realism and constructivism: Merging research paradigms for a deeper qualitative study. *Qualitative Research in Organizations and Management: An International Journal*. Published online ahead of print. https://doi.org/10.1108/QROM-06-2019-1778

Brewster, C., Wood, G., & Brookes, M. (2008). Similarity, isomorphism or duality? Recent survey evidence on the human resource management policies of multinational corporations. *British Journal of Management*, *19*(4), 320–342. https://doi.org/10.1111/j.1467-8551.2007.00546.x

Buchanan, D. A., & Hällgren, M. (2019). Surviving a zombie apocalypse: Leadership configurations in extreme contexts. *Management Learning*, *50*(2), 152–170. https://doi.org/10.1177/1350507618801708

Budhwar, P. S., Varma, A., & Patel, C. (2016). Convergence-divergence of HRM in the Asia-Pacific: Context-specific analysis and future research agenda. *Human Resource Management Review*, *26*(4), 311–326. https://doi.org/10.1016/j.hrmr.2016.04.004

Bumochir, D. (2020). *The state, popular mobilisation and gold mining in Mongolia: Shaping 'neoliberal' policies.* UCL Press.

Caniëls, M. C., Semeijn, J. H., & Renders, I. H. (2018). Mind the mindset! The interaction of proactive personality, transformational leadership and growth mindset for engagement at work. *Career Development International, 23*(1), 48–66. https://doi.org/10.1108/CDI-11-2016-0194

CEIC Data. (2020). *Mongolia Foreign Direct Investment (2009–2020).* https://www.ceic-data.com/en/indicator/mongolia/foreign-direct-investment

Chen, M. J., & Miller, D. (2011). The relational perspective as a business mindset: Managerial implications for East and West. *Academy of Management Perspectives, 25*(3), 6–18.

Clapp-Smith, R., & Lester, G. V. (2014). Defining the 'mindset' in global mindset: Modeling the dualities of global leadership. In M. Li, Y. Wang, & J. S. Osland (Eds.), *Advances in global leadership* (Vol. 8, pp. 205–228).Emerald Group Publishing Limited.

Cunha, M. P., & Clegg, S. (2019). Improvisation in the learning organization: A defense of the infra-ordinary. *The Learning Organization, 26*(3), 238–251. https://doi.org/10.1108/TLO-07-2018-0126

Cunha, M. P., Gomes, E., Mellahi, K., Miner, A. S., & Rego, A. (2020). Strategic agility through improvisational capabilities: Implications for a paradox-sensitive HRM. *Human Resource Management Review, 30*(1), 100695–100613. https://doi.org/10.1016/j.hrmr.2019.100695

De Villa, M. A., & Rajwani, T. (2013). The mirror trap – Do managerial perceptions influence organizational responses to crises? *Academia Revista Latinoamericana de Administración, 26*(1), 170–188. https://doi.org/10.1108/ARLA-05-2013-0044

DeFacto. (2019). *The internal democracy index of Mongolian political parties.* De Facto, Indpendent Research Institute. https://www.researchgate.net/publication/337335984_THE_INTERNAL_DEMOCRACY_INDEX_OF_MONGOLIAN_POLITICAL_PARTIES_2019

Demirbag, M., & Wood, G. (Eds.). (2018). *Comparative capitalism and the transitional periphery: Firm centred perspectives.* Edward Elgar Publishing.

Dibben, P., Brewster, C., Brookes, M., Cunha, R., Webster, E., & Wood, G. (2017). Institutional legacies and HRM: Similarities and differences in HRM practices in Portugal and Mozambique. *The International Journal of Human Resource Management, 28*(18), 2519–2537. https://doi.org/10.1080/09585192.2016.1164225

Dweck, C. S. (1986). Motivational processes affecting learning. *American Psychologist, 41*(10), 1040–1048. https://doi.org/10.1037/0003-066X.41.10.1040

Dweck, C. S. (2006). *Mindset: The new psychology of success.* Random House.

Edwards, P., Ram, M., & Smith, V. (2008). Introduction to special issue: Workers, risk and the new economy. *Human Relations, 61*(9), 1163–1170. https://doi.org/10.1177/0018726708094908

Edwards, T., Schnyder, G., & Fortwengel, J. (2019). Mapping the impact of home- and host-country institutions on human resource management in emerging market multinational companies: A conceptual framework. *Thunderbird International Business Review, 61*(3), 531–544. https://doi.org/10.1002/tie.22036

Edwards, T. (2017). Mongolian leader urged to resign after party's loss in presidential vote. *Reuters.* [Online]. https://www.reuters.com/article/us-mongolia-politics/mongolian-leader-urged-to-resign-after-partys-loss-in-presidential-vote-idUSKCN1B51AC

Garavan, T., McCarthy, A., Sheehan, M., Lai, Y., Saunders, M., Clarke, N., Carbery, R., & Shanahan, V. (2019). Measuring the organizational impact of training: The need for greater methodological rigor. *Human Resource Development Quarterly, 30*(3), 291–309. https://doi.org/10.1002/hrdq.21345

Glesne, C. (2011). *Becoming qualitative researchers: An introduction* (4th ed.). Pearson.

Gronow, A. (2008). Not by rules or choice alone: A pragmatist critique of institution theories in Economics and Sociology. *Journal of Institutional Economics, 4*(3), 351–373. https://doi.org/10.1017/S1744137408001124

Guest, G., Bunce, A., & Johnson, L. (2006). How many interviews are enough? An experiment with data saturation and variability. *Field Methods, 18*(1), 59–82. https://doi.org/10.1177/1525822X05279903

Halkier, B. (2011). Methodological practicalities in analytical generalization. *Qualitative Inquiry, 17*(9), 787–797. https://doi.org/10.1177/1077800411423194

Han, S. J., & Stieha, V. (2020). Growth mindset for human resource development: A scoping review of the literature with recommended interventions. *Human Resource Development Review, 19*(3), 309–323. https://doi.org/10.1177/1534484320939739

Herdin, T. (2012). Deconstructing typologies: Overcoming the limitations of the binary opposition paradigm. International *Communication Gazette, 74*(7), 603–618. https://doi.org/10.1177/1748048512458557

Holtbrügge, D. (2013). Indigenous management research. *Management International Review, 53*(1), 1–11. https://doi.org/10.1007/s11575-012-0160-1

Hutchins, H. M., & Wang, J. (2009). Organizational crisis management and human resource development: A review of the literature and implications to HRD research and practice. *Advances in Developing Human Resources, 10*(3), 310–330. https://doi.org/10.1177/1523422308316183

ILO. (2019, April). *Accelerating the 2030 Sustainable Development goals through decent work. SDG monitoring and country profile for Mongolia.* [factsheet]. https://www.ilo.org/beijing/what-we-do/publications/WCMS_687934/lang–en/index.htm

Johnson, P., & Duberley, J. (2000). *Understanding management research: An introduction to epistemology.* Sage Publications.

Jordaan, B. (2019). Leading organisations in turbulent times: Towards a different mental model. In J. Kok & S. Van den Heuvel (Eds.), *Leading in a VUCA world—Integrating leadership, discernment and spirituality* (pp. 59–75). Springer Open.

Kaynak, E. M., Demirbag, M., & Tatoglu, E. (2007). Determinants of ownership-based entry mode choice of MNEs: Evidence from Mongolia. *Management International Review, 47*(4), 505–530. https://doi.org/10.1007/s11575-007-0028-y

Keating, L. A., & Heslin, P. A. (2015). The potential role of mindsets in unleashing employee engagement. *Human Resource Management Review, 25*(4), 329–341. https://doi.org/10.1016/j.hrmr.2015.01.008

Kutaula, S., Gillani, A., & Budhwar, P. (2019). An analysis of employment relationships in Asia using psychological contract theory. A review and research agenda. Human Resource *Management Review,* 100707. https://doi.org/10.1016/j.hrmr.2019.100707

Lowe, S., Kainzbauer, A., Tapachai, N., & Hwang, K. S. (2015). Ambicultural blending between Eastern and Western paradigms: Fresh perspectives for international management research. *Culture and Organization, 21*(4), 304–320. https://doi.org/10.1080/14759551.2014.901324

Magnani, G., & Zucchella, A. (2018). Uncertainty in entrepreneurship and management studies: A systematic literature review. *International Journal of Business and Management, 13*(3), 98–133. https://doi.org/10.5539/ijbm.v13n3p98

Mamman, A., & Al Kulaiby, K. Z. (2014). Is Ulrich's model useful in understanding HR practitioners' roles in non-western developing countries? An exploratory investigation across private and public sector organizations in the Sultanate Kingdom of Oman. *The International Journal of Human Resource Management, 25*(20), 2811–2836. https://doi.org/10.1080/09585192.2014.914053

Marshall, B., Cardon, P., Poddar, A., & Fontenot, R. (2013). Does sample size matter in qualitative research: A review of qualitative interviews in IS research. *Journal of Computer Information Systems, 54*(1), 11–22. https://doi.org/10.1080/08874417.2013.11645667

McGaughey, S. L., Kumaraswamy, A., & Liesch, P. W. (2016). Institutions, entrepreneurship and co-evolution in international business. *Journal of World Business, 51*(6), 871–881. https://doi.org/10.1016/j.jwb.2016.07.003

McSweeney, B. (2012). Constitutive contexts: The myth of common cultural values. In G. Wood & M. Demirbag (Eds.), *Handbook of institutional approaches to international business* (pp. 142–172). Glos and Northampton, Massachusetts: Edward Elgar.

Meyer, K. E., & Xin, K. R. (2018). Managing talent in emerging economy multinationals: Integrating strategic management and human resource management. *The International Journal of Human Resource Management, 29*(11), 1827–1855. https://doi.org/10.1080/09585192.2017.1336362

Murphy, M. C., & Dweck, C. S. (2010). A culture of genius: How an organization's lay theory shapes people's cognition, affect, and behavior. *Personality & Social Psychology Bulletin, 36*(3), 283–296. https://doi.org/10.1177/0146167209347380

Polsa, P. (2013). The crossover-dialog approach: The importance of multiple methods for international business. *Journal of Business Research, 66*(3), 288–297. https://doi.org/10.1016/j.jbusres.2011.08.008

Psychogios, A., Szamosi, L. T., Prouska, R., & Brewster, C. (2020). Varieties of crisis and working conditions: A comparative study of Greece and Serbia. *European Journal of Industrial Relations, 26*(1), 91–106. https://doi.org/10.1177/0959680119837101

Pudelko, M., Tenzer, H., & Harzing, A. W. (2015). Cross-cultural management and language studies within international business research – Past and present paradigms and suggestions for future research. In N. Holden, S. Michailova, & S. Tietze (Eds.), *The routledge companion to cross-cultural management* (pp. 85–94). Routledge.

Punch, K. F. (2014). *Introduction to social research: Quantitative and qualitative approaches* (3rd ed.). Sage.

Ramamurti, R. (2009). What have we learned about emerging market MNEs? In R. Ramamurti & J. V. Singh (Eds.), *Emerging multinationals in emerging markets* (pp. 399–426). Cambridge University Press.

Rathbun, B. C. (2007). Uncertain about uncertainty: Understanding the multiple meanings of a crucial concept in International Relations Theory. *International Studies Quarterly, 51*(3), 533–557. https://doi.org/10.1111/j.1468-2478.2007.00463.x

Reiche, B. S., Lee, Y.-t., & Quintanilla, J. (2018). Cultural perspectives on comparative HRM. In C. Brewster, W. Mayrhofer, & E. Farndale (Eds.), *Handbook of research on comparative human resource management* (2nd ed., pp. 48–64). Edward Elgar.

Saunders, M. K., & Townsend, S. (2016). Reporting and justifying the number of interview participants in organization and workplace research. *British Journal of Management, 27*(4), 836–852. https://doi.org/10.1111/1467-8551.12182

Schneider, S. C., & De Meyer, A. (1991). Interpreting and responding to strategic issues: The impact of national culture. *Strategic Management Journal, 12*(4), 307–320. https://doi.org/10.1002/smj.4250120406

Scott, W. R. (2014). *Institutions and organizations – Ideas, interests and identities* (4th ed.). Sage Publications.

Serafini, G. O., & Szamosi, L. T. (2015). Five star hotels of a Multinational Enterprise in countries of the transitional periphery: A case study in human resources management. *International Business Review, 24*(6), 972–983. https://doi.org/10.1016/j.ibusrev.2014.12.001

Sparrow, P. R., & Hiltrop, J. M. (1997). Redefining the field of European human resource management: A battle between national mindsets and forces of business transition? *Human Resource Management, 36*(2), 201–219. https://doi.org/10.1002/(SICI)1099-050X(199722)36:2<201::AID-HRM3>3.0.CO;2-0

Stokes, P., Liu, Y., Smith, S., Leidner, S., Moore, N., & Rowland, C. (2016). Managing talent across advanced and emerging economies: HR issues and challenges in a Sino-German strategic collaboration. *The International Journal of Human Resource Management, 27*(20), 2310–2338. https://doi.org/10.1080/09585192.2015.1074090

Storgaard, M., Tienari, J., Piekkari, R., & Michailova, S. (2020). Holding on while letting go: Neocolonialism as organizational identity work in a multinational corporation. *Organization Studies*. Published online ahead of print. https://doi.org/10.1177/0170840620902977

Swidler, A. (1986). Culture in action: Symbols and strategies. *American Sociological Review, 51*(2), 273–286. https://doi.org/10.2307/2095521

Teece, D., & Leih, S. (2016). Uncertainty, innovation, and dynamic capabilities: An introduction. *California Management Review, 58*(4), 5–12. https://doi.org/10.1525/cmr.2016.58.4.5

Teece, D., Peteraf, M., & Leih, S. (2016). Dynamic capabilities and organizational agility: Risk, uncertainty, and strategy in the innovation economy. *California Management Review, 58*(4), 13–35. https://doi.org/10.1525/cmr.2016.58.4.13

Tsang, E. W. K. (2014). Case studies and generalization in information systems research: A critical realist perspective. The *Journal of Strategic Information Systems, 23*(2), 174–186. https://doi.org/10.1016/j.jsis.2013.09.002

Ulrich, D. (1997). *Human resource champions: The next agenda for adding value and delivering results.* Harvard Business School Press.

Ulrich, D., & Brockbank, W. (2005). *The HR value proposition.* Harvard Business School Press.

Vu, M. C., & Gill, R. (2019). Fusion leadership: A transcultural interpretation and application. *International Journal of Cross Cultural Management, 19*(2), 140–159. https://doi.org/10.1177/1470595819847229

Welch, C., Piekkari, R., Plakoyiannaki, E., & Paavilainen-Mäntymäki, E. (2011). Theorising from case studies: Towards a pluralist future for international business research. *Journal of International Business Studies, 42*(5), 740–762. https://doi.org/10.1057/jibs.2010.55

Whitley, R. (2005). Developing transnational organizational capabilities in multinational companies: Institutional constraints on authority sharing and careers in six types of MNC. In G. Morgan, R. Whitley, & E. Moen (Eds.), *Changing capitalisms? Internationalization, institutional change, and systems of economic organization* (pp. 235–276). Oxford University Press.

Wicks, A. C., Keevil, A., & Parmar, B. (2012). Sustainable business development and management theories: A mindset approach. *Business and Professional Ethics Journal, 31*(4), 375–398. https://doi.org/10.5840/bpej2012313/420

Williams, T. A., Gruber, D. A., Sutcliffe, K. M., Shepherd, D. A., & Zhao, E. Y. (2017). Organizational response to adversity: Fusing crisis management and resilience research streams. *Academy of Management Annals, 11*(2), 733–769. https://doi.org/10.5465/annals.2015.0134

Wood, G., Cooke, F. L., Demirbag, M., & Kwong, C. (2018). Introduction to Special Issue on: International human resource management in contexts of high uncertainties. *The International Journal of Human Resource Management, 29*(7), 1365–1373. https://doi.org/10.1080/09585192.2018.1477547

World Bank. (2020, April 8). *The World Bank in Mongolia – Overview*. https://www.worldbank.org/en/country/mongolia/overview

Yan, Z. J., Zhu, J. C., Fan, D., & Kalfadellis, P. (2018). An institutional work view toward the internationalization of emerging market firms. *Journal of World Business, 53*(5), 682–694. https://doi.org/10.1016/j.jwb.2018.03.008

Yari, N., Lankut, E., Alon, I., & Richter, N. F. (2020). Cultural intelligence, global mindset, and cross-cultural competencies: A systematic review using bibliometric methods. *European Journal of International Management, 14*(2), 210–250.

Breaking away or holding on to the past? Exploring HRM systems of export-oriented SMEs in a highly uncertain context: insights from a transition economy in the periphery

Dilshod Makhmadshoev and Knut Laaser

ABSTRACT

This article advances understanding of the interplay between high levels of environmental uncertainty and HRM challenges and practices of exporting SMEs in the garment industry of Kyrgyzstan. Uncertainty in this post-Socialist country emanates from the complex, conflict-ridden and ongoing process of transition from planned to market-based economy, resulting in a volatile institutional environment with under-developed formal institutions at its core. Drawing on qualitative data and framed by a novel theoretical framework consisting of HRM systems theory, North's institutional approach and the concept of path-dependency, the article advances knowledge of the distinctive set of HRM challenges faced by SMEs and the contrasting HRM systems adopted by them. The article draws particular attention to how the embeddedness of socialist-era norms and the diffusion of new market-oriented institutional features influence the utilisation of HRM systems in SMEs, whilst also revealing their evolutionary nature in a transition economy context. The article contributes by extending the scope of HRM research to the little-explored transitional periphery of Central Asia and adds to the nascent body of knowledge on HRM in SMEs by offering a more nuanced understanding of HRM systems in exporting SMEs in a highly uncertain context.

Introduction

Research on Human Resource Management (HRM) in environments characterized by high levels of uncertainty is scant. This is particularly true, as the call for papers for this special issue suggests, for the "people management side of crisis and volatility" (Wood et al., 2018:1367).

This article responds to this call and provides an exploration and analysis of HRM challenges and systems in internationally oriented small and medium-sized enterprises (SMEs) in the garment industry of Kyrgyzstan. Uncertainty in this Central Asian country emanates from the complex and ongoing process of institutional transformation from socialism to market-based economy, resulting in a context that is socially, economically and politically volatile (Makhmadshoev et al., 2015; Tudoroiu, 2007). As such, environmental uncertainty in this research is reflected in the uncertainty of the institutional context. While SMEs in general and exporting SMEs in particular are central for jobs and economic growth in developed and emerging countries (ILO, 2015), their role in transition economies for employment generation, reduction of poverty and facilitation of trade through integration and participation in regional and global value chains is paramount (Mcguire and Laaser, 2018; Makhmadshoev et al., 2015; Williams & Vorley, 2017; Wood & Demirbag, 2015). As SMEs face a range of challenges, for example limited resources, weak institutional support and, more generally, a high level of context sensitivity, HRM in general and people management in particular are considered crucial for their survival and success (Bacon and Hoque, 2005; Barrett & Mayson, 2007; Cunningham, 2010; Huang & Gamble, 2011). It is therefore surprising that research on HRM in SMEs has been neglected for some time and only in the last decade has this field received more systematic attention (Psychogios & Prouska, 2019).

The emerging literature in this area provides important insights, especially pointing towards the distinctiveness of HRM in SMEs compared to larger organisations, encapsulated in the high degree of informal HRM practices and specific challenges in light of high level of vulnerability to contextual factors (Psychogios & Prouska, 2019). Therein, important gaps in understanding HRM in SMEs exist, in particular why SMEs utilize specific bundles of HRM (Harney & Nolan, 2014), what HRM systems they utilize (Borda et al., 2019), whether the utilized HRM practices and systems differ or converge between countries and industries (Zhu et al., 2012), and how different socio-economic environments and their particular institutional structures, including informal norms and traditions, impact on HRM in SMEs (Cunningham & Rowley, 2008). Furthermore, as the majority of research on HRM in SMEs is conducted in developed and emerging economies (Cunningham, 2010; Cunningham & Rowley, 2008; Zhu et al., 2012), a gap of knowledge exists concerning HRM in SMEs in transition economies, particularly regarding how environments characterized by high levels of uncertainty impact on HRM (Marchington, 2015; Psychogios & Prouska, 2019; Zhu et al., 2012). This article addresses these calls by presenting an exploratory qualitative case study of the interplay between high levels of environmental uncertainty and HRM challenges and systems in exporting SMEs in the internationalised garment industry of Kyrgyzstan. This inquiry is embedded in a novel theoretical framework consisting of HRM systems theory, North's informal institutions approach and the concept of path-dependency. The article argues that this theoretical framework allows for a rich analysis of how dominant features of a highly uncertain environment impact on HRM in SMEs, creating particular sets of HRM challenges, and how SMEs react by deploying specific HRM systems.

This article makes three key contributions to theory and knowledge on HRM in SMEs. First, the article captures through the theoretical frameworks of institutional theory and HRM systems theory the unique HRM challenges that emerge against the backdrop of high levels of institutional uncertainty in Kyrgyzstan. This addresses a substantial evidence gap concerning how HRM in SMEs is confronted with distinctive challenges that are shaped by extreme forms of environmental uncertainty in a transition economy (Psychogios & Prouska, 2019). Second, this article addresses the gap of research on HRM systems in SMEs (Borda et al., 2019; Zhu et al., 2012) by identifying and analysing two contrasting HRM systems deployed by SMEs in Kyrgyzstan. The article draws special attention to the importance of informal institutions and how the embeddedness of old and the diffusion of new institutional features shape the dynamic utilization of HRM systems in SMEs. Informal institutions, encompassing norms, values and expectations (North, 1990), have been conceptually and empirically neglected in research on HRM in SMEs and this article showcases the importance of this approach (Cunningham & Rowley, 2008; Psychogios & Prouska, 2019). Third, the article contributes to the discussion regarding the convergence, divergence and hybridization of western HRM practices in emerging and transition economies. This responds to discussion of Warner (2009) and Rowley et al. (2017) and Zhu et al. (2012) where it is argued that HRM systems in large organisations are primarily characterized by within-country and between country variations. A contribution is offered by providing evidence of a within-industry variation of HRM systems that reflects the changing and uncertain nature of the institutional context in Kyrgyzstan. A particular theoretical contribution pertains to the ways the usefulness of the HRM system approach for SMEs is showcased and a new hybrid HRM system is introduced. Practical implications point towards the centrality of context sensitivity of HRM in SMEs and the influence of the co-existing old and new institutional structures in shaping how business and people management is executed in an uncertain transition environment.

The article commences with a synthesis of research addressing the nature of HRM and its challenges in SMEs based on which research gaps are identified and research questions are formulated. Next, the conceptual framework of HRM systems and institutional theory are presented and linked to the specifics of the institutional environment of Kyrgyzstan. This is followed by a discussion of the research context and research methodology. The analysis of empirical data is provided next and this is followed by discussion of key findings, outlining the theoretical, empirical and practical contributions of this article.

Literature review and research questions

HRM in SMEs and its challenges

A prominent theme in the literature on HRM in SMEs stresses that a key difference between HRM in large organizations and SMEs is the degree of formality (Bacon et al., 1996; Edwards & Ram, 2006; Harney, 2015; Nguyen & Bryant, 2004). It is argued that while HRM in large organizations features high levels of formality, encapsulated in documentation, systematization and institutionalization of HR practices (Nguyen & Bryant, 2004), informal HRM, characterized by "unwritten customs and the tacit understandings that arise out of the interaction of the parties at work" (Ram et al., 2001:846), prevails in SMEs (Psychogios & Prouska, 2019). Research illustrates that informality is embodied in recruitment practices that rely on word of mouth, lack of formal job descriptions, ad-hoc on the job-training, unstructured reward and pay systems and a heavy involvement of the owner in HRM practices (Barrett & Mayson, 2007; Behrends, 2007; Cooke, 2005; Dietz et al., 2006; Edwards & Ram, 2006). Case studies point towards the central role of the owner in designing HRM practices, setting and communicating performance targets and organisational objectives to employees (Cunningham & Rowley, 2008; Marlow & Patton, 2002). In contrast to research on HRM in large organisations that stresses the importance of understanding coherent bundles of HRM practices as reflecting specific strategic HRM systems, research on HRM practices in SMEs and their fit within an HRM system is scant (Borda et al., 2019), despite the importance of functioning HRM systems for firm performance (Hauff et al., 2014).

HRM in SMEs has been linked with a wide range of challenges. A key challenge stems from SMEs' heightened vulnerability to political, economic and institutional uncertainty due to their constrained financial resources, relatively small customer bases, dependence on larger organisations in supply chains and limited bargaining power with stakeholders (Edwards & Ram, 2006; Psychogios & Prouska, 2019; Smallbone & Welter, 2001). Therein, high levels of uncertainty are perceived to threaten SMEs existence and narrow HRM practices to ad-hoc interventions. It is argued that formal institutions, encoded in official rules, laws and contracts that are underpinned by regulative frameworks and formal policies are pivotal for SMEs and HRM as they shield firms from uncertainty (Harney, 2015; Matten & Geppert, 2004; Zhu et al., 2012). In this light, research on the interplay of institutions and HRM in SMEs point towards SMEs' context dependency. This perspective suggests that SMEs are embedded in their national institutional context, which extends from legal to social and cultural to political fields and shapes their practices and strategies to cope with HRM challenges (Barringer & Milkovich, 1998; Rosenzweig & Nohria, 1994; Wright & McMahan, 1992).

Concerning HRM practices, Marlow and Patton (2002) suggest that a key challenge relates to coping with disciplinary, grievance and equality issues. They argue that due to the high level of informality of HRM and the lack of formal policies and channels, discipline and grievance problems are inadequately dealt with by SMEs, heightening conflict and workers experience of ill-treatment at work. In a similar vein, Nguyen and Bryant (2004) argue that HRM in SMEs is characterized by the conflict between fostering a positive and collaborative-oriented environment and establishing practices that maintain discipline and cope with grievances. These findings are more broadly reflected by Edwards and Ram (2006) and Wilkinson (1999), who state that HRM in SMEs tends to face the challenge of being in conflict with employees' interest in consistency, equality and fair treatment due to the personalized, ad-hoc and informal nature of HRM (Edwards & Ram, 2006; Wilkinson, 1999). Another significant HRM challenge relates to attracting qualified workers, due to labour market participants perception of SMEs offering less attractive employment conditions while being more vulnerable to negative market dynamics in comparison to large organisations (Festing et al., 2013; Psychogios & Prouska, 2019; Storey et al., 2010). As a consequence, SMEs tend to experience shortage of qualified workers, while also experiencing higher levels of worker turnover. Tightly interwoven with the prevalence of informal HRM practices in SMEs are the challenges Hudson et al. (2001) and Garengo et al. (2005) identified concerning performance management in SMEs. Here, SMEs face the challenge that most performance management systems (PMS) are designed for large organisations, resulting in inadequate adoptions of PMS, while PMS is also undermined by the ad-hoc management approach of SMEs that is in conflict with mid-to long term planning.

Research questions

While providing invaluable insights, the majority of literature on HRM in SMEs is conducted in developed countries, and increasingly in relatively stable large emerging economies like China (Cunningham, 2010; Cunningham & Rowley, 2008; Zhu et al., 2012). Yet, HRM in SMEs in transition countries have received scant attention. In order to provide a more nuanced understanding of HRM in SMEs in general and how environments characterized by high levels of uncertainty impact on HRM in particular, calls for research on HRM in SMEs in transition economies have been issued (Borda et al., 2019; Marchington, 2015; Psychogios & Prouska, 2019). Furthermore, this literature review also established that an understanding of HRM systems in SMEs has been neglected. This article addresses these calls by presenting a qualitative case study of HRM challenges and systems in exporting SMEs in the garment industry of Kyrgyzstan. Against the backdrop of the literature review and the identified research gaps, this article explores the following three research questions:

1. What HRM challenges do SMEs face in an environment characterized by high levels of environmental uncertainty?
2. What HRM systems are utilized by SMEs to cope with HRM challenges?
3. How do high levels of environmental uncertainty shape these HRM systems?

The analysis that addresses these research questions is informed by the theoretical framework that combines HRM systems theory with an institutional approach. The theory of HRM systems allows an analysis of bundles of HRM practices, while the institutional theory approach enables an exploration of how the prevalence of informal institutional norms and practices in highly uncertain environments shape HRM in SMEs.

HRM in SMEs through the lens of HRM systems

The most prominent feature of the HRM systems debate is the traditional distinction between control and commitment HRM systems (Guest, 1987; Jackson et al., 2014; Storey, 1992; Thompson, 2011; Truss et al., 1997). Organizations that utilize commitment HRM systems aim to create "conditions for employees to become highly involved in the organisation and identify with its overall goals" (Wood & de Menezes, 1998: 487). Grounded in an unitarist HRM approach, commitment HRM systems aim to achieve this goal by fostering consent-based relations converging employee interests and organisational goals (Geare et al., 2006). This is reflected in particular sets of HR practices, such as flexible job design, job rotation, direct communication and reduction in hierarchy, career ladders, employment security and individual as well as team performance-based compensation (Hendry & Pettigrew, 1990; Storey, 1992). In this light Thompson notes that commitment HRM systems understand workers' efforts "as discretionary if it is directed from within rather than the result of sanctions or external pressure" (Thompson, 2011:358).

In contrast, the control HRM system focusses on the strategic link between HRM practices and organisational strategies (Guest, 1987), aiming to heighten labour efficiency while reducing labour costs (Hauff et al., 2014). Here, HRM is driven by a top-down decision-making process in which workers' performance and behaviour is closely monitored and framed by extensive formal rules and procedures (Guest, 1987; Storey, 1992). As this system is traditionally associated with low-skill and low-discretion workplaces, high levels of labour specialisation and division of labour goes in tandem with low levels of employment security and limited investment in training and career mobility (Walton, 1985). Control HRM systems incentivize workers primarily *via* performance-based remuneration practices that are based on extensive measurement of quantified output criteria (Legge, 2005). Compliance is secured by controlling and motivating workers *via* internal competition, financial incentives, weeding out strategies and external labour market as a disciplinary force (Purcell, 1993).

Conceptualisations of HRM systems are rooted in Western HRM debates and interlinked with specific features of large organisations (Guest, 1987; Hauff et al., 2014). As an increasing number of Western MNEs operating in Asia aim to "(…) globally benchmark HRM 'best practices'" (Rowley et al., 2017:2) and apply HRM system throughout the supply chain, the applicability of Western HRM systems in emerging countries have been subject to discussions. Two contrasting positions dominate the debate: on the one hand it is argued that a standardized HRM system is crucial for efficient and lasting supply chain relationships between developed and emerging economies (e.g. Nohria & Ghoshal, 1997). On the other, IHRM research on large-scale organisations in emerging countries suggest that HRM systems are mainly characterized by within-country and between country variations. Here, research points towards varying levels of convergence, divergence and hybridization of control and commitment HRM systems, depending on the particularities of contextual factors of countries and sectors that impact on HRM in large organisations (Horwitz & Budhwar, 2015; Rowley et al., 2017;

Warner, 2009). While the debate marches on, the vast majority of this research focusses on HRM systems in large organisations based in developed economies. Thus, analysis of HRM bundles in small firms is neglected in general, and insights on HRM systems of exporting SMEs in transition economies that tend to be characterized by higher levels of uncertainty remain particularly scant (Borda et al., 2019; Psychogios & Prouska, 2019). This article argues that a focus on HRM systems in SMEs is important in achieving a more nuanced picture that goes beyond an interpretation of HRM practices as informal and ad-hoc, offering an acknowledgement of how HRM practices in SMEs follow particular strategic HRM systems to cope with HRM challenges. The following section introduces informal institutions and the concept of path-dependency that inform the exploration of the impact of high levels of institutional uncertainty and change on HRM challenges and systems in SMEs.

HRM in SMEs through the lens of informal institutions and path-dependency

North's (1990) institutional theory and its particular focus on the importance and endurance of informal institutions is increasingly utilized in HRM research (e.g. Child & Tse, 2001; Gooderham et al., 2019; Huang & Gamble, 2011). Informal institutions include values, beliefs, conventions and social norms of behaviour that are influenced by various factors such as culture, history, traditions, social expectations and moral obligations (North, 1990). In this way, informal institutions are distinctive to individual societies, making them a context-specific variable in any institutional analysis. The importance of informal institutions for organisations is heightened when formal institutions are weak, lack legitimacy or are in the process of radical transformation, which corresponds to environmental features prominent in post-Socialist countries (Makhmadshoev, 2018). Indeed, firms operating in such uncertain environments tend to face high transaction costs, weak protection of property rights and ineffective enforcement of contracts (North, 1990; Peng & Luo, 2000). Here, informal social and cultural institutions become prominent for reducing SMEs uncertainty by providing structure and meaning to firm activities and practices (Puffer et al., 2010).

Connected to the concept of informal institutions is the notion of path-dependency that informs the focus of this article to explain distinguishing features of HRM in SMEs that have evolved in the context of high levels of institutional uncertainty and change. Path-dependency points to the incremental change of institutions, especially informal ones, in light of major external social and economic transformations (Delbridge et al., 2011; Dibben et al., 2017). Path-dependency suggests that institutional change is characterized by the enduring influence of past institutional arrangements on contemporary institutions and economic practices (Campbell, 2004; Zhu et al., 2012). Thus, path-dependency captures HRM practices that are informed by social norms and values that are associated with previous institutional regimes in times of uncertainty and radical change (Dibben et al., 2017; Sydow et al., 2009; Whitley, 1999; Williams & Vorley, 2017). Complementing path-dependency in understanding institutional uncertainty and change is the concept of path-break that, in contrast, suggests a move away from legacy institutions and re-orientation towards new institutional arrangements, economic principles and associated systems of norms and values (Williams & Vorley, 2017). This concept is particularly useful in understanding contexts that experienced radical forms of change, particularly the post-Socialist states where the new liberal market-based institutions are being implanted through path-breaking reforms to replace the old socialist-era institutional framework (Tamilina & Tamilina, 2017). At the firm level, path-break suggests that economic actors and their practices will gradually align with and reflect the key features embodied in the logic of market institutions (Williams & Vorley, 2017).

Indeed, it is increasingly argued that understanding the nuances of SMEs and HRM practices they utilize requires an understanding of how SMEs are socially embedded in their particular national institutional contexts (Harney, 2015; Rowley et al., 2017). Transition in post-Socialist countries entails not only a change of economic model from central-planning to marketisation, but also, as summarised in Table 1, a shift in socio-political system from a form of paternalistic state socialism to a liberal democracy where state no longer officially acts as a benefactor but more as a guarantor of the rule of law (Lane & Myant, 2007). Paternalistic socialism can be described as a political system where the state acts as a supreme authority and a father-like figure and enters into a social contract with its citizens to undertake various provisions in exchange for control and decision-making (Zhu et al., 2012). According to institutional theory, institutional transition entails change in informal institutions reflected in tendencies to move away from embedded paternalistic norms and expectations towards marketisation values and mechanisms. This gives rise to national institutional contexts wherein Soviet-inherited structures of values and social norms co-exist, interact and potentially conflict with newly developed market-based rules and principles (Buck et al., 2003).

Exposure of post-Socialist economies to path-breaking market reforms encompassing liberalisation of prices, market competition and privatisation

Table 1. Relevant features of old and new institutional systems in transition economies.

Comparative dimensions and features	Old/Socialist-era institutional features	New/Post-Socialist era institutional features
Economic system	• state-planned economy • centrally controlled prices • prohibition of private entrepreneurship activities and profit seeking motives	• market-based economy • price liberalisation • centrality of private enterprise activity, competition, efficiency and profit seeking motives
Socio-political system	• social paternalism • limited individual freedom • state cares for all and acts in the interest of all • individuals are part of the collective	• market capitalism • focus on individual and economic freedoms • state acts as provider of rules and laws • people are autonomous actors
Value orientation	• group-oriented culture • collectivistic value system	• individual-oriented culture • individualistic value system
Dominant organisational type and roles	• state-owned enterprises • dominated by paternalistic management tradition • key role to provide jobs and social/non-wage benefits to workers	• privately-owned enterprises • focus on transactional management practices • key role to achieve profitability

Complied by authors from insights from multiple sources: Buck et al. (2003); Lane and Myant (2007); Myant and Drahokoupil (2011); Zhu et al. (2012); Morley et al. (2018).

(Wood & Demirbag, 2018) suggests that traces of new market-oriented HRM in these countries are being gradually implanted and diffused (Morley et al., 2018). These transformations can be captured by the concept of marketization that refers to the expansion of market forces into previously non-market or heavily regulated social and economic spheres (Williams, 2006). Yet, in highlighting the path-dependency perspective and the embeddedness of informal institutions and norms, Buck et al. (2003: 532) state that firms in transition economies "will still try to rely on HRM practices inherited or modified from their central planning past". Such changing conditions, where new market-oriented institutional practices are gradually gaining ground but old ones inherited from the Socialist era are likely to persist, can lead to institutional arrangements that are grounded in different norms and values, potentially leading to HRM strategies that encompass institutional hybridization (Bjerregaard & Lauring, 2012; Zhu et al., 2012). Above discussion suggests that exploration of the impact of institutions on HRM in Kyrgyzstan requires explicit recognition the country's evolving institutional framework.

Context and methodology

Study context: Kyrgyzstan's uncertain environment

It is widely acknowledged that firms in transition economies face an institutional environment which is "far more extreme than that experienced (…) in more developed economies" (Puffer & McCarthy, 2001: 30). Reflecting this, we selected Kyrgyzstan, a post-Soviet transition

economy in the periphery and with a particularly turbulent recent institutional setting, as a suitable context for our study. Kyrgyzstan gained independence in 1991 as a result of the collapse of the USSR. This represented
the first major period of environmental uncertainty as extensive and path-
breaking institutional reforms were required to its political, economic and
social systems. However, several years of unrests culminated in an unprecedented uprising, namely the Tulip Revolution or the First Kyrgyz
Revolution, which resulted in the overthrow of the first president Askar
Akayev's regime in 2005 (Tudoroiu, 2007). The new government, headed by
the former prime minister Kurmanbek Bakiyev, vowed to strengthen the
rule of law and fight corruption. However, five years later his regime too
was overthrown in the Second Kyrgyz Revolution of 2010. These events
reinforced the notion of an environmentally unstable setting, with institutional uncertainty and change at its core.

Research suggests that uncertainty in post-crisis Kyrgyzstan remains high,
as firms continue to deal with the consequences of socio-political turmoil
and regime discontinuities of 2005 and 2010 (Makhmadshoev et al., 2015).
We argue that this backdrop presents an appropriate context to examine
HRM challenges faced by SME exporters and analyse the impact of institutional uncertainty in particular on HRM practices and systems. Our study
focuses on Kyrgyzstan's burgeoning garment sector, which is primarily
dominated by exporting SMEs integrated in regional and global value chains
governed by MNEs. The choice of this industry reflects its status as a major
sector with significant impacts on economic development, exports, and
employment (ILO, 2012). A report by Asian Development Bank suggests
that garments made in Kyrgyzstan account for 5% of all garment imports
in Russia, making Kyrgyz SMEs the fifth largest garment exporters to the
Russian market, behind China, Turkey, Germany and Italy (ADB, 2013).
Others estimate that the sector employs around 150,000 people, or up to
300,000 including those employed in the informal sector, which corresponds
to 6.5% and 13% of total labour force in the country, respectively (ADB,
2013; Birkman et al., 2012; OECD, 2014).

Research method

The data used in this paper was collected as part of a research project
that explored SME challenges and management strategy in Kyrgyzstan.
The fieldwork was conducted by one of the authors in Kyrgyzstan
between April and May of 2018, utilizing a qualitative single country
case-study research design (Creswell, 2007; Yin, 2003). A qualitative case
study approach is a well-established research strategy in the fields of
IHRM (Cooke, 2002; Cunningham & Rowley, 2008) and IB (Ghauri,

2004; Gligor et al., 2016) and is particularly suitable for studying firm activities in transition economies given that such environments manifest increased dynamism and instability and require deeper engagement and understanding of the context in which economic actors operate (Luthans & Ibrayeva, 2006). Indeed, the case study was preferred for its flexibility in allowing the use of data from several sources, namely semi-structured interviews, field observations and published reports. Firms are taken as the main unit of analysis, which is in line with this study's research aim of exploring HRM challenges and practices from the firm perspective (Yin, 2003).

A purposive sampling approach was utilized (Miles & Huberman, 1994) to gather data from firms in the same industry and with internationalisation experience, typically reflected in their participation in regional or global value chains as manufacturers and exporters of garment products. Suitable SMEs were initially identified through official databases of registered firms held by the Ministry of Economy and national business associations, with snowball sampling technique, based on recommendations, subsequently used to expand the pool of respondents. In addition, the named author's personal connections in Kyrgyzstan were also utilised to help facilitate access to firms. Using personal connections to negotiate research access is not uncommon in transition economies as entrepreneurs and firm managers often demonstrate reluctance to participate in academic studies due to high political sensitivities and suspicious attitudes towards interviews (Cooke, 2002; Cunningham, 2010).

In total, 21 firms participated in the study and interviews were conducted with key decision makers. In most cases these were firm owners or co-founders who held key managerial roles. Semi-structured in-depth qualitative interviews were used as the main method of gathering data. Most interviews took place on firm premises and recorded with the consent of interviewees. Given Kyrgyzstan's politically sensitive context, participants were assured that their identities and those of their companies will remain anonymous. All interviews were conducted in Russian by the first author who is fluent in that language and lasted between 50 and 150 min during which a range of topics and issues were discussed. They were subsequently transcribed verbatim by an external organisation and a sample was later cross-checked by the same author. After the completion of formal interviews, the author was frequently granted permission to tour firm facilities under the guidance of shop-floor managers. This resulted in further observational evidence from informal discussions with employees, including middle managers and shop-floor workers (seamstresses). All firms were based in the capital city of Bishkek or its periphery where the garment manufacturing sector is largely concentrated. The workforce in most firms comprised predominantly of female employees. All firms were established between 1994 and 2015, but to respect their anonymity exact founding years are not indicated (Table 2).

Interviews were framed around a series of thematic areas, ranging from general management challenges to perceptions of institutions and policy. In terms of HRM, emphasis was placed to encourage managers to describe their people management practices, challenges they faced in this regard and strategies they adopted in dealing with them. Managers were not only asked to highlight particular problems they faced, but also to reflect and elaborate how they addressed them in the context of wider institutional and political uncertainty in the country. Due to the open-ended nature of the questions asked, respondents often raised issues which were pertinent but not necessarily included originally in the interview programme. The flexibility of semi-structured interviews allowed for follow-up questions to be asked in order to explore these emergent themes further and include them in subsequent interviews.

Transcribed interviews were organized in relevant topics and coded and analysed thematically. Whilst this study adopted an exploratory approach due to paucity of HRM studies in the context of Central Asian transition countries, the data analysis was informed by relevant literature on institutions and HRM. Specifically, the former suggested a broad distinction between formal and informal institutions, whilst the latter highlighted differences between control and commitment HRM approaches. These themes provided a provisional guide to code and analyse our findings, whilst also allowing new themes to emerge from the data. Following the review of interview transcripts, key emergent themes relating to our research questions were identified and relevant parts of interview transcripts were coded to each emergent theme. In line with our stated aims, some themes were based on prior literature and theory, whereas others, specifically concerning the impact of environmental and institutional uncertainty on HRM practices in SMEs emerged from the data (Eisenhardt & Graebner, 2007). This means that while provisional themes from the literature allowed to distinguish and categorize particular HRM challenges and practices in SMEs, specific explanations in support and extension of each theme emerged from the data. The analysis of findings is provided below.

Findings and analysis

This section consists of two parts. The first presents and analyses our findings on key HRM challenges highlighted by study firms. The second

Table 2. Firm characteristics.

Firm No.	No. of workers	Product specialization	Export markets	Interviewee position	Location of the firm
Firm 1	12	Garments and footwear	Russia, Kazakhstan	Co-founder	Bishkek
Firm 2	35–50	Garments	Russia, Kazakhstan, Uzbekistan, Tajikistan	Owner & Manager	Bishkek
Firm 3	100–120	Garments	Russia, Kazakhstan, Uzbekistan	Owner and manager	Outskirts of Bishkek
Firm 4	60–80	Garments	Russia, Kazakhstan, Uzbekistan, Tajikistan	Owner and manager	Bishkek
Firm 5	30–50	Garments	Uzbekistan, Kazakhstan. Russia	Owner and manager	Bishkek
Firm 6	55–80	Garments	Russia, Kazakhstan, Germany, Mongolia	Owner and manager	Bishkek
Firm 7	15–25	Garments	Kazakhstan, Tajikistan, Russia, Uzbekistan	Owner and manager	Bishkek
Firm 8	50–60	Garments	Russia	Managing director	Bishkek
Firm 9	500	Garments	Kazakhstan, Russia	Co-founder and manager	Outskirts of Bishkek
Firm 10	8–10	Garments	Kazakhstan	Owner and manager	Bishkek
Firm 11	60–70	Garments	Kazakhstan, Russia	Managing director	Outskirts of Bishkek
Firm 12	32	Garments	Russia	Owner and manager	Outskirts of Bishkek
Firm 13	40–50	Garments	Russia, Kazakhstan	Owner and manager	Bishkek
Firm 14	8–12	Garments	Kazakhstan, Russia, South Africa	Owner and manager	Bishkek
Firm 15	8–10	Garments	Kazakhstan	Owner and manager	Bishkek
Firm 16	30–50	Garments	Russia	Owner and manager	Bishkek
Firm 17	50	Garments	Russia, Kazakhstan, Armenia	Managing director	Outskirts of Bishkek
Firm 18	6–10	Garments	Russia, Kazakhstan, Dubai, EU countries	Owner and manager	Bishkek
Firm 19	500	Garments	Russia and Kazakhstan	Co-owner and general manager	Bishkek
Firm 20	30	Garments	Russia, Dubai, EU countries	Owner and manager	Bishkek
Firm 21	30–40	Garments	Russia	Owner and manager	Outskirts of Bishkek

part focuses on HRM systems and explores and analyses how SMEs cope with HRM challenges by utilizing bundles of HRM practices that tend to represent either a control or commitment HRM system. We compare the two HRM systems identified in SMEs by focussing on three specific bundles of HRM practices through which differences in HRM systems, and norms and traditions they are embedded in, become visible.

HRM challenges in an environment of high institutional uncertainty

All SMEs reported high levels of labour turnover, which is perceived to be a major challenge that threatens their survival and growth. Managers argue that due to the unregulated labour market and the existence of a significant shadow economy, it is quite common for workers to terminate their engagement without prior notice. This problem is intensified by the scarcity of qualified workforce in the industry. In this light, a firm owner states as follows:

> We don't have enough good and experienced workers, that's the first issue … The second and more important is that the turnover is very high, it is very difficult to hold on to good workers, incredibly difficult … they dictate their own terms. (Firm 2)

Ample evidence suggests that high levels of labour turnover in combination with periods of labour shortage and labour poaching undermine mid- to long-range planning in SMEs, heightening uncertainty regarding timely fulfilment of orders for overseas customers and MNE counterparts in regional markets and thereby threaten the survival of SMEs. Coping with uncertainty over labour staffing is therefore a key HRM challenge, as illustrated by this quote:

> … You know that you have a hundred people working for you, you accept a big order from a multinational retail chain for 24,000 items on the assumption that you have 100 workers … and one day you come to work to find out that you have only 4 people left on the factory floor! And when you inquire you find out that other firms, many in the informal sector, are offering more money because it is a high season … then of course you are unable to fulfil the order, half of your buyers stop working with you. (Firm 13)

SME managers also highlight that relationships between workers and managers tend to be conflict-ridden, embodied in low levels of commitment, frequent unapproved absences and unstable performance and regular organisational misbehaviour, such as name calling and shouting on both sides. This points to a more fundamental HRM challenge faced by SMEs that relates to a recent increase in workers' power position which has been reinforced by the rapid growth and internationalisation of the Kyrgyz garment sector and increased migration of skilled and semi-skilled labour overseas. These circumstances exacerbate labour shortage and present a serious challenge for SMEs, particularly in relation to attraction and retention of labour. This is evident from the following excerpt:

> …one female worker did not come to work for three days and then was suddenly at her desk again, without telling me what happened. If I would give her a formal warning for her absence, she would just leave… (Firm 5)

Therein, the shortage of labour supply causes chronical understaffing, especially during peak seasons when SMEs in the shadow economy attract labour for higher salaries that SMEs in the formal sector cannot match. The above firm owner continues their narrative by comparing the lack of effective formal rules and regulations with the Soviet past that is considered to be more orderly:

> In the Soviet times all workers had a workbook. In order to get a new job your previous employer had to indicate in this book the reason you left them. And if the reason was poor behaviour, or theft, or something of that sort, then finding a new job would be very difficult. Our government doesn't introduce these kinds of documents. But we need something like this… (Firm 5)

This section analysed findings in relation to the first research question. It is suggested that the key features of the context in which SMEs are embedded are characterized by high levels of institutional uncertainty. This uncertainty is encoded in unregulated labour market, frequently changing regulations, weak enforcement of formal rules and a powerful shadow economy. In such conditions high labour turnover in combination with labour shortage and wider difficulties concerning the implementation of efficient reward and disciplinary practices for workers are identified as key HRM challenges for SME exporters. The following section suggests that SMEs aim to overcome these HRM challenges by utilizing two contrasting HRM systems. Importantly, it is argued that these HRM systems are shaped in different ways by distinctive elements of the old and new institutional structures and practices against the wider backdrop of rapidly changing and highly uncertain institutional landscape.

HRM control system: The prevalence of individual and transactional reward practices

Impersonal management and tight job control
SMEs belonging to this cluster cope with the above discussed HRM challenges by organizing and managing the labour process in a way that increases replaceability and status of the workforce as a commodity, with the aim of making management less dependent on individual workers. SMEs provide tightly defined jobs and associated tasks that are framed

by a set of rules, behavioural norms and procedures. For example, breaks from work are standardized and deviation from the norm needs to be explained to management, putting workers under constant pressure to finish tasks within a given time set. The tight structural control is aligned with direct managerial control, as most SMEs in this cluster installed a dedicated shop floor supervisor whose task is to ensure that workers fulfil their individual quota and perform the standardized practices in time. Some SMEs even installed video cameras on the shop floor to have an additional opportunity to monitor and control workers. Here, the relationship between worker and management is described as impersonal and characterized by low levels of trust. Indeed, Lepak et al. (2006) suggest that replaceability and low-trust relations are core characteristics of control HRM systems. These dimensions are central leitmotifs in the following reflection of SME manager on their management approach.

> We are an economic unit and I need to make sure we fulfil orders. How do I accomplish that when the workers come and go? I make sure that the ones who are showing up fulfil their duties. That is why I have video cameras on the shop-floor. I hardly know everyone's name and I don't know if they are here tomorrow, how can I trust them? They are monitored and that is why they work hard. They get paid for it, so it is a fair deal ... (Firm 7)

This quote aptly captures perspectives of the majority of interviewed managers who tend to utilise this HRM system in the way that low trust-based relations in combination with a high control oriented approach are justified with a heightened marketization of the political economy in the country. This informs a focus on work as a pure economic exchange, triggered by competitive pressures, fluctuating demands, unregulated labour market and weak law enforcement.

Performance management and incentive system

The HRM challenge of implementing effective disciplinary and reward practices is tackled by a deeply individualized system that renders the employment arrangement as a short-term transactional and monetary driven exchange. Here, individual incentive components were key for rewarding, motivating and retaining labour. This represents a path-breaking change and therefore a distinct deviation from the traditional Soviet-inherited system of norms and values which placed emphasis on collective performance and offered collective bonuses and non-wage benefits based on seniority, rank of workers and group performance (Buck et al., 2003; Zhu et al., 2012). Marketization elements of competition, transactional exchange and individualization are deeply interwoven in narratives about performance management practices, as captured in the following quote:

> ... an attractive financial package is the most important thing to keep workers
> happy. But workers do not get that just for being here. They need to deliver and
> the more they deliver the better are the ... incentives. (Firm 9)

Generally, these SME managers prioritize the market-driven performance management practice over the traditional and more egalitarian payment system, as it builds on the more individualized and economic rationality driven employment arrangement in the unregulated labour market, instead of fighting it. This is also inherent in the following reflection:

> ... there are no contracts, it is uncertain who will be here in a month. So I had
> to adopt and implement individual work effort based pay. Why and how should I
> reward teams when they change? (Firm 4)

Emphasis on HRM practices that focus on monetary incentives and individual performance-based renumeration is a reflection of how informal institutions pertaining to norms and values of the new market-based economic system are becoming gradually influential in the Kyrgyz export SME context. This demonstrates traces of managerial thinking and commitment to new institutional norms in managing labour and as such represent a shift or break away from social norms and principles that are associated with the previous socialist system.

Investment in workers

The "headcount resource" (Storey, 1992:29) approach and the aim to increase the replaceability of labour (Lepak et al., 2006) suggests reduced investment by SMEs in their workers. Indeed, notable incentives beyond individual performance pay are not offered to workers and as such seniority is rarely rewarded. In a similar vein, SME owners in this cluster minimize investment in training and focus exclusively on inexpensive and short-term task-related training. The transactional approach that informs training and skill formation practices in SMEs has little interest in developing human resources but focusses more on attracting and replacing labour swiftly given the high levels of turnover. Indeed, on-the-job training for new seamstress recruits is provided that typically lasts between two days and a week. A key element of training is the informal practice of work shadowing, where new recruits work under the guidance of an experienced worker who is selected by management based on the criteria of performance. The aim of this short-term training is to prepare employees for their job as fast as possible and socialize them into an individualized performance culture.

> Workers come and go. Why should I spend much on training? Spending money
> on someone who leaves after 10–12 weeks?! I don't think so. They learn on the
> job how to use this sewing machine. (Firm 8)

... given the high turnover it is important to make sure they hit the ground running as soon as possible ... Ideally, workers are on machines after a couple of days of work shadowing. (Firm 4)

In summary, the control oriented HRM practices in the Kyrgyz garment industry culminate in the way that the individual worker is managed on an instrumental basis, with economic incentives being the principal source of recognition for workers' performance and loyalty. The reward practices utilized by SMEs in this cluster are primarily quantitative, calculative and tend to treat workers as a commodity. SMEs utilizing this HRM system cope with the uncertainty and the HRM challenges it poses by minimizing reliance on workers, making them exchangeable. Here, a marketized approach to the employment relationship is adopted, conceptualizing it as a short-term economic exchange. The following quote candidly summarizes the market-oriented control approach and illustrates the path-break that embeds the control HRM system in the increasingly marketized and short-term oriented environment:

> Some SMEs operate as if we are still living in the Soviet times. They focus on loyalty, seniority rules and so on. But it is the 21st century now, the market economy has changed everything, firms are competing, it is about the survival of the fittest ... you cannot try to fulfil social obligations as a firm here, these norms have changed ... (Firm 5)

HRM commitment system: commitment through reciprocal exchange and managerial paternalism

Bundles of HRM practices in SMEs belonging to this cluster co-mingle marketization elements with selective values and behavioural norms stemming from the Socialist past, highlighting selective path-dependency and thereby the importance of embedded informal institutions. We dub this hybrid system a 'commitment-paternalist HRM system'.

Personalized management and paternalism

SMEs that pursue a commitment oriented HRM system organize work *via* formal descriptions, rules and procedures. Here, a distinct characteristic of this approach is visible in the prevalence of 'responsible autonomy', embodied by the move from explicit external control over performance to more self-control and team control (Paauwe & Boselie, 2008). SME management control the output of all workers on a daily basis and visit regularly the shop floor. Observations portray these shop floor visits as primarily informal, encapsulated in short chats between management and workers about work as well as non-work aspects. The importance of 'responsible autonomy' that grants workers pockets of discretion in the relatively standardized labour process, while focussing on the disciplining character of team and internal control, is discussed by the following narratives:

> I don't think that someone watching over workers' shoulders every minute of the day helps. If I have the impression that there is a worker who is not pulling their weight, I will have an eye on her, but generally I let them do their job and if there are problems the teams often solve it amongst themselves… I am not interfering with their work unless performance is constantly poor. (Firm 2).

> … as long as the output at the end of the day meets the expectations, I do not closely monitor workers. Of course, attendance is checked, but how long they spend at lunch and if they have to take a call while at work is not my concern… If there are problems with someone taking advantage of others by doing less, the workers themselves tend to regulate that. (Firm 12).

Therein, SMEs in this cluster are characterized by less direct managerial control and workers act in semi-autonomous workgroups who are given a degree of flexibility in certain aspects so long as the performance is sufficient for the manager.

Performance management system: Egalitarian pay and collective bonuses

Another distinctive characteristic of SMEs using commitment and paternalist HRM strategies is the utilization of egalitarian wages in combination with collective bonuses for workers based on group performance and the performance of the company. Here, path-dependency is evident as egalitarian wages that have little relationship to individual performance were a key characteristic of personnel management under the socialist regime (Buck et al., 2003; Zhu et al., 2012). Indeed, performance and pay practices of SMEs in this cluster mix egalitarian wages with a combination of efficiency and group performance wages. As the narratives below show, there are two key dimensions to this remuneration practice. First, collective financial bonuses that exist for all workers are coupled with collective productivity targets, thereby strengthening the importance of collective effort in combination with heightening workers interest to perform team control, a key aspect of commitment HRM system (Hauff et al., 2014). Second, annual holiday vacations are offered to all workers. This incentive is collectively organized, and the aim is that workers spent time with their colleagues, families and management. Here, path-dependency is again evident in the way collective incentives for exceeding performance expectations, a modern commitment HRM practice (Storey, 1992), is combined with paternalist practices that portray the firms as organisations that care about their workers, highlighting a fatherly and benevolent management approach:

I don't believe in paying individual bonuses to workers, I think it is counterproductive, it creates more problems than solutions. I prefer to reward the collective so that everyone benefits as we all work together... Sharing responsibility is key. (Firm 14).

I buy them and their families holiday trips to Issyk-Kul (a holiday resort) every year. When they worked so hard all year as a collective and reached our aims, they deserve it. This strengthens ties, boosts their morale and creates a real cohesion, and for me too - I get to know workers and their families better. (Firm 3).

More broadly, the impact of path-dependent informal institutions was strongly evident among this group of SME owners in that they frequently and often evocatively recalled socialist era norms and practices, particularly in relation to the role of organisations in caring for workers and providing social or non-wage benefits such as housing or holidays that went beyond financial rewards, and workplaces being regarded as having a greater sense of belonging. It was indicated that some workers still expected firms to continue with such practices. As suggested by Minbaeva et al. (2007), provision of social benefits by enterprises under the old socialist system was considered a norm as well as an expectation, which points to the contextual embeddedness of this sentiment. This showcases that inherited norms and traditions continue to shape SME managers' HRM approach today.

Investment in workers

A crucial practice that showcases the co-mingling of commitment and paternalism *via* investment in workers is represented in the decision of some SMEs in this cluster to install sewing machines in homes of experienced workers who had caring responsibilities. As the following testimonial of a manager illustrates, the decision to install sewing machines in the home of workers represents an attempt to facilitate the convergence of workers' interests and organizational goals. The organisational goal is represented in the aim to reduce turnover, maintain experienced workers and establish a ground for mutual reciprocity which is a key ingredient of the paternalist HRM management (Zhu et al., 2012). Furthermore, workers who had stayed with the SME for a minimum of 12 months, and who were perceived by the manager to be reliable and hard-working, were allowed to work from home. This novel practice is also a strategy that aims to offer seniority benefits in exchange for loyalty, aiming to make up for lack of career progression in this sector.

I am caring about workers and some of them have family commitments that conflict with coming here and working in the factory. So, I decided to install sewing machines in their homes and allowing them to work from home (...) and what I found is that my "home-workers" are much more reliable. I learned that you have to invest, you have to trust and commit to them in order for them to commit to you. (Firm 6)

As alluded earlier, social programmes and non-wage benefits for workers are historically anchored in the old socialist system in which organisations acted as a small society, providing exclusive benefits such as healthcare, education, recreational holiday trips and housing (Buck et al., 2003; Minbaeva et al., 2007; Zhu et al., 2012). After the collapse of the Soviet regime and the start of a radical institutional and political change that went in tandem with marketization and transition towards (a form of) capitalism, some SMEs continued to offer scaled-down but nonetheless a distinctive set of social programmes to their workers. This approach which places emphasis on providing social benefits to the collective can be seen to be explicitly shaped by past institutional norms and practices. For example, a number of SMEs offer workers and their families assistance in renting and buying affordable homes, while also providing workers with personal loans in times of need. As the following quotes highlight, these HRM practices combine the ambition to meet workers needs with the aim to strengthen workers loyalty through establishing a HRM system that rests on values of mutual reciprocity and care. These practices showcase how the commitment HRM system is interwoven with values and norms that stem from informal and cultural institutions that are anchored in the past, further highlighting the path-dependency of institutional change that contributes to the hybridity of this HRM system in SMEs. This is illustrated further in the following excerpts:

> We grew up in the Soviet Union with a different value system, so I can't ignore the social welfare of my workers. Focussing on workers needs is crucial, such thinking is embedded in us ... I can't grow on my own, but I can if they grow together with me, like a family. (Firm 13)

> Things were different in the past, workers were more loyal but companies also cared more, it wasn't just about earning money. And some workers still expect that and when you treat them appropriately, with respect, why would they leave? (Firm 2)

> I want to provide them an opportunity to bring their kids with them and live here in company-sponsored housing ... This is my way to help them socially, but I benefit too because they will stay with me for at least 5 years ... (Firm 3)

In summary, the two sections above analysed findings in relation to the second and third research questions. Our findings identify two distinct HRM systems employed by exporting SMEs in Kyrgyzstan, namely the *control HRM* characterised by establishing commitment through individual and transactional reward practices and *commitment-paternalist*

HRM which focuses on reciprocal exchange and managerial paternalism. The two models diverge on three key aspects, namely management and job control, performance management and incentive system, and training and worker investment. While some firms tend to employ practices and strategies that seem consistent with key principles of the control HRM system, others tend to adopt practices and measures that combine commitment with paternalistic management strategies, which is identified here as a hybrid form of commitment HRM. A further key finding is that while the control HRM system is seemingly shaped by elements of the new market-oriented institutions, the commitment HRM system is influenced by the old socialist-era institutional structures. While exposure to market reforms and almost three decades of economic liberalisation reflect progress in terms of transition towards the path-breaking market institutions which is captured in the control HRM model, the path-dependent institutions and norms from the socialist era also seemingly persist and appear to continue to influence HRM practices as reflected by the commitment-paternalist HRM model. We now discuss the implications of these findings.

Discussion, conclusions and implications

This article answers calls for research on HRM in SMEs located in transition economies that are characterized by high levels of environmental uncertainty and contributes to the gap of knowledge on HRM systems in SMEs (Borda et al., 2019; Cunningham, 2010; Marchington, 2015; Psychogios & Prouska, 2019). Informed by evidence from exporting SMEs located in the garment industry of Kyrgyzstan, the article utilises the theory of HRM systems in combination with institutional theory and the concept of path-dependency and provides new insights into HRM challenges and HRM systems in SMEs against the backdrop of an environment characterized by high levels of institutional uncertainty. This article offers three key contributions to the empirical and theoretical literature on HRM in SMEs.

First, the article highlights the importance of institutional approaches in combination with HRM systems theory for understanding HRM in SMEs located in highly uncertain environments. The article stresses that the institutional theory of informal institutions and the concept of path-dependency are well-suited to analyse the ingredients of uncertainty for SMEs and HRM challenges they pose by understanding institutional change in transition economies as characterized by change and continuity, incrementalism and rupture (North, 1990). Indeed, focusing on the contested, radical and on-going transition from socialism to market-based system has enabled the article to capture the high levels of uncertainty in Kyrgyzstan, embodied in unregulated labour market, weak property and labour law enforcement and a strong shadow economy. Against this uncertain backdrop, exporting SMEs in the garment industry encountered unique HRM challenges, ranging from the constant threat of labour shortages, high levels of labour turnover to problems of implementing efficient discipline and reward policies.

Thereby, this article adds to the literature on HRM in SMEs a distinct set of fundamental HRM challenges, supporting the thesis that SMEs are highly vulnerable to environmental uncertainty (Edwards & Ram, 2006; Festing et al., 2013; Storey et al., 2010). The majority of HRM research on SMEs is conducted in relatively stable political and economic environments that are characterized by higher levels of environmental and institutional certainty. Here, HRM challenges in SMEs are often of technical and strategic in nature, explained with the lack of HRM expertise and specialism (Harney, 2015). This article underlines the discussion of the importance of contextualising HRM to understand the interplay between SMEs and the wider environment on the one hand, and particular HRM challenges that emerge from this environment on the other (Cunningham, 2010; Delbridge & Keenoy, 2010; Horwitz & Budhwar, 2015; Psychogios & Prouska, 2019).

The second key contribution of this article is that it addresses the gap of research on HRM systems in SMEs (Borda et al., 2019; Psychogios & Prouska, 2019) and identifies and analyses two contrasting HRM systems in Kyrgyz SMEs. First, the article identifies a control HRM system among some SMEs that deploy transactional, individualized and low-trust HRM practices (Guest, 1987; Hauff et al., 2014; Storey, 1992). These HRM practices aim to solve the distinctive HRM challenges by heightening the replaceability of labour and tightening managerial control and thus represent the core characteristic of control HRM. The combination of HRM system theory with institutional theory enhances understanding of the embeddedness of HRM system in an uncertain context while also allowing to analyse some of the reasoning behind deploying the control HRM system. Here, the article offers novel insights into how SME managers adopting this HRM system refer to market forces of the newly introduced market-based institutional system. This is incorporated in the logic of individualised competition and low trust-based transactional exchanges that informs their decision to adopt a path-break approach with traditional values of informal institutions and deploy a control HRM system that aligns more with contemporary market economy values and thereby enables them to adapt to external environmental uncertainty.

In contrast, a novel hybrid commitment HRM system that this article coins 'commitment-paternalist HRM system' is also identified among some SMEs. They tend to utilize practices that are associated with HRM commitment systems such as responsible autonomy for workers, personal and direct communication between workers and management and investment in workers (Guest, 1987; Storey, 1992; Wilkinson et al., 1992). Yet, the article suggests that strong notions of paternalism accompany commitment practices. Paternalism is visible in the fatherly and benevolent managerial approach that aims to establish reciprocal exchange, loyalty and moral ties between management and workers in order to elicit control from inside the worker and strengthen loyalty to the firm (Thompson, 2011; Zhu et al., 2012). The focus on the legacy of informal institutions situates the commitment-paternalist HRM system approach within its broader institutional context, pointing to the influence of path-dependent institutions. Indeed, this article showcases how some SMEs consciously merge values and behavioural norms that stem from informal institutions that are anchored in the Soviet past with modern HRM commitment system practices. This is reflected in SME managers' belief that a collective and reciprocal approach to labour management is key to overcome the perennial HRM challenges in an environment with high institutional uncertainty.

This supports Zhu et al. (2012) and Psychogios and Prouska (2019) emphasis on the importance of exploring informal institutions and the path-dependency of SMEs in transition economies in order to fully understand the nature of HRM in SMEs and their strategies. Following on from this, the article supports Buck et al. (2003) and Morley et al. (2018) suggesting that it is not only important to understand path-dependent change, but also to capture path-breaking change in order to unravel the diverse and distinctive types of HRM that emerge as a result of the co-existence of strong market forces and the continuing importance of informal institutions and "ideational legacies" from the past (Morley et al., 2018: 473). Therein, our study also highlights that the process of change from socialism to capitalism is not straightforward but is rather riddled with uncertainties, complexities and contradictions, including in terms of HRM practices. This is reflected in our findings which reveal the evolutionary nature of HRM systems in a transition economy context. The existence of a hybrid HRM system further strengthens the usefulness and applicability of HRM systems in exploring HRM in SMEs. Indeed, discussions about hybrid HRM systems are a key debate in the literature on HRM in large organisations (Hauff et al., 2014) and this article suggests this discussion to be extended to the field of HRM in SMEs (Borda et al., 2019).

Lastly, the article contributes to the discussion regarding the convergence, divergence and hybridization of western HRM practices in emerging and transition countries. This paper is among the first studies to focus on HRM issues in the Central Asian transitional periphery more generally, and on HRM practices of exporting SMEs in this region in particular, thereby highlighting a valuable empirical contribution by extending HRM literature to new grounds. Warner (2009) and Rowley et al. (2017) and Zhu et al. (2012) have argued that HRM systems in large organisations are primarily characterized by within-country and between country variations. This article contributes to this discussion by providing evidence of a within-industry variation of HRM systems that go back to the different ways that SME managers tackle HRM challenges. In this way, the variability and yet coherence of HRM practices even in highly uncertain environments is illustrated and explained with the differing set of values and norms that stem from new and past institutions in a context that has experienced radical and on-going change and uncertainty. Supporting Psychogios and Prouska (2019) and Rowley et al. (2017), this article suggests that in order to understand variations of HRM in organisations, and particularly in internationally oriented SMEs in transition economies, the concepts of informal institutions and path-dependency are well equipped to contextualize HRM theory, allowing to capture and explain variations and hybridization. Yet, more research needs to be done on HRM systems and their embeddedness in formal and informal institutions in order to illustrate a nuanced portrayal of the variety of HRM practices, systems and strategic choices, including in contexts that are characterized by high levels of uncertainty.

Practical implications, limitations and future research

The peripheral transition economies in Central Asia are endowed with natural resources and rapidly growing markets, making them attractive but so far relatively unexplored destinations for international businesses (Minbaeva et al., 2007; Wood & Demirbag, 2015). This study offers rare empirical insights into the state of HRM in this "historically" under researched region (Morley et al., 2018: 469) and suggests that firms that are currently active in, or are seeking entry into Kyrgyzstan need to be aware of the co-existence of older and newer institutional structures that run counter to the assumption that institutional environments in transitional periphery may be homogenous. The article provides implications for practice by developing awareness of how the co-existence of path-dependent and path-breaking institutional change shapes HRM systems in different ways. HRM concepts and tools have been dominated by

Western discourses and developed and tested in MNEs. The article argues that firms entering Kyrgyzstan should be aware that Western HRM models tend to reflect an "individualistic context" (Rowley et al., 2017:11), whose ideals of behaviour emphasize individual accomplishments, individual incentives and individual development. These ideals, while gradually being set in place, may still be in conflict with deeply embedded values and behavioural norms of many labour market participants, although not all of them as evidenced in this paper. Furthermore, the study suggests that academics and practitioners need to be sensitive towards the particular contexts and past and present formal and informal institutions that shape HRM practices in transition economies (Delbridge & Keenoy, 2010). The illustration of two different HRM systems also offers an understanding of how firms in transition economies manage people in unique and novel ways against the backdrop of context specific HRM challenges. It adds to the prevalence of the dualistic control and commitment HRM system focus in the literature a contextualized social and political focus, suggesting that control and commitment systems are used in non-Western contexts in hybrid forms. Thus, understandings of hybrid HRM systems allows practitioners to develop an understanding of the reality of HRM in different contexts and supports the development of new place-based models and interventions to help firms improve their practices and achieve better performance and strategic outcomes. Such a contextualised approach will help practitioners and policy makers alike to avoid the drawbacks of 'one-size-fits-all' type recommendations on HRM.

Lastly, it remains to acknowledge the present paper's limitations in the context of which its findings should be viewed. It is important to highlight that the firms included in this study are exposed to international markets and the particular approaches to HRM identified may, in part, also reflect the pressures they face from exposure to international competition. Thus, caution is advised in applying the findings of this study as they may not be generalisable to firms with no internationalisation experience. Future research can, for instance, complement the findings of this study by examining the state of HRM in domestically oriented firms and whether such firms adopt a similar mix of HRM systems or whether their practices reflect greater commitment to older or newer institutional structures. Additionally, it has not been the focus of this paper to address how owner-specific characteristics such as background, age, education, generation and entrepreneurial orientation, among others, impact HRM approaches at the firm level. While addressing these questions was beyond the scope of this study, they also represent potentially promising and similarly understudied avenues that future researchers can address to gain a more complete understanding of the micro and macro-level factors impacting HRM in transition contexts. Lastly, the study's methodological approach and in particular its singular focus on the garment industry also constrains the wider generalisability of its findings. Future research is advised to adopt more cross-industry efforts to add to the findings of this study.

Disclosure statement

No potential conflict of interest was reported by the author(s).

References

Asian Development Bank (ADB). (2013). *Private sector assessment update: The Kyrgyz Republic*. Asian Development Bank (ADB).

Bacon, N., & Hoque, K. (2005). HRM in the SME sector: valuable employees and coercive networks. *The International Journal of Human Resource Management*, 16(11), 1976–1999. https://doi.org/10.1080/09585190500314706

Bacon, N., Ackers, P., Storey, J., & Coates, D. (1996). It's a small world: Managing human resources in small businesses. *The International Journal of Human Resource Management*, 7(1), 82–100. https://doi.org/10.1080/09585199600000119

Barrett, R., & Mayson, S. (2007). Human resource management in growing small firms. *Journal of Small Business and Enterprise Development*, 14(2), 307–320. https://doi.org/10.1108/14626000710746727

Barringer, M. W., & Milkovich, G. T. (1998). A theoretical exploration of the adoption and design of flexible benefit plans: A case of human resource innovation. *The Academy of Management Review*, 23(2), 305–324.

Behrends, T. (2007). Recruitment practices in small and medium size enterprises: An empirical study among knowledge-intensive professional service firms. *Management Revue*, 18(1), 55–74.

Birkman, L., Kaloshkina, M., Khan, M., Shavurov, U., & Smallhouse, S. (2012). *Textile and apparel cluster in Kyrgyzstan*. Harvard Kennedy School and Harvard Business School.

Bjerregaard, T., & Lauring, J. (2012). Entrepreneurship and institutional change: Strategies of bridging institutional contradictions. *European Management Review*, 9(1), 31–43.

Borda, D. G., Hansen, N., & Gore, J. (2019). Control and commitment HRM systems in SME family firms. *Academy of Management Proceedings*, 2019(1), 1–39.

Buck, T., Filatotchev, I., Demina, N., & Wright, M. (2003). Insider ownership, human resource strategies and performance in a transition economy. *Journal of International Business Studies*, 34(6), 530–549. https://doi.org/10.1057/palgrave.jibs.8400065

Campbell, J. L. (2004). *Institutional change and globalisation*. Princeton University Press.

Child, J., & Tse, D. (2001). China's transition and its implications for international business. *Journal of International Business Studies*, 32(1), 5–21. https://doi.org/10.1057/palgrave.jibs.8490935

Cooke, F. L. (2002). Ownership change and reshaping of employee relations in China: A study of two manufacturing companies. *Journal of Industrial Relations*, 44(1), 19–40.

Cooke, F. L. (2005). *HRM, work and employment in China*. Routledge.

Creswell, J. W. (2007). *Qualitative inquiry and research design: Choosing among five approaches.* Sage Publications, Inc.

Cunningham, L. X. (2010). Managing human resources in SMEs in a transition economy: Evidence from China. *The International Journal of Human Resource Management, 21*(12), 2120–2141.

Cunningham, X. L., & Rowley, C. (2008). The development of Chinese small and medium enterprises and human resource management: A review. *Asia Pacific Journal of Human Resource, 46*(3), 353–379.

Delbridge, R., & Keenoy, T. (2010). Beyond managerialism? *The International Journal of Human Resource Management, 21*(6), 799–817.

Delbridge, R., Hauptmeier, M., & Sengupta, S. (2011). Beyond the enterprise: Broadening the horizons of international HRM. *Human Relations, 64*(4), 483–505.

Dibben, P., Brewster, C., Brookes, M., Cunha, R., Webster, E., & Wood, G. (2017). Institutional legacies and HRM: Similarities and differences in HRM practices in Purtugal and Mozambique. *The International Journal of Human Resource Management, 28*(18), 2519–2537. https://doi.org/10.1080/09585192.2016.1164225

Dietz, G., Wiele, T., Iwaarden, J., & Brosseau, J. (2006). HRM inside UK e-commerce firms. *International Small Business Journal: Researching Entrepreneurship, 24*(5), 443–470. https://doi.org/10.1177/0266242606067267

Edwards, P., & Ram, M. (2006). Surviving on the margins of the economy: Working relationships in small, low-wage firms. *Journal of Management Studies, 43*(4), 895–916.

Eisenhardt, K. M., & Graebner, M. E. (2007). Theory building from cases: Opportunities and challenges. *Academy of Management Journal, 50*(1), 25–32.

Festing, M., Schäfer, L., & Scullion, H. (2013). Talent management in medium-sized German companies: An explorative study and agenda for future research. *The International Journal of Human Resource Management, 24*(9), 1872–1893. https://doi.org/10.1080/09585192.2013.777538

Garengo, P., Biazzo, S., & Bititci, U. S. (2005). Performance measurement systems in SMEs: A review for a research agenda. *International Journal of Management Reviews, 7*(1), 25–47. https://doi.org/10.1111/j.1468-2370.2005.00105.x

Geare, A., Edgar, F., & McAndrew, I. (2006). Employment relationships: Ideology and HRM practice. *International Journal of Human Resource Management, 17*(7), 1190–1208.

Ghauri, P. (2004). Designing and conducting case studies in international business research. In R. Piekkari & C. Welch (Eds.), *Handbook of qualitative research methods for international business.* Edward Elgar.

Gligor, D. M., Esmark, C. L., & Golgeci, I. (2016). Building international business theory: A grounded theory approach. *Journal of International Business Studies, 47*(1), 93–111.

Gooderham, P. N., Mayrhofer, W., & Brewster, C. (2019). A framework for comparative institutional research on HRM. *The International Journal of Human Resource Management, 30*(1), 5–30.

Guest, D. (1987). Human resource management and industrial relations. *Journal of Management Studies, 24*(5), 503–521.

Hauff, S., Alewell, D., & Hansen, N. K. (2014). HRM systems between control and commitment: Occurrence, characteristics and effects on HR outcomes and firm performance. *Human Resource Management Journal, 24*(4), 424–441.

International Labour Organization (ILO). (2012). *Skills for trade and economic diversification in the Kyrgyz garment sector* (Employment Report No.19). International Labour Organization.

International Labour Organization (ILO). (2015). *Small and medium-sized enterprises and decent and productive employment creation*. Report IV. International Labour Conference, 104th session, International Labour Office.

Harney, B. (2015). HRM and SMEs: Contextualizing significance, neglect and meaning in an international context. In C. Machado (Ed.), *International human resources management and industrial engineering* (pp. 109–122). Springer.

Harney, B., & Nolan, C. (2014). HRM in small and medium-sized firms. In B. Harney & K. Monks (Eds.), *Strategic HRM: Research and practice in Ireland* (pp. 153–169). Blackhall/Open Press.

Hendry, C., & Pettigrew, A. (1990). Human resource management: An agenda for the 1990s. *International Journal of Human Resource Management, 1*(1), 17–44.

Horwitz, F. M., & Budhwar, P. (2015). *Handbook of human resource management in emerging markets*. Edward Elgar.

Huang, Q., & Gamble, J. (2011). Informal institutional constraints and their impact on HRM and employee satisfaction: Evidence from China's retail sector. *The International Journal of Human Resource Management, 22*(15), 3168–3186.

Hudson, M., Smart, A., & Bourne, M. (2001). Theory and practice in SME performance measurement systems. *International Journal of Operations & Production Management, 21*(8), 1096–1115. https://doi.org/10.1108/EUM0000000005587

Jackson, S. E., Schuler, R. S., & Jiang, K. (2014). An aspirational framework for strategic human resource management. *Academy of Management Annals, 8*(1), 1–56.

Lane, D., & Myant, M. (2007). (Eds) *Varieties of capitalism in post-communist countries*. Palgrave.

Legge, K. (2005). *Human resource management: Rhetorics and realities; Anniversary Edition*. Palgrave Macmillan.

Lepak, D. P., Liao, H., Chung, Y., & Harden, E. E. (2006). A conceptual review of human resource management systems in strategic human resource management research. *Research in Personnel and Human Resource Management, 25*, 217–271.

Luthans, F., & Ibrayeva, E. S. (2006). Entrepreneurial self-efficacy in Central Asian transition economies: Quantitative and qualitative analyses. *Journal of International Business Studies, 37*(1), 92–110.

Makhmadshoev, D., Ibeh, K., & Crone, M. (2015). Institutional influences on SME exportersunder divergent transition paths: Comparative insights from Tajikistan and Kyrgyzstan. *International Business Review, 24*(6), 1025

Makhmadshoev, D. (2018). Expanding the boundaries of institutional analysis in the transitional periphery. In M. Demirbag and G. Wood (Eds.), *Comparative capitalism and the transitional periphery: Firm centred perspectives*. Edward Elgar

Marchington, M. (2015). Human resource management (HRM): Too busy looking up to see where it is going longer term? *Human Resource Management Review, 25*(2), 176–187.

Marlow, S., & Patton, D. (2002). Minding the gap between employers and employees: The challenge for owner-managers or smaller manufacturing firms. *Employee Relations, 24*(5), 523–539.

Matten, D., & Geppert, M. (2004). Work systems in heavy engineering: The role of national culture and national institutions in multinational corporations. *Journal of International Management, 10*(2), 177–198.

Mcguire, D., & Laaser, K. (2018). You have to pick': Cotton and state-organized forced labour in Uzbekistan. *Economic and Industrial Democracy*, Epub ahead of print August 2018, https://doi.org/10.1177/0143831X18789786

Miles, M. B., & Huberman, A. M. (1994). *Qualitative data analysis: An expanded source-book*. Sage Publications.

Minbaeva, D. B., Hutchings, K., & Thomson, S. B. (2007). Hybrid human resource management in post-Soviet Kazakhstan. *European Journal of International Management*, *1*(4), 350–371.

Morley, M. J., Minbaeva, D., & Michailova, S. (2018). HRM in the transition states of Central and Eastern Europe and former Soviet Union. In C. Brewster, W. Mayrhofer & E. Farndale (Eds.), *Handbook of research on comparative human resource management*. Edward Elgar.

Myant, M. & Drahokoupil, J. *Transition Economies: Political Economy in Russia*, Eastern Europe, and Central Asia. San Francisco, CA: Wiley.

Nguyen, T., & Bryant, S. (2004). A study of the formality of human resource management practices in small and medium-size enterprises in Vietnam. *International Small Business Journal: Researching Entrepreneurship*, *22*(6), 595–618. https://doi.org/10.1177/0266242604047412

Nohria, N., & Ghoshal, S. (1997). *The differentiated network: Organizing multinational corporations for value creation*. Jossey-Bass.

North, D. C. (1990). *Institutions, institutional change, and economic performance*. Cambridge University Press.

Organisation for Economic Co-operation and Development (OECD). (2014). Expanding the garment industry in the Kyrgyz Republic. *Private sector development, policy handbook*. OECD Eurasia Competitive Program.

Paauwe, J. & Boselie, P. (2008). HRM and social embeddedness. In P. Boxall, J. Purcell, and P.M. Wright (Eds.), *The Oxford handbook of HRM*, Oxford: Oxford University Press.

Peng, M. W., & Luo, Y. (2000). Managerial ties and firm performance in a transition economy: The nature of micro-macro link. *The Academy of Management Journal*, *43*(3), 486–501.

Puffer, S. M., & McCarthy, D. J. (2001). Navigating the hostile maze: A framework for Russian entrepreneurship. *Academy of Management Executive*, *15*(4), 24–36.

Puffer, S. M., McCarthy, D. J., & Boisot, M. (2010). Entrepreneurship in Russia and China: The impact of formal institutional voids. *Entrepreneurship Theory and Practice*, *34*(3), 441–467.

Purcell, J. (1993). The challenge of human resource management for industrial relations research and practice. *International Journal of Human Resource Management*, *4*(3), 511–527.

Psychogios, A., & Prouska, R. (2019). *Managing people in small and medium enterprises in turbulent contexts*. Routledge.

Ram, M., Edwards, P., Gilman, M., & Arrowsmith, J. (2001). The dynamics of informality: Employment relations in small firms and the effects of regulatory change. *Work Employment and Society*, *15*(4), 845–861.

Rosenzweig, P. M., & Nohria, N. (1994). Influences on human resources development practices in multinational corporations. *Journal of International Business Studies*, *25*(2), 229–251.

Rowley, C., Bae, J., Horak, S., & Bacouel-Jentjens, S. (2017). Distinctiveness of human resource management in the Asia Pacific region: Typologies and levels. *The International Journal of Human Resource Management*, *28*(10), 1393–1408.

Smallbone, D., & Welter, F. (2001). The role of government in SME development in transition economies. *International Small Business Journal: Researching Entrepreneurship*, *19*(4), 63–77.

Storey, J. (1992). *Development in the Management of Human Resources*. Oxford: Blackwell.

Storey, D. J., Saridakis, G., Sen-Gupta, S., Edwards, P. K., & Blackburn, R. A. (2010). Linking HR formality with employee job quality: The role of firm and workplace size. *Human Resource Management, 49*(2), 305–329. https://doi.org/10.1002/hrm.20347

Sydow, J., Schreyogg, G., & Koch, J. (2009). Organizational path dependence: Opening the black box. *Academy of Management Review, 34*(4), 1–21.

Tamilina, L., & Tamilina, N. (2017). Post-communist transition as a path-break: Comparing legal institutional effects on economic growth between path-breaking and path-drifting institutional reforms. *Journal of Applied Economic Research, 11*(3), 315–347.

Thompson, P. (2011). The trouble with HRM. *Human Resource Management Journal, 21*(4), 355–367.

Truss, C., Gratton, L., Hope-Hailey, V., McGovern, P., & Stiles, P. (1997). Soft and hard models of human resource management: A reappraisal. *Journal of Management Studies, 34*(1), 53–73.

Tudoroiu, T. (2007). Rose, orange, and tulip: The failed post-Soviet revolutions. *Communist and Post-Communist Studies, 40*(3), 315–342.

Walton, R. (1985). From control to commitment in the workplace. Harvard Business Review, March–April, 77–84.

Warner, M. (2009). "Making sense" of HRM in China: Setting the scene. *The International Journal of Human Resource Management, 20*(11), 2169–2193.

Whitley, R. (1999). *Divergent capitalisms*. Oxford University Press.

Wilkinson, A. (1999). Employment relations in SMEs. *Employee Relations, 21*(3), 206–217.

Wilkinson, A., Marchington, M., Goodman, J., & Ackers, P. (1992). Total quality management and employee involvement. *Human Resource Management Journal, 2*(4), 1–20.

Williams, C. C. (2006). Beyond marketization: rethinking economic development trajectories in Central and Eastern Europe. *Journal of Contemporary European Studies, 14*(2), 241–254. https://doi.org/10.1080/14782800600892283

Williams, N., & Vorley, T. (2017). Fostering productive entrepreneurship in post-conflict economies: The importance of institutional alignment. *Entrepreneurship and Regional Development, 29*(5–6), 444–466.

Wood, G., Cooke, F. L., Demirbag, M., & Kwong, C. (2018). International Journal of Human Resource Management (IJHRM) special issue on: International human resource management in contexts of high uncertainties. *The International Journal of Human Resource Management, 29*(7), 1365–1373.

Wood, G., & Demirbag, M. (2015). Business and society on the transitional periphery: Comparative perspectives. *International Business Review, 24*(6), 917–920.

Wood, G., & Demirbag, M. (2018). Introduction. In M. Demirbag & G. Wood (Eds.), *Comparative capitalism and the transitional periphery: Firm centred perspectives* (pp. 1–11). Edward Elgar.

Wood, S., & de Menezes, L. (1998). High commitment management in the UK: Evidence from the workplace industrial relations survey, and employers' manpower and skills practices survey. *Human Relations, 51*(4), 485–515.

Wright, P. M., & McMahan, G. C. (1992). Theoretical perspectives for strategic human resource management. *Journal of Management, 18*(2), 295–320.

Yin, R. K. (2003). *Case study research: Design and methods*. Sage Publications.

Zhu, C. J., Zhang, M., & Shen, J. (2012). Paternalistic and transactional HRM: the nature and transformation of HRM in contemporary China. *The International Journal of Human Resource Management, 23*(19), 3964–3982.

Variations and differences in the application of HR policies and practices by US hotel multinational firm's subsidiaries across coordinated and transitional periphery economies: a case approach

Giovanni Oscar Serafini (iD) and Leslie Thomas Szamosi (iD)

ABSTRACT

In this study, we explore how, and to what extent, home country effects on HR practice in hotel industry MNEs might diminish when host country institutional mediation is weak or uneven. This study centres on the case of luxury hotel chain subsidiaries of a US multinational firm operating across advanced coordinated and transitional periphery economies. It focuses on employee resourcing, training, reward and performance management practices, and draws on in-depth interviews, participant observation and document analysis thereby enabling triangulation of results. Through qualitative analysis, we conclude that the reduction in home country effects in subsidiaries operating in uncertain environments of transitional periphery economies reflects not only the extent to which prominent foreign players may be subject to closer regulatory scrutiny even when enforcement capabilities are weak but also the operation of extended clan-based networks of support.

Introduction

This study focuses on host country effects by comparing variations and differences of HR practice across a US luxury hotel multinational enterprise's (MNE) overseas subsidiaries in mature, advanced coordinated market economies (CMEs) of Germany and Switzerland with transitional peripheral economies (TPEs) of the Caucasus and Central Asia, namely Azerbaijan and Kyrgyzstan. Despite the international expansion of hotel chains and the subsequent globalisation of the human resource management (HRM) function, a closer examination of local contexts demonstrates the existence of unique institutional challenges which require HR policies and practices of overseas subsidiaries to adapt accordingly (Naama et al., 2008). Indeed, Boxall (1995) argues that differences in labour markets, workforce capability and employment systems affect HRM, thus suggesting the need for accommodating and adapting HRM policies and practices to the local context.

Although the post state socialist world has commonly been categorised as comprising 'transitional' economies, it has become clear that there is significant diversity within it. The primary focus of the existing research has been on the relatively developed post state socialist economies of Central and Eastern Europe (CEE) or Russia (Arslan et al., 2015; Topalli & Ivanaj, 2016), but there is also an emerging body of literature on the more peripheral ones of Central Asia and the Caucasus (Demirbag et al., 2015). It has been argued that the post-Soviet economies of the Caucasus and Central Asia constitute a variety of capitalism (VoC) in their own right, the TPEs (Wood & Demirbag, 2015). Despite more than eight decades of Soviet rule, the latter's collapse has revealed historical legacies dating back to the pre-colonial period. These have persisted including the role of clans in coordinating political and economic life (Collins, 2006). It can be argued that a key difference between the CEE and TPE countries was that liberalisation was much more rapid – and comprehensive – in the former than the latter (Aslund, 2013).

Research aim and contribution

Our aim is to explore the extent to which the high uncertainty, post state, socialist contexts of Azerbaijan and Kyrgyzstan, featuring weaker institutions and fluid institutional mediation, may provide firms with fewer (or greater) opportunities to depart from specific country of domicile ways of doing business. Consequently, this study examines variations in HR practice within the subsidiaries of a US MNE straddling the divide between both CMEs and TPEs, the differences in how diverging or persistently unlike types of non-market orientated national institutions might mould HR practice, and whether institutional weakness or fluidity opens or decreases opportunities for innovation. Much of the international HRM (IHRM) literature on home and host country effects compares a limited cross-section of national contexts, comprising the most advanced societies and a limited number of large emerging markets (Brewster et al., 2016; Tarique & Schuler, 2010). The original contribution of this research rests in terms of understanding both mature and under-investigated markets on the transitional periphery thus enabling an examination of how and why any shared country of origin effects or embedded organisation wide practices may be diluted according to differing countries of domicile. Ultimately, we aim to reveal what type of host country effects (if any), weak or poorly coupled institutions in high uncertainty contexts, might impose on the HR practices of MNEs.

Literature review

Despite the dearth of research on TPEs, we attempt to profile the high uncertainty contexts covered in this study, Azerbaijan and Kyrgyzstan. Lately there is a very strong movement in HRM studies which considers context as a key aspect of the application of HRM practices (Budhwar et al., 2016; Farndale & Sanders, 2017; Prouska & Psychogios, 2018; Psychogios et al., 2020). The slow and erratic pace of change in the TPEs reflects not only the continued influence of former members of the Soviet elite (Sievers, 2013) but also the pervasive and disruptive influence of informal clan and client based networks (Minbaeva et al., 2007; Schatz, 2004). Not only did the latter long predate Soviet rule but such networks also interpenetrated and manipulated the local communist parties and associated state structures. Members of such networks both have incentives to leverage their present strengths to capture more spoils in a time of crisis and to seek to entrench their position (Gould & Sickner, 2008; López & Santos, 2014).

The high uncertainty TPE context: Azerbaijan and Kyrgyzstan

MNEs operating in transitional settings are exposed to a wide array of challenges that require organisations to handle them as crises (Pearson & Clair, 1998, table 1, p. 60). The high uncertainty affecting the Caucasus and Central Asia states relates to the political and economic volatility which reflect on institutional arrangements appearing to be 'stable outside, fragile inside' (Kavalski, 2016, p. 4). Early moves to democracy were superseded by 'the establishment of super-presidential political systems under autocratic rulers' (Pomfret, 2012, p. 400) which have mobilised clan resources to secure their position while being likely associated with high levels of corruption. Namely, according to Transparency International's Corruption Perception Index 2018 (Transparency International, 2019), Azerbaijan and Kyrgyzstan rank respectively 152 and 132 out of 180 nations; other countries in the Caucasus and Central Asia region perform similarly or worse. Foreign hotel chains entering such setting would have to find ways of adapting and accommodating this, and risk being compromised themselves; however, corruption may mean that local rules and regulations may be quite 'negotiable'. A climate of weak and erratic regulation may impel similar fluidity in practice, or

Table 1. Coding and themes.

Main themes (third level)	Sub-themes (second level)	Codes (first level)
Employee resourcing	Autonomy of subsidiary in relation to HRM decisions	Internal recruitment
		External recruitment
	Influence of home country on HRM decisions	Resourcing through recommendations and connections
	Host-country HRM determinants	Extended informal networks
	Regulatory scrutiny	Incumbent employees' social network
Employee training	Informal training	On the job training
	Formal training	Apprenticeship
		Traineeship
		Career development
Employee reward	Compensation fairness	Nationwide collective work agreement
	Market value	Industry sector collective work agreement
		Minimum wage
		Pay scales
Performance management	Favouritism	Key employees
	Relevance	Low-skilled jobs
		Control
		Communication
		Internal politics

the negotiation of a space within which the organisation adopts the kind of practices it deems optimal (cf. Kouznetsov et al., 2014).

Institutional effects on internal organisational practice

Broadly, scholars of international and comparative HRM have tended to favour either the cultural (D'Annunzio-Green, 2002; Romani, 2004) or the institutional approach (Hotho & Pedersen, 2012; Sorge, 2004) to explain the economic dynamics and outcomes of societies and their actors. According to proponents of the cultural approach (Hofstede, 1980, 1984, 1993; Hofstede & McCrae, 2004; Trompenaars & Woolliams, 2002), different national cultural contexts distinctively influence the way business is conducted by overseas subsidiaries of MNEs. Since HRM is concerned with an organisation's human asset, the role of culture is capital in order to understand the way employees behave and thus perform. In fact, according to Hofstede (1984), a prominent researcher in the field, culture is mainly built around values and is defined as being the 'collective programming of the mind which distinguishes the members of one human group from another' (p. 21).

Hofstede (1980) and Zhang (2003) identified that HRM policies and practices may not be valid across different countries because of divergence from local laws, customs and cultures. Equally, cultural differences could affect how the HR function is deployed across borders by global organisations. Supporters of the cultural oriented approach argue that it attempts to explain or foresee human behaviour where, in practical contexts, the mere consideration of economic, political or institutional factors may reveal inadequacies (Hofstede, 2002). As Chapman maintains (Chapman, 1996), the virtue of the cultural approach is that it crucially points to the effects of culture on business and management. Indeed, Amable et al. (2008) recognise the mediating effect of culture on business systems and organisational capabilities through its influence, for instance, on behavioural norms (p. 781) or the perception of fairness (p. 783). Drawing from the work of Hofstede, the subsequent GLOBE cross-cultural research project (House et al., 2004) provides a complementary framework to interpret societal values and practices within the context of business leadership (Grove, 2015, p. 835). Furthermore, this study offers additional evidence of cultural dimensions permeating 62 societies throughout the world (Shi & Wang, 2011).

Critics of the cultural approach (McSweeney, 2002a, 2002b; Smith, 2006) remark, however, its inherent limitations in addressing the complexity of denoting national cultures. Further, doubts are cast on reliability and generalisability of the cultural approach with its universalistic assertions (Oyserman et al., 2002). In fact, this approach claims to be able to analyse national cultures while its research population base is not only narrow but also homogenised. Specifically, Hofstede's seminal work draws from studies of intra-company IBM employee surveys, thus revealing inadequacies in the research methodology (McSweeney, 2002b). Again, the homogeneity critique applies to the GLOBE project since it engages with middle managers across a small sample of corporations (Terlutter et al., 2006, p. 434). Additionally, Shenkar (2001) recognises that the culture-orientated approach tends to be deficient for two main reasons. First, it ignores the existence of corporate culture which further compounds the national culture construct as these reciprocally influence each other. Second, cultural distance is a very sensitive concept because it is reduced or boosted by a variety of factors such as globalisation and inevitable cultural frictions. Nonetheless, the most determining critique to the cultural framework is that the set polarities of cultural dimensions are fixed thus implying that cultures remain predominantly unchanged over time (Ess & Sudweeks, 2005). An individual belonging to a particular national context should fit exclusively into the cultural characteristics identifiable with the related nation's culture. Consequently, while this viewpoint does not consider the fluidity of cultural exchanges occurring nowadays, it also 'runs the risk of oversimplification, if not stereotyping' (ibid., p. 184).

In the final analysis since cultural explanations fail to properly '"capture" the social reality' (Ailon, 2008, p. 898) they attempt to describe, the institutional theory is better set to consider and interpret the nuances of contemporary society (Brookes et al., 2011).

Consequently, this study applies the institutional approach to undertake a comparative analysis of HRM applied across subsidiaries of luxury hotel MNE.

There is an extensive body of literature highlighting institutional effects on internal organisational practice which compares differences in practice between MNEs and indigenous firms (Farndale et al., 2008; Ferner et al., 2005; Rugman & Oh, 2013). This body of literature can be divided into two camps: on the one hand, those merely focussing on the extent to which institutions may interfere with or facilitate firms adopting those sets of practices proven to maximise returns irrespective of the setting (Guler & Guillén, 2010; Michailova, 2002; North, 1990; Peng, 2003; Pissarides et al., 2003). On the other, those arguing that institutions may confer competitive advantage in many different ways, and may steer or incentivise firms towards those sets of solutions best suited to working in a particular setting (Barbopoulos et al., 2014; Hall & Soskice, 2001; McCarthy & Puffer, 2016).

What links these different strands of literature is a primary concern in comparing liberal markets with more coordinated, peripheral or emerging ones. This is typically either to explore the relative superiority or dominance of liberal markets and associated modes of practice (Ferner & Quintanilla, 1998; Parry et al., 2008), or to make the case for viable alternative paths to national economic development (Kalleberg, 2009; Meelen et al., 2017). Whilst it has often been assumed that institutional arrangements associated with emerging markets are likely to converge towards the liberal market model (cf. Hall & Soskice, 2001; Peng, 2003), it is increasingly clear that such markets have retained distinct features which, as historical institutionalists remind us, are developed and embedded in specific and relatively unusual ruptures or departures within the path of national development (Aoki, 2010). What this suggests is that in venturing into high uncertainty contexts of the transitional periphery, the ability of MNEs to pioneer new practices that disrupt existing institutional models and dominant existing modes of practices may be somewhat less than commonly assumed (cf. Dore, 2008).

Institutions and firm practice

Perhaps the most influential contemporary account that seeks to explain the nature and degree of national differences is the dichotomous model which divides mature VoCs (Dore, 2002; Hall & Soskice, 2001) into two main categories defined by the extent of their market coordination. On the one hand are the liberal market economies (LMEs) where firms reflect the decisions and desires of stock market investors (Godard, 2002) and, on the other hand, the business-CMEs which filter such pressures (Culpepper, 2005). The former are characterised by light market regulation, a strong focus on private property rights and arms-length contracting (i.e., the Anglo-Saxon advanced economies; Kinderman, 2012; Marens, 2012). The latter feature extensive market coordination and denser ties between key players (e.g., the Rhineland economies, Scandinavia and Japan; Emmenegger, 2015).

In LMEs, employees typically assume responsibility and ownership for their own career development and seek to accommodate their skills to the positions and functions made available; firms rely on the external labour market to solve skills gaps to a greater extent than in CMEs (Hall & Soskice, 2001). On the other hand, depending on the characteristics of the labour force, firms in CMEs typically adjust selection criteria, and target training and development programs to maximise employee performance. They seek to develop the skills and capabilities of their staff over many years in a climate of relatively high mutual commitment (Busemeyer & Schlicht-Schmälzle, 2014). This, ultimately, reveals the extent to which the financial capital utilises the human capital in distinct national corporate regimes (Psychogios et al., 2010). Hence, CMEs feature a solid industry base strengthened by top-level specialisation, industry-based development of vocational training standards and technology transfer and diffusion, whose highly skilled employees benefit from job security obtained through industry-defined union representation. This is particularly conducive to incrementally innovative manufacturing. In LMEs, flexible labour markets and a focus on generic skills, along with the ready availability of short term capital, is conducive to areas of high technology but is also associated with the development of large areas of low value-added service activity (Hall & Soskice, 2001).

Given the extensive range of institutional mediation in CMEs, MNEs are more likely to come under particular pressure to fit into the local ways of doing things (Jackson & Deeg, 2008). Even in LMEs, MNEs would have incentives to emulate their local counterparts to reap the benefits that might flow from context specific complementarities (Boussebaa et al., 2012). Where does this leave the hospitality industry? If LMEs are conducive to low cost labour intensive service sector activities, hotels in CMEs would have to accommodate extensive labour market regulation, without necessarily reaping the same range of benefits that might flow from it than would a traditional manufacturing firm (i.e., a workforce with high levels of industry specific technical skills). Hence, hotel MNEs would, on the one hand, have to abide by extensive rules, but on the other hand, might have strong incentives to push against them, find ways to evade them or push for systemic reform (Chowdhury & Mahmood, 2012).

The hotel industry context

Traditionally, the international business literature neglected the hotel industry (King et al., 2011; Serafini & Szamosi, 2015) in favour of manufacturing firms (Lafontaine et al., 2017), service industries, mining and engineering and information technology companies (Kundu & Lahiri, 2015). A key reason lies in the hotel industry being a relatively closed sector where research has been mainly focused on industry specific issues (Kusluvan et al., 2010). Indeed, it could be argued that the industry is quite introverted in its willingness to engage with the research community as opposed to the extraversion found in other sectors (e.g., pharmaceuticals; King et al., 2011). Still, the hotel industry is one of the most globalised, capital-intensive, service sectors playing a key role in the development of travel and tourism (Martorell et al., 2013). It has a high level of location boundedness since it needs to be where customers are (Dunning & McQueen, 1982). Research on hotel MNEs is in its infancy when compared to, for example, the manufacturing sector. Interestingly, it has been recognised that models developed to understand manufacturing MNEs may be less relevant for service sector firms (León-Darder et al., 2011). Further, the evidence base related to the impact of international hotels on host country economies remains incomplete (Niewiadomski, 2015).

It has only been over the past few years, that there has been an increase in research on HRM in hotels (Baum, 2015; Hoque, 2013). Given that much of the work is labour-intensive, low-skilled and around-the-clock, HRM is likely to place a strong emphasis on cutting costs (Serafini & Szamosi, 2018); this has led to allegations of endemically poor HRM (Knox, 2014). In fact, competition, flexibility and technological change are named as key reasons for the sector's 'decent work deficits and (…) reputation of poor working conditions' (Boardman et al., 2015, p. 49). In turn, this has been associated with high employee dissatisfaction and turnover rates (Bakkevig Dagsland et al., 2015). Hence, Bakkevig Dagsland et al. (2015) argue that the industry has failed to generate those conditions that would motivate early career hires to stay within the industry towards building sector relevant knowledge and skills. This has led to industry concerns of shortages in skilled and experienced staff (Davidson & Wang, 2011; Kim, 2014). There are, however, organisations shifting towards more strategic HRM application as it occurs in large hotel MNEs (Hoque, 2013). The limited body of work on variations in HR practice in hotel MNEs has mostly explored the effects of cultural differences (Assaf et al., 2015).

IHRM and HRM applied at national level by subsidiaries

Since this article focuses on topics mostly studied in the IHRM literature (see Cooke et al., 2019, p. 65, table 5), it centres on how MNEs
resource, train and reward employees as well as manage their performance to best exploit them internationally (Peltonen & Vaara, 2012).
According to the seminal work of Perlmutter (1969), the international
strategy of a MNE defines its orientation to IHRM. Depending on the
strategic approach to HRM applied in its subsidiaries, a MNE could be
classified as ethnocentric, polycentric or geocentric. Research demonstrates
that country of origin determines the IHRM strategic approach of hotel
MNEs. In particular, US MNEs favour ethnocentrism reflecting a home
country dominance approach (Dowling et al., 2008; Dunning & Lundan,
2008). While HRM at the subsidiary level gravitates around the same
functions as IHRM, it is compelled to respond to the local context and
adapt to differentiated needs affecting the application of HR policies and
practices in host countries (Brewster et al., 2016). Starting with employee
resourcing, much of the extant research focuses on expatriates (McNulty
& Brewster, 2017). Yet, local subsidiaries crucially depend on the availability and identification of appropriate local candidates. As Wood and
Szamosi (2016) contend, employee sourcing is a pivotal function because
it impacts on a range of interlinked HR areas spanning from training to
reward and performance management. Furthermore, research indicates
that differing national institutional settings related to education affect the
training approach across subsidiaries. Thus, the type of economy is likely
to impact on the training offered in MNE subsidiaries (Peretz &
Rosenblatt, 2011). In terms of rewards, the rhetoric of ethnocentric US
MNEs tends to emphasise commonalities on pay across countries
(Edwards et al., 2016). Nonetheless, as research shows that pay practices
vary across national contexts (ibid.), HRM at subsidiary level needs to
take into account the institutional context in shaping the approach to
employee reward. Lastly, performance management is another HR function
that US MNEs tend to deploy with a customary 'one size fit all' approach
resulting from a preconception towards American HRM practices considered to be 'best practices' (Ananthram & Chan, 2013, p. 226). Apart from
its inherent limitations caused, among others, by subjectivity bias and politics (Mackenzie et al., 2019; Rosen et al., 2017; Trost, 2017; van
Woerkom & de Bruijn, 2016), the application of performance appraisal is
further challenged by the need to consider the national context (Farndale,
2017). Hence, this study attempts to shed light on the global versus local
question in relation to IHRM by focussing on key HRM functions carried
out within US MNE hotel chain independent subsidiaries located in
CMEs and TPEs.

Institutional arrangement strength and differences in country of domicile practice: propositions

There is a wide body of literature on home and host country effects on the HR practices of MNE subsidiaries (Brewster et al., 2008; Meyer et al., 2011). As Geppert and Dorrenbacher (2011) note, it is not only the strategic choices of actors that matter but also the relative stage of the host countries historical development, which helps shape the space available to adopt new practices or to benefit from established ways of doing things.

All settings allow some space for innovation, but at the same time, the scale and scope for departing from dominant local practices will be bound with local dynamics (Meyer et al., 2011). Although it has been often assumed that, in the interests of internal coherence and affinity with home country practices, there are strong pressures to align practices with what goes on in the home country (Tempel et al., 2006), research evidence suggests that MNEs often opt for a hybrid approach (Brewster et al., 2008). In turn, this may reflect the relative importance and autonomy of the subsidiary and the strategic choices of local managers (Ahlvik et al., 2016).

Morgan (2012) argues that MNEs are only partially rooted in any single institutional domain; they are less committed to any particular setting and have incentives and disincentives to adopt practices from countries of origin, domicile, or, indeed, from emerging transnational practices. MNEs seek to enter particular settings for the competitive advantages they confer (Morgan, 2012). Mature economies have stronger institutional arrangements; firms have similarly strong incentives to fit in with these to gain the benefits of associated complementarities (Whitley, 1999). For example, if legally obliged to provide stronger tenure security, firms may incentivise employees to develop organisational specific skills to make the best usage of a workforce that is not readily interchangeable (Hall & Soskice, 2001). Again, by applying existing mechanisms of workplace participation, they can harness workers' insider knowledge, and hence enhance quality and productivity (Hall & Soskice, 2001; Whitley, 1999). In emerging markets, where complementarities are less developed, the incentives for fitting in are much weaker. Again, it can be argued that when local institutions are less effective and/or complementarities less developed there is more room to follow proven country of origin recipes, or indeed, global best practice (Almond et al., 2005). Thus, we posit the following:

> Proposition 1: In CMEs there is likely to be stronger concurrence with local formal and informal regulations and conventions regarding HR practice than in TPEs.

Alternatively, it can be argued that in high uncertainty countries with weak formal institutions, informal networks and inter-personal ties assume greater importance. As the literature on institutional voids alerts us, actors may respond to institutional shortfall through relying more on personal networks, which can impart an element of predictability and reciprocity in the absence of effective formal mediation (Miller et al., 2009). Building on this, there is an extensive body of literature on the role of informal networks in emerging markets (Darbi et al., 2018; Filatotchev et al., 2007). They are often seen as playing a vital role in building social capital and in helping players access resources and opportunities that would otherwise be denied owing to formal systemic shortfalls (Woolcock & Narayan, 2000). More pessimistic accounts suggest that the networks may represent the extension of informal peasant based mechanisms of support, and drain the modern economy of resources in favour of personal family networks, rendering much more difficult to infuse more modern practices from abroad (Hydén, 1980). At the same time, such networks are quite difficult for outsiders to decode or forge accommodations with (ibid.); they represent ways in which marginalised groupings may access resources, but at the same time, may undermine more formal policies, practices and procedures. Rather than compensating for institutional voids, personal ties and networks may capitalise on systemic weaknesses to maximise their personal rents, worsening existing systemic shortfalls.

In TPEs, a long history of institutional ruptures means that key social strata are divided on clan and regional lines (Demirbag et al., 2015) making it difficult for outsiders to disentangle or circumnavigate. Hence, MNEs may come under strong pressures to adjust their practices in line with such realities; it is much harder to evangelise new practices than might be the case in developed economies with more established formal institutional arrangements (cf. Dore, 2008). In CMEs, there are strong pressures for liberal market style reforms opening up opportunities for actors to pioneer new practices that challenge established ways of doing things (Streeck, 2009); in contrast, in TPEs, it can be argued that turbulence in the 1990s has done much to discredit or undermine practices associated with Western LMEs and has further strengthened the power of informal networks (Demirbag et al., 2015). On the one hand, it could be argued that the operation of informal networks may render formal rules meaningless. On the other hand, it could be argued that the primary effect will be in their coverage; outside players will have to adhere to both formal regulations and informal conventions, whilst smaller and indigenous players may be better equipped to evade them (ibid.). Further, nor will an adherence to formal regulations insulate MNEs from the effects of informal networks who may seek to interpenetrate the firm and shape who it locally contracts with (Wood et al., 2011). Thus, we posit the following alternative proposition:

Proposition 2: In TPEs there is likely to be stronger concurrence with local formal and informal regulations and conventions regarding HR practice than in CMEs.

Methodology

This research focuses on countries of domicile and explores overseas subsidiaries of a US luxury hotel MNE (cf. Yin, 2009) which, to safeguard anonymity, is hereafter referred to as HotelChain. The subsidiaries pertaining to CMEs are located in Germany (3) and Switzerland (1) while those belonging to TPEs operate in Azerbaijan (1) and Kyrgyzstan (1). Given the dearth of research in TPEs, this study has implemented an exploratory approach by utilising a qualitative methodology (cf. Eisenhardt, 1989). The following paragraphs illustrate and explain the methodological decisions taken.

Case study design

Our research revolves around a case study focussing on subsidiary HR managers who are generally seen as the key 'actors' affecting HR policies and practices in their respective subsidiaries. As Wooldridge and Floyd (2017, pp. 61–62) contend, this managerial category belongs to the 'Senior Team Leader' typology characterised by a direct reporting line to top management. While being internally focused, subsidiary hotel HR managers cover a pivotal role in '(...) supporting the firm's internal functions and managing high-level internal relationships' (Wooldridge & Floyd, 2017, p. 61) while developing, coordinating and leading strategic initiatives and activities through, also, creative solutions. The advantage of obtaining input from HR managers lies in their comprehensive awareness of both intended and applied HR (e.g., Huselid et al., 1997). Involving them, as such, in this study helps to ensure that respondents thoroughly understand the research topics. In fact, not only are participants informed and possess specialised knowledge but also, since the research is relevant to their profession, they may be more motivated to contribute.

The sample under examination represents the totality of wholly owned and operated properties on the continent by the HotelChain's European division. There is a distinctive benefit in focusing on subsidiaries onto which the MNE in question exerts the strongest form of control because of it being the exclusive owner and operator (cf. León-Darder et al., 2011). Furthermore, Contractor and Kundu (1998) argue that in lower income nations such as those in the transitional periphery, hotel chains often opt for equity investments. Despite the business uncertainty involved, the key reasons behind this preference are the prospected higher growth rate and revenues owing to weaker competition in such frontier markets. The decision to exclude other types of business arrangements such as franchising and management contract agreement stems from the need of the researchers to avoid considering hotels oper-ating under business relationships in which the role of HotelChain is reduced because it may be more heavily influenced by third parties. In fact, it is quite common for franchised and contracted properties to experience operational disagreements between franchisor and franchisee, and management company and owner, respectively (Pine et al., 2000). Owing to the relative dearth of research on a rather closed industry (King et al., 2011) operating in both advanced CMEs and highly uncer-tain TPEs, this study has applied an exploratory case study approach emphasising depth over breadth (cf. Eisenhardt, 1989).

Collection of data

This research is founded on three complementary methods: semi-struc-tured interviews, participant observation and document analysis. It is recognised that, on their own, qualitative interviews are an insufficient basis on which to advance meaningful conclusions (Malina et al., 2011). Hence, the research is reliant on two further sources, both as a basis of corroboration and in providing additional supportive evidence. Further corroboration was sought by examining publicly available documents related to HotelChain while featuring a participant observer thereby add-ing internal validity. Consequently, the most robust methodological fea-ture presented in this study is the application of triangulation to inductively derive meaning from evidence through a multiple, structured approach (Rothbauer, 2008). Interestingly, the combined application of research methods featuring extensive document analysis and participant observation has rarely been found in the MNE literature (Bainbridge & Lee, 2014). Even within qualitative research, however, biases may affect data collection and analysis, which could emerge because of personal experiences as well as participant stress (Bernard, 2017). The researchers' implementation of the ethical standards outlined by the Academy of Management (AOM, 2017) ensured the rigour required from a partici-pant-observation perspective.

The main advantage of featuring participant observation derives from the attainment of an insider perspective of the social group (cf. Robson, 2003, p. 311). Unlike a pure observer who utilises an observation instru-ment to research, here the participant observer represents the very research instrument itself (Hammersley & Atkinson, 2007). This is par-ticularly true for management studies whereby the researcher, in order to examine business reality in depth, needs to relate with organisations as if they were tribes (Roy, 1952); hence, the link with anthropology and soci-ology. Participant observation then becomes a most critical source of val-idation (Adler & Adler, 1994) as it represents a solid and legitimate point of reference to the researcher corroborated by direct knowledge and judgment (Adler, 1987) that can be used to complement and contrast other research techniques (Yin, 2009).

Having experienced the HotelChain environment directly, the researcher is thus able to examine complex situations while untying themselves from depending on the honesty of respondents (Douglas, 1976). In particular, this study benefits from a combination of roles seldom found in academic research (Hodson, 1998; Locke, 2011) which qualify the participant observer to conduct the research without bias. In fact, at the time the study was conducted, the participant observer was a doctoral researcher but as well in a senior HRM role within the organisation under investigation. According to Agar (1983), knowledge from within allows the participant observer to elaborate on nuances that may be missed by an outsider. In fact, since the latter would inevitably incur in 'breakdowns' (Agar, 1983, p. 32), they would be prevented from digging deeper into the emerging social world's evidence and thus reveal connections and implications (Becker & Geer, 1978). It results, therefore, that an observational study critically builds on experiencing and inductively investigating the social world in which the researcher is immersed rather than testing hypotheses about an organisation not known a priori (cf. Becker, 1958, p. 653). Besides the juxtaposition of scientifically valid and reliable investigation (Glaser & Strauss, 2009; Kuhlmann, 1992; Wiseman, 1974), it offers the grounds for 'collaborative research' (Angrosino & Mays de Pérez, 2000, p. 675) by establishing a dialogue between the researcher and the study respondents. The approach adopted here reflects the 'mixed method' research (Tashakkori & Teddlie, 1998, p. 3) which is further enriched by three main elements. First, the advantage offered by a small sample size; second, the under-studied industrial sector operating in high uncertainty TPEs that are mostly terra incognita for scholars (Arslan et al., 2015); and, finally, the unique status of an author as researcher, practitioner, participant, observer and interviewer at once, thus offering multiple viewpoints which can strengthen the inductive research process (Patton, 2015).

Once consent was obtained, the participant observer recorded and transcribed the six interviews each lasting nearly 90 min. These involved hotel HR managers who are host country nationals: they are identified by the acronym of the relevant business system combined with an ordinal letter corresponding to the subsidiary (A, B, C, D, E and F).

Research participants: demographics

The typical participant was a female local employee aged between 36 and 40 who, besides holding a university degree, had also attained an additional professional qualification in HRM. This reflects what earlier research has revealed in terms of the domination of the HRM profession by females (cf. Minbaeva et al., 2007). In terms of seniority, the average respondent had been working in the assigned hotel property for between 6 and 10 years. Relatively with total years of service at HotelChain, the mean period was 10 years. Thus, it is inferred that the average participant had been working most of their career with HotelChain in the same overseas subsidiary. This observation reveals that sample HotelChain HR managers were not particularly mobile, which is an aspect coinciding with evidence supported by literature (cf. Dowling et al., 2008). To the contrary, other senior hotel operational positions shift properties more frequently such as in the Kitchen, Food & Beverage Service and Front Office departments (Brotherton, 2012; Sims, 2003). Overall, there is evidence suggesting that in the hospitality industry 'turnover rates can reach as high as 200 or 300 percent in rank-and-file positions, and management turnover, at least at the operations level, can approach 100 percent in some organisations' (Riegel, 2011, p. 449).

Consequently, another fundamental rationale as to why the researcher surveyed HR professionals exclusively, is grounded on the premise that these are much more likely to stay longer with HotelChain and, particularly, with their assigned property. Since all other employee categories are affected by high turnover rates, it is quite reasonable to assume that these potential respondents would not have had the necessary deep and broad experience with HR policies and practices at HotelChain as required by the study.

The designated HR manager respondents covered the same jobs across the sampled TPE and CME locations involving typical HR activities gravitating around hiring employees, people processes and related administration. Furthermore, the sampled HR managers were engaged in long-term key roles as partners in the deployment of business strategy. They were duly informed in advance about their colleague's role as researcher and participant observer (cf. Gold, 1958) as well as the research aims. Consequently, the researcher was able to further enhance authentic communication patterns with the respondents which were already established through 'pre-existing relations of trust' (Lofland, 1971, p. 71). The resulting three key benefits are noteworthy, especially when considering the high 'refusal rate' in management research (Gill & Johnson, 2002, p. 135). First, this research accesses the 'real world' of HRM application at the level of luxury hospitality MNE overseas subsidiaries in high-uncertainty contexts. Second, evidence was gathered by involving the most qualified professionals. Third, the hierarchical proximity between the researcher and respondents as well as the awareness of the latter about the role of the former as participant observer, allowed for more analytical reflection (Robson, 2003). These advantages are certainly no simple matter because studies of management urge the researcher to penetrate the secrecy covering organisations and particularly their sensitive managerial functions such as HRM. Furthermore, the specific industrial sector explored has a reputation of not being particularly open to academic research. The fact that HotelChain gave permission only to approach HR managers is not surprising because, as also maintained by Kusluvan et al. (2010), traditionally only management participates in hotel-related HRM research.

Analysis of data

Primary evidence was gathered and examined qualitatively through one-on-one semi-structured interviews based on an interview guide drawing from Whitley's (1999) defining features of HRM practice: employer–employee interdependence and delegation to employees. These semi-structured in-depth interviews, thus, enabled the researcher to reveal and understand the why of things in what Saunders, Lewis, and Thornhill refer to as obtaining 'explanations and meanings' (Saunders et al., 2007, p. 326). The careful reading and interpretation of transcripts highlighted emergent ideas (Spencer et al., 2014, p. 271) eventually leading to the categorisation of main themes and patterns (Ritchie & Lewis, 2003; see Table 1).

    After applying content analysis leading to the identification of a coding scheme, transcripts were then rearranged and compared (Miles & Huberman, 1994). An ensuing process of detailed comparisons not only guaranteed the research's rigour but also unearthed additional patterns and themes. These include the influence of home country on HRM decisions, the pressure to recruit through recommendations and connections, compensation fairness and favouritism. Here, the participant observer's privileged insider view as a professional allowed for the appreciation of nuances in the respondents' inputs and further reinforced sense-making of the evidence garnered (Patton, 2008).

    Furthermore, analysis of both HotelChain and HotelChain-related documents centres on material openly available on the Internet. These documentary secondary data sources, which represent a specific category of artefacts (Robson, 2003) and can be either recent or historical, are particularly instrumental because they illustrate the HotelChain country of origin viewpoint (cf. Bryman, 2005, p. 189). In fact, according to Krippendorff (1980) the analysis of the documents' content should assist in establishing 'valid inferences from data to their context' (p. 21). Thus, further supporting information on HotelChain corporate practices can be obtained from organisational and industry association documents, notices, letters, the corporate internet homepage, blogs and popular media such as newspaper and magazines (Hakim, 1982; Sleeman, 2002).

On the positive side, this type of analysis presents three key strengths: first, it is stable because it may be examined any time without the risk of corrupting the source (Altheide et al., 2010). Second, as documents are created independently from the case study, they are unobtrusive providers of exact details which usually cannot be manipulated to affect the research outcomes (Love, 2003). Third, as documents could encompass a vast array of informative resources, a broad longitudinal coverage may be attained in terms of both time and space (Hakim, 2004).

In terms of drawbacks, document analysis may present a problem of confidentiality. Since organisations are often restive to divulge internal documents, researchers may be prevented access to documents which otherwise may add to the study (Yin, 2014). Further, the availability of company documentary material to examine is influenced by two biasing elements, namely 'selective deposit' and 'selective survival' (Gray, 2009, p. 267). The former refers to the storage and disposing of records according to company directives. The latter, instead, concerns the degree according to which employees actually abide by such directives. Again, as Finnegan (2006) notes, the researcher's bias needs to be taken into account as this affects the very selection of documents to analyse, their relevance to the research topic, and the researcher's ability to interpret the meaning of the documentary data.

Findings and discussion

This section presents research findings in terms of themes that emerged during the final stage of data analysis, namely employee resourcing, training, reward and performance management. Overall, in TPE subsidiaries it was felt that the firm was held to closer regulatory scrutiny than indigenous players, something that did not emerge from the evidence provided by CME research participants. According to TPE respondents' input which is further corroborated by participant observation, the officials in charge of regulatory oversights and labour law enforcement wielded considerable power. While the enforcement of labour law in the TPE countries under review remains uneven and patchy (cf. Demirbag et al., 2015), from the point of view of HotelChain it was perceived as strict and arbitrary thus pointing to one set of rules for local players and another for foreigners.

Employee resourcing

According to participant observation, HotelChain advised overseas subsidiary HR managers to be particularly supportive of corporate rhetoric towards promoting from within, as corroborated by document analysis (HotelChain, 2012). Triangulation shows that external recruitment purportedly occurred whenever there were no suitable internal candidates. If external recruitment was necessary, HotelChain resorted to recommendations originated by employees because by knowing the organisation from within and through their diverse social network, they were apparently able to attract the best talent (HotelChain, 2012). Hence, respondents distinguished between two recruitment streams: the internal (employee referral) and external. The former related to endorsements originated internally which involved employees recommending a candidate from their personal social network such as an acquaintance, friend or even a relative (cf. Shinnar et al., 2004). This seems to be the norm in TPE based subsidiaries, indicating that personal staff contacts played a key role, even if with some dubious results at times. In fact, as commented by a TPE respondent:

> Employee recommendation award systems boost the number of candidacies: however, as for its assistance to select quality employees, on this there are mixed feelings.

(TPE/E)

As further shared by another TPE respondent, recruitment through social networks involved also using indigenous business partners and local authorities, which were considered as

> (…) an alternative avenue for recruitment.

(TPE/F)

Since the process seemingly drew on extended informal networks (cf. Myloni et al., 2004), this underlines the importance of personal ties and recommendations in subsidiaries located in high uncertainty host countries featuring fluid and weak institutional settings. There, subsidiaries adapt to local customs by giving importance to recommendations because these may not only provide a guarantee about the quality of the candidate but also be part of a broader mechanism within a society where clientelism and quid-pro-quo exchanges are rooted. This is especially important in TPEs where the clan system and the resulting pervasive tribal solidarity is deeply established and rooted in the fabric of society (cf. Temirkoulov, 2004; Wolters, 2012). The role and effect of such influence emerges as both TPE representatives agree over the weak head office effect over non-financial HRM aspects. As one respondent puts it:

> The [head office] influence is not really much: there are certain guidelines towards which we need to move; however, these are not particularly prescriptive and

limiting. There is more or less full autonomy as long as we are moving towards the same goals. (...) Mainly, we are influenced by the local culture that determines how we do things, especially because the *overwhelming majority of employees are local* [emphasis added].

(TPE/F)

Consequently, the local context influences would seemingly encompass having to deal with clan networks linking existing and prospective staff.

Training

In TPE subsidiaries, the usage of internal recruitment reflected a strong emphasis on informal, on the job, training. As one TPE respondent indicated:

Internal recruitment is very critical, especially as the local workforce education is clueless on world-class hospitality standards: thus, it is important to develop the labour force from within.

(TPE/E)

This was done on an informal basis and compensated for shortfalls in national training institutions. Contrariwise, in CME processes were less orientated towards personal recommendations and more through formal employment procedures. According to a CME respondent:

Who is recommended is directed through the conventional selection process.

(CME/A)

Further in CMEs, internal promotion is built on formal training programmes with a perspective to the career development of apprentices. For example:

At our property, internal recruitment is particularly common in situations whereby trainees are promoted to cover standard line positions.

(CME/B)

If new staff passed the probation phase, they were given priority over external applicants in covering non-managerial positions and could ultimately look forward to a management career. CME subsidiaries emphasised employee development and thus assured a constant stream of apprenticeship level applicants being developed (cf. Briscoe & Schuler, 2004). In TPEs, the traineeship system was by no means as developed as the sector wide CME vocational training system, and this, in turn, impacted on both career prospects and quotidian capabilities (cf. Tatoglu et al., 2016).

Reward

In comparing institutional environments, it became clear that nationwide and hotel industry-sector collective work agreements moulded industrial relations in CMEs, but not TPEs. Thus, as declared by a CME participant in relation to line positions:

> Collective work agreement for hotels is applied and complied to.

> (CME/C)

Conversely, in TPEs there was no industry-sector collective work agreements to abide by; there was the obligation to pay, at least, a minimum wage set by law (cf. Bosch & Weinkopf, 2013). Thus, as commented by a TPE respondent:

> The laws in this respect are particularly simplified. There are no sector collective work agreements and organisations are expected to respect the minimum wage set on a yearly basis by the Labour Ministry.

> (TPE/E)

In CMEs, respondents resorted to market value considerations only for managerial level positions; again, although pay was individually set, this imparted a collective dimension. As summarised by a CME participant:

> Industry survey pay scales are applied for managerial positions. For all other positions these are irrelevant because we pay according to the hotel collective work agreements.

> (CME/D)

As indicated by a CME respondent, equity in compensation practices was ensured by:

> (…) complying with the guidelines of the collective work agreement for hotels.

> (CME/A)

In contrast, the input of a TPE respondent accorded more attention to the internal and external environments:

> Pay scales are defined particularly for managerial positions by considering internal and external market conditions. This enables the retention of managers and high potential key employees.

> (TPE/F)

Respondents agreed that consistency in the administration of compensation was maintained through pay scales that, while taking into account legal constraints as analysed previously, also integrated market considerations in order for the subsidiaries to feature competitive salaries fitting into the business context. Yet, the highly uncertain economic settings of TPEs presented unique challenges due to pay precariousness linked, among others, to inflation:

> External surveys are used to assess where this subsidiary stands compared to other business. However, the big challenge is the very high inflation rate which increases year after year and compensation *cannot keep pace* [emphasis added].

(TPE/F)

Through corporate rhetoric underlining that the most valuable asset were talented employees (HotelChain, 2012, 2017), HotelChain urged subsidiary HR managers to retain this employee category through appropriate, consistent and fair compensation, while considering the dynamics of the local labour market. Nonetheless, in the fluid and lightly regulated TPEs the exclusive points of reference were the minimum wages set by law and/or what subsidiaries felt they could get away with. The absence of unions gave management the flexibility to set pay according to scales which needed to be attractive to talented candidates for core positions yet allowed for cost cutting in other areas. As noted by participant observation, the HotelChain HR system provided for measures to define attractive compensation packages for core managerial employees, while blue-collar workers were not accorded the same degree of attention, and without benefitting from sectoral collective bargaining. Ultimately, where CMEs differed from TPEs was that the former was associated with a greater recourse to procedurality, and the latter with cost reduction.

Performance management

According to participant observation, performance management at HotelChain gravitated around a highly structured performance appraisal system to be applied consistently across subsidiaries. Despite the HotelChain's rhetoric emphasising the importance of performance appraisal, crucial doubts emerged around this practice (cf. Biron et al., 2011; Pulakos & O'Leary, 2011). First, workforce segmentation separating core employees with career prospects from blue-collar workers undertaking low-skilled jobs rendered performance appraisal fundamentally irrelevant to the latter. Second, senior managers and supervisors who might have reached a career bottleneck or ceiling were likely to perceive the performance appraisal procedure as insignificant because they had developed themselves through competence. To complicate things, participants acknowledged the presence of favouritism in the performance appraisal process requiring tight control as it harms workplace trust (cf.

Harrington & Rayner, 2011). A CME respondent maintained that the professedly articulate HotelChain model appeared to be effective in stemming this negative phenomenon:

> [Favouritism is] a human tendency, however the sound HotelChain culture, clear guidelines and open communication work to limit its manifestation and possible negative effects.

(CME/B)

Hence, in CME subsidiaries a strong focus emerged on adhering to organisational rules and procedures. In the case of TPE subsidiaries, it appears there was a stronger emphasis on informal checks and balances relying on individual discretion:

> Fairness and the reduction of favouritism is safeguarded through close checking [of performance appraisals] – one by one by the HR leader and their team. If there is any question, things are followed up with the assessors. HR does not instruct the procedure execution – however, there is close monitoring.

(TPE/E)

Indeed, existing research has demonstrated the central role of internal politics in appraisals, leading to evaluation inequity (cf. Dhiman & Maheshwari, 2013). Subjectivity emerges in all evaluations owing to the cognitive and motivational conditions of raters resulting in the inconsistent application of standards (cf. Ibrahim et al., 2014). As experienced by the participant observer and as emerged in the document analysis, triangulation reveals that the HR Manual and training material addressed these interferences to the performance appraisal processes reminding appraisers about the need to conduct performance evaluations in an objective manner (HotelChain, 2012).

Discussion

Echoing the existing literature, we encountered variations in HR practices reflecting differences in institutional forms; however, and somewhat counter-intuitively, we found that stronger and more comprehensive institutional mediation made for weaker, rather than stronger, country of domicile pressures. In other words, proposition 1 is not confirmed while proposition 2 is confirmed. Particularly, in CMEs we found that practices represented a mix of home and host country pressures (cf. Brewster et al., 2008).

In the case of recruitment, there was a tendency to use existing staff member contacts in TPE subsidiaries, and more formal recruitment policies in CME ones. The former represents a common practice in many emerging markets (cf. Wood et al., 2011). The operation of the clan system, however, would mean that new staff would be embedded within the clan networks of existing staff. While this may help in the induction and socialisation of new staff as well as in internal communication, it can also mean that the capturing of key aspects of hotel subsidiary activity to help them serve a means of dispensing clan patronage would be reinforced. In other words, in adjusting policies to fit local circumstances, the process is one of accommodation which serves to reinforce existing systemic distortions rather than building on strengths.

Relatively with training, in the case of CMEs fitting in involved the usage of local vocational training systems, topping them up with skills specific to the hotel group; an emphasis was placed on the sustained and incremental development of skills. Contrariwise, in TPEs there was no similar recourse to national training institutions; rather, training was purely of the on the job 'learning with Nellie' variety. Although this may seem akin to the training provided in low end service work in LMEs, a key difference is that in the hotel – and, indeed, many other large LME firms – less emphasis was placed on formal induction closely adhering to fixed company procedures, and more on informality; it was felt that such training was more appropriate in nurturing the 'correct' approach to working in a Western hotel chain. Again, country of domicile effects seemed to predominate in both types of economy, but that, once more, in CMEs, it appeared to be focused on harnessing systemic strengths, while in TPEs, compensating for weaknesses.

As with reward systems, country of domicile practices appeared to be predominant within both capitalist archetypes; however, in CMEs, this involved the usage of formalised procedures, and in TPEs accommodating informal social networks; engaging with the latter, however, would involve significant departures from central company policy. Host country effects included wage setting, which followed prevailing collective bargaining arrangements (cf. Kim & Sakamoto, 2008). In TPEs, wage setting followed host country practices, but rather than building on specific complementarities, they veered to a default position of either offering employees the bare minimum or trimming practices to fit local dynamics (cf. Özcan, 2016). In TPEs, pay rates for managers were similarly set with an eye to the prevailing 'going rates' for specific jobs but, in practice, pay setting often lagged behind inflation. Meanwhile, rank and file pay was simply imposed unilaterally, paying the bare minimum the external labour market could afford.

Lastly, in the case of CMEs formal company procedures were adopted regarding the administration of appraisals; here, home country effects predominated. Company policies were closely adhered to with a focus on supporting company promotion policies and in identifying talented individuals for careers. In TPEs, appraisals were viewed as ineffective; even in the case of poor performance, it was difficult to take effective action. Rather, informal solutions were followed for performance management focusing on agreeing to ad hoc outcomes.

Managerial and theoretical implications

Whilst CME practices represented a mix of country of domicile and origin practices (cf. Brewster et al., 2008), a set of key TPE practices represented a significant departure from what might be encountered in developed world subsidiaries, most notably in terms of informal recruitment practices and appraisals. Indeed, practices encountered in TPEs represented a mix of cost cutting and the devising and rolling out of ad hoc solutions taking account of local realities, including the clan system. At times, the practices adopted – informally agreed mechanisms for recruitment and performance management – as enabled by organisational policy would confirm the earlier literature on institutional voids, which suggests that, rather than providing room to innovate, such settings forced firms to adopt a range of compensatory practices (cf. Miller et al., 2009). As Cantwell et al. (2010) explained, '(…) dynamic institutional environments put pressure on MNE subsidiaries to develop novel responses in their local operating environment' (p. 580).

Although this was not a study of clans, our evidence highlights effects which are likely to be the consequence of clan based networks, most notably in terms of recruitment policy and practice; indeed, such areas of HRM will be likely to be of acute interest to clan members wishing to dispense patronage and fulfil commitments to fellow members. Hence, a key managerial implication is that the influence of clanism is particularly felt in the recruitment and selection process which reinforces research findings by Minbaeva and Mouratbekova-Touron (2013, p. 136) in relation with the context of nearby Kazakhstan in Central Asia.

An even more important effect of the system was the extent to which, as an outside player, the firm had to closely adhere to formal regulations which were elsewhere more commonly honoured in the breach. As the literature on the liability of foreignness alerts us, MNEs have to adopt different strategies to compensate for it because they lack the ties and profile associated with their domestic counterparts (Calhoun, 2002). However, what this study highlights is this liability may, in fact, constrain the room for strategic decision making and result in a default position that centres on a narrow interpretation of the law. Indigenous competitors would, of course, have an incentive to ensure foreign competitors closely adhered to regulations in order to seize the competitive advantage that may be conferred by their own ability to circumnavigate them. Again, the challenges of working in the highly uncertain Caucasian and Central Asian environments made it very difficult to implement policies and practices set by head office even in areas not covered by formal regulation. In this sense, the firm was pulled in different directions: towards close conformity with formal regulations, and to devising ad hoc locally appropriate solutions in areas it did not. Therefore, by linking back to Perlmutter's (1969) notions related to the management of overseas subsidiaries, we observe the emergence of a hybrid approach which, as evidence suggests, in non-ethnocentric.

This raises two theoretical questions. The first is whether this would be true for many emerging markets where there is a strong emphasis on informal, extended, networks of support. Whilst theoretical explanations for the latter tend to be generic, it is worth noting that the clan system is firmly embedded on spatial grounds; other extended networks (e.g., the guanxi system) can be rather more flexible, less closed and more capable of operating on a global scale (cf. Hydén, 1980). Again, the clan system is characterised by clear lines of internal authority, centring on elders; in practical terms, this means that whilst clan networks serve a redistributive function, much of the value generated ends back in the hands of local power holders (Özcan, 2016). Although it was not possible to explore this dimension, it is worth underscoring that little value devolved down to the workforce, which may have contributed to the noted productivity and quality problems. A possible area for further theorising would be around the identification of defining features of different types of network of support, and variations in internal authority, space and scale, and in the nature of the redistribution of value.

The second issue is around how we understand institutional voids. Although the practices encountered in TPEs were largely compensatory, it should not be concluded that such circumstances are only characterised by market distortions. Rather, informal regulations may deter firms from simply defaulting to universally hard-line HR practices; the study revealed that the firm was restrained by the need to heed both unevenly forced regulations, and local networks of support. In turn, such a system provided some protection for individuals; again, firms could benefit from a more stable workforce, allowing more room for the long-term development of human capabilities, potentially making for greater productivity. Even if large scale complementarities may be elusive, firm and sector specific complementarities of this type may leave both parties somewhat better off than might be the case had the firm a completely free hand.

In summary, it can be seen that weaker and less encompassing formal institutions characterising high-uncertainty contexts made for greater, rather than lesser, departures, from head office policies and practices, disproving Proposition 1, but confirming Proposition 2. Although such departures, to a large extent, reflected attempts to compensate for systemic distortions, they may also have allowed for localised and small-scale complementarity: in other words, the ability to secure localised solutions that yield better results than an assessment of the context might suggest. In further developing the literature on institutional voids (cf. McCarthy & Puffer, 2016), it would be worth further considering ways in which such systems sometimes lead to opportunities for, or confirm benefits on, firms, rather than simply viewing such circumstances only in terms of the challenges and costs they impose.

Disclosure statement

No potential conflict of interest was reported by the authors.

Funding

This research was not supported by any grants or other external funding sources.

ORCID

Giovanni Oscar Serafini (iD) http://orcid.org/0000-0002-3147-8467
Leslie Thomas Szamosi (iD) http://orcid.org/0000-0003-0470-7671

Data availability statement

The authors confirm that the data supporting the findings of this study are available within the article.

References

Adler, P. A. (1987). *Membership roles in field research*. SAGE.
Adler, P. A., & Adler, P. (1994). Observational techniques. In N. K. Denzin & Y. S. Lincoln (Eds.), *Handbook of qualitative research* (pp. 377–392). SAGE.
Agar, M. H. (1983). Ethnographic evidence. *Journal of Contemporary Ethnography*, *12*(1), 32–48.
Ahlvik, C., Smale, A., & Sumelius, J. (2016). Aligning corporate transfer intentions and subsidiary HRM practice implementation in multinational corporations. *Journal of World Business*, *51*(3), 343–355. https://doi.org/10.1016/j.jwb.2015.04.003
Ailon, G. (2008). Mirror, mirror on the wall: Culture's consequences in a value test of its own design. *Academy of Management Review*, *33*(4), 885–904. https://doi.org/10.5465/amr.2008.34421995
Almond, P. H. I. L., Edwards, T. O. N. Y., Colling, T., Ferner, A., Gunnigle, P., Müller-Camen, M., Quintanilla, J., & Wächter, H. (2005). Unraveling home and host country effects: An investigation of the HR policies of an American multinational in four

European countries. *Industrial Relations: A Journal of Economy and Society*, *44*(2), 276–306. https://doi.org/10.1111/j.0019-8676.2005.00384.x

Altheide, D., Coyle, M., DeVriese, K., & Schneider, C. (2010). Emergent qualitative document analysis. In S. N. Hesse-Biber & P. Leavy (Eds.), *Handbook of emergent methods* (pp. 127–154). Guilford Press.

Amable, B., Audretsch, D. B., & Dore, R. (2008). Richard Whitley business systems and organizational capabilities: The institutional structuring of competitive competences. The heterogeneity of competing capitalisms and business systems. *Socio-Economic Review*, *6*(4), 771–775. https://doi.org/10.1093/ser/mwn017

Ananthram, S., & Chan, C. (2013). Challenges and strategies for global human resource executives: Perspectives from Canada and the United States. *European Management Journal*, *31*(3), 223–233. https://doi.org/10.1016/j.emj.2012.12.002

Angrosino, M. V., & Mays de Pérez, K. A. (2000). Rethinking observation: From method to context. In *Handbook of qualitative research* (pp. 673–702). SAGE.

Aoki, M. (2010). *Corporations in evolving diversity: Cognition, governance, and institutions*. Oxford University Press.

AOM. (2017). *Code of ethics*. Retrieved December 17, 2017, from http://aom.org/About-AOM/AOM-Code-of-Ethics.aspx

Arslan, A., Tarba, S. Y., & Larimo, J. (2015). FDI entry strategies and the impacts of economic freedom distance: Evidence from Nordic FDIs in transitional periphery of CIS and SEE. *International Business Review*, *24*(6), 997–1008. https://doi.org/10.1016/j.ibusrev.2015.03.004

Aslund, A. (2013). *How capitalism was built: The transformation of Central and Eastern Europe*. Cambridge University Press.

Assaf, A. G., Josiassen, A., & Agbola, F. W. (2015). Attracting international hotels: Locational factors that matter most. *Tourism Management*, *47*, 329–340. https://doi.org/10.1016/j.tourman.2014.10.005

Bainbridge, H. T. J., & Lee, I. (2014). Mixed methods in HRM research. In K. Sanders (Ed.), *Research methods for human resource management* (pp. 15–33). Routledge.

Bakkevig Dagsland, Å. H., Mykletun, R. J., & Einarsen, S. (2015). "We're not slaves – we are actually the future!": A follow-up study of apprentices' experiences in the Norwegian hospitality industry. *Journal of Vocational Education & Training*, *67*(4), 460–481.

Barbopoulos, L., Marshall, A., MacInnes, C., & McColgan, P. (2014). Foreign direct investment in emerging markets and acquirers' value gains. *International Business Review*, *23*(3), 604–619. https://doi.org/10.1016/j.ibusrev.2013.10.003

Baum, T. (2015). Human resources in tourism: Still waiting for change?. *Tourism Management*, *50*, 204–212. https://doi.org/10.1016/j.tourman.2015.02.001

Becker, H. S. (1958). Problems of inference and proof in participant observation. *American Sociological Review*, *23*(6), 652–660. https://doi.org/10.2307/2089053

Becker, H. S., & Geer, B. (1978). Participant observation and interviewing: A comparison. In J. C. Manis & B. N. Meltzer (Eds.), *Symbolic interaction: A reader in social psychology* (pp. 76–82). Allyn and Bacon.

Bernard, H. (2017). *Research methods in anthropology: Qualitative and quantitative approaches*. Rowman & Littlefield.

Biron, M., Farndale, E., & Paauwe, J. (2011). Performance management effectiveness: Lessons from world-leading firms. *The International Journal of Human Resource Management*, *22*(6), 1294–1311. https://doi.org/10.1080/09585192.2011.559100

Boardman, J., Johns, A., & Petre, D. (2015). Sectoral studies on decent work in global supply chains: Tourism. *International Labour Office: Geneva, Switzerland*, 43–101.

Bosch, G., & Weinkopf, C. (2013). Transnational labour markets and national wage setting systems in the EU. *Industrial Relations Journal*, *44*(1), 2–19. https://doi.org/10.1111/irj.12006

Boussebaa, M., Morgan, G., & Sturdy, A. (2012). Constructing global firms? National, transnational and neocolonial effects in international management consultancies. *Organization Studies*, *33*(4), 465–486. https://doi.org/10.1177/0170840612443454

Boxall, P. (1995). Building the theory of comparative HRM. *Human Resource Management Journal*, *5*(5), 5–17. https://doi.org/10.1111/j.1748-8583.1995.tb00386.x

Brewster, C., Mayrhofer, W., & Smale, A. (2016). Crossing the streams: HRM in multinational enterprises and comparative HRM. *Human Resource Management Review*, *26*(4), 285–297. https://doi.org/10.1016/j.hrmr.2016.04.002

Brewster, C., Wood, G., & Brookes, M. (2008). Similarity, isomorphism or duality? Recent survey evidence on the human resource management policies of multinational corporations. *British Journal of Management*, *19*(4), 320–342. https://doi.org/10.1111/j.1467-8551.2007.00546.x

Briscoe, D. R., & Schuler, R. S. (2004). *International human resource management: Policy and practice for the global enterprise*. Routledge.

Brookes, M., Croucher, R., Fenton-O'Creevy, M., & Gooderham, P. (2011). Measuring competing explanations of human resource management practices through the Cranet survey: Cultural versus institutional explanations. *Human Resource Management Review*, *21*(1), 68–79. https://doi.org/10.1016/j.hrmr.2010.09.012

Brotherton, B. (2012). *International hospitality industry*. Routledge.

Bryman, A. (2005). *Research methods and organization studies*. Routledge.

Budhwar, P. S., Varma, A., & Patel, C. (2016). Convergence-divergence of HRM in the Asia-Pacific: Context-specific analysis and future research agenda. *Human Resource Management Review*, *26*(4), 311–326. https://doi.org/10.1016/j.hrmr.2016.04.004

Busemeyer, M. R., & Schlicht-Schmälzle, R. (2014). Partisan power, economic coordination and variations in vocational training systems in Europe. *European Journal of Industrial Relations*, *20*(1), 55–71. https://doi.org/10.1177/0959680113512731

Calhoun, M. A. (2002). Unpacking liability of foreignness: Identifying culturally driven external and internal sources of liability for the foreign subsidiary. *Journal of International Management*, *8*(3), 301–321. https://doi.org/10.1016/S1075-4253(02)00072-8

Cantwell, J., Dunning, J. H., & Lundan, S. M. (2010). An evolutionary approach to understanding international business activity: The co-evolution of MNEs and the institutional environment. *Journal of International Business Studies*, *41*(4), 567–586. https://doi.org/10.1057/jibs.2009.95

Chapman, M. (1996). Social anthropology, business studies, and cultural issues. *International Studies of Management & Organization*, *26*(4), 3–29.

Chowdhury, S. D., & Mahmood, M. H. (2012). Societal institutions and HRM practices: An analysis of four European multinational subsidiaries in Bangladesh. *The International Journal of Human Resource Management*, *23*(9), 1808–1831. https://doi.org/10.1080/09585192.2011.610339

Collins, K. (2006). *Clan politics and regime transition in Central Asia*. Cambridge University Press.

Contractor, F. J., & Kundu, S. K. (1998). Franchising versus company-run operations: Modal choice in the global hotel sector. *Journal of International Marketing*, *6*(2), 28–53. https://doi.org/10.1177/1069031X9800600207

Cooke, F. L., Wood, G., Wang, M., & Veen, A. (2019). How far has international HRM travelled? A systematic review of literature on multinational corporations (2000–2014). *Human Resource Management Review*, *29*(1), 59–75. https://doi.org/10.1016/j.hrmr.2018.05.001

Culpepper, P. D. (2005). Institutional change in contemporary capitalism: Coordinated financial systems since 1990. *World Politics*, *57*(2), 173–199. https://doi.org/10.1353/wp.2005.0016

D'Annunzio-Green, N. (2002). An examination of the organizational and cross-cultural challenges facing international hotel managers in Russia. *International Journal of Contemporary Hospitality Management*, *14*(6), 266–273.

Darbi, W. P. K., Hall, C. M., & Knott, P. (2018). The informal sector: A review and agenda for management research. *International Journal of Management Reviews*, *20*(2), 301–324. https://doi.org/10.1111/ijmr.12131

Davidson, M. C. G., & Wang, Y. (2011). Sustainable labor practices? Hotel human resource managers views on turnover and skill shortages. *Journal of Human Resources in Hospitality & Tourism*, *10*(3), 235–253.

Demirbag, M., McGuinnness, M., Wood, G., & Bayyurt, N. (2015). Context, law and reinvestment decisions: Why the transitional periphery differs from other post-state socialist economies. *International Business Review*, *24*(6), 955–965. https://doi.org/10.1016/j.ibusrev.2015.03.003

Dhiman, A., & Maheshwari, S. K. (2013). Performance appraisal politics from appraisee perspective: A study of antecedents in the Indian context. *The International Journal of Human Resource Management*, *24*(6), 1202–1235. https://doi.org/10.1080/09585192.2012.706816

Dore, R. (2008). Best practice winning out?. *Socio-Economic Review*, *6*(4), 779–784.

Dore, R. P. (2002). Stock market capitalism: Welfare capitalism Japan and Germany versus the Anglo-Saxons. *Journal of International Business Studies*, *33*(1), 195–197.

Douglas, J. D. (1976). *Investigative social research: Individual and team field research*. SAGE.

Dowling, P., Festing, M., & Engle, A. D. (2008). *International human resource management: Managing people in a multinational context*. South Melbourne, Cengage Learning.

Dunning, J. H., & Lundan, S. M. (2008). *Multinational enterprises and the global economy*. Edward Elgar Publishing.

Dunning, J. H., & McQueen, M. (1982). Multinational corporations in the international hotel industry. *Annals of Tourism Research*, *9*(1), 69–90. https://doi.org/10.1016/0160-7383(82)90035-4

Edwards, T., Sánchez-Mangas, R., Jalette, P., Lavelle, J., & Minbaeva, D. (2016). Global standardization or national differentiation of HRM practices in multinational companies? A comparison of multinationals in five countries. *Journal of International Business Studies*, *47*(8), 997–1021. https://doi.org/10.1057/s41267-016-0003-6

Eisenhardt, K. M. (1989). Building theories from case study research. *Academy of Management Review*, *14*(4), 532–550. https://doi.org/10.5465/amr.1989.4308385

Emmenegger, P. (2015). The politics of job security regulations in Western Europe. *Politics & Society*, *43*(1), 89–118.

Ess, C., & Sudweeks, F. (2005). Culture and computer-mediated communication: Toward new understandings. *Journal of Computer-Mediated Communication*, *11*(1), 179–191. https://doi.org/10.1111/j.1083-6101.2006.tb00309.x

Farndale, E. (2017). Two-country study of engagement, supervisors and performance appraisal. *Journal of Asia Business Studies*, *11*(3), 342–362. https://doi.org/10.1108/JABS-07-2015-0105

Farndale, E., & Sanders, K. (2017). Conceptualizing HRM system strength through a cross-cultural lens. *The International Journal of Human Resource Management*, *28*(1), 132–148. https://doi.org/10.1080/09585192.2016.1239124

Farndale, E., Brewster, C., & Poutsma, E. (2008). Coordinated vs. liberal market HRM: The impact of institutionalization on multinational firms. *The International Journal of Human Resource Management*, *19*(11), 2004–2023. https://doi.org/10.1080/09585190802404247

Ferner, A., & Quintanilla, J. (1998). Multinationals, national business systems and HRM: The enduring influence of national identity or a process of "Anglo-Saxonization." *The International Journal of Human Resource Management*, *9*(4), 710–731. https://doi.org/10.1080/095851998340973

Ferner, A., Almond, P., Colling, T., & Edwards, T. (2005). Policies on union representation in US multinationals in the UK: Between micro-politics and macro-institutions. *British Journal of Industrial Relations*, *43*(4), 703–728. https://doi.org/10.1111/j.1467-8543.2005.00480.x

Filatotchev, I., Strange, R., Piesse, J., & Lien, Y.-C. (2007). FDI by firms from newly industrialized economies in emerging markets: Corporate governance, entry mode and location. *Journal of International Business Studies*, *38*(4), 556–572. https://doi.org/10.1057/palgrave.jibs.8400279

Finnegan, R. (2006). Using documents. In R. Sapsford & V. Jupp (Eds.), *Data collection and analysis* (pp. 138–152). SAGE.

Geppert, M., & Dorrenbacher, C. (2011). Introduction. In C. Dorrenbacher & M. Geppert (Eds.), *Politics and power in multinational corporations* (pp. 3–38). Cambridge University Press.

Gill, J., & Johnson, P. (2002). *Research methods for managers*. SAGE.

Glaser, B. G., & Strauss, A. L. (2009). *The discovery of grounded theory: Strategies for qualitative research*. Transaction Publishers.

Godard, J. (2002). Institutional environments, employer practices, and states in liberal market economies. *Industrial Relations: A Journal of Economy and Society*, *41*(2), 249–286. https://doi.org/10.1111/1468-232X.00245

Gold, R. L. (1958). Roles in sociological field observations. *Social Forces*, *36*(3), 217–223. https://doi.org/10.2307/2573808

Gould, J. A., & Sickner, C. (2008). Making market democracies? The contingent loyalties of post-privatization elites in Azerbaijan, Georgia and Serbia. *Review of International Political Economy*, *15*(5), 740–769. https://doi.org/10.1080/09692290802408923

Gray, D. E. (2009). *Doing research in the real world*. SAGE.

Grove, C. N. (2015). Value dimensions: GLOBE study. In J. M. Bennett (Ed.), *The SAGE encyclopedia of intercultural competence* (pp. 835–841). SAGE.

Guler, I., & Guillén, M. F. (2010). Institutions and the internationalization of US venture capital firms. *Journal of International Business Studies*, *41*(2), 185–205. https://doi.org/10.1057/jibs.2009.35

Hakim, C. (1982). *Secondary data analysis in social research*. Allen & Unwin.

Hakim, C. (2004). Research analysis of administrative records. In M. Hammersley (Ed.), *Social research: Philosophy, politics and practice* (pp. 131–145). SAGE.

Hall, P., & Soskice, D. (2001). *Varieties of capitalism: The institutional foundations of comparative advantage*. Oxford University Press.

Hammersley, M., & Atkinson, P. (2007). *Ethnography: Principles in practice*. Routledge.

Harrington, S., & Rayner, C. (2011). Whose side are you on? Trust and HR in workplace bullying. In R. Searle & D. Skinner (Eds.), *Trust and human resource management* (pp. 223–246). Edward Elgar Publishing.

Hodson, R. (1998). Organizational ethnographies: An underutilized resource in the sociology of work. *Social Forces*, 76(4), 1173–1208. https://doi.org/10.2307/3005832

Hofstede, G. (1980). Motivation, leadership, and organization: Do American theories apply abroad?. *Organizational Dynamics*, 9(1), 42–63. https://doi.org/10.1016/0090-2616(80)90013-3

Hofstede, G. (1984). *Culture's consequences: International differences in work-related values*. SAGE.

Hofstede, G. (1993). Cultural constraints in management theories. *Academy of Management Executive*, 7(1), 81–94.

Hofstede, G. (2002). Dimensions do not exist: A reply to Brendan McSweeney. *Human Relations*, 55(11), 1355–1361. https://doi.org/10.1177/0018726702055011921

Hofstede, G., & McCrae, R. R. (2004). Personality and culture revisited: Linking traits and dimensions of culture. *Cross-Cultural Research*, 38(1), 52–88. https://doi.org/10.1177/1069397103259443

Hoque, K. (2013). *Human resource management in the hotel industry: Strategy, innovation and performance*. Routledge.

HotelChain. (2012). Corporate HR manual. Retrieved from website (accessed 17 September 2017).

HotelChain. (2017). Corporate information. Retrieved from website (accessed 27 September 2017).

Hotho, J., & Pedersen, T. (2012). Institutions and international business research: Three institutional approaches and recommendations for future research. In R. Van Tulder, A. Verbeke, & L. Voinea (Eds.), *New policy challenges for European multinationals (Progress in International Business Research* (Vol. 7, pp. 135–152). Emerald Group Publishing Limited.

House, R. J., Hanges, P. J., Javidan, M., Dorfman, P. W., & Gupta, V. (Eds.). (2004). *Culture, leadership, and organizations: The GLOBE study of 62 societies*. SAGE.

Huselid, M. A., Jackson, S. E., & Schuler, R. S. (1997). Technical and strategic human resource management effectiveness as determinants of firm performance. *Academy of Management Journal*, 40(1), 171–188.

Hydén, G. (1980). *Beyond Ujamaa in Tanzania: Underdevelopment and an uncaptured peasantry*. University of California Press.

Ibrahim, J., Macphail, A., Chadwick, L., & Jeffcott, S. (2014). Interns' perceptions of performance feedback. *Medical Education*, 48(4), 417–429. https://doi.org/10.1111/medu.12381

Jackson, G., & Deeg, R. (2008). From comparing capitalisms to the politics of institutional change. *Review of International Political Economy*, 15(4), 680–709. https://doi.org/10.1080/09692290802260704

Kalleberg, A. L. (2009). Precarious work, insecure workers: Employment relations in transition. *American Sociological Review*, 74(1), 1–22. https://doi.org/10.1177/000312240907400101

Kavalski, E. (Ed.). (2016). *Stable outside, fragile inside?: Post-Soviet statehood in Central Asia*. Routledge.

Kim, C., & Sakamoto, A. (2008). The rise of intra-occupational wage inequality in the United States, 1983 to 2002. *American Sociological Review*, 73(1), 129–157. https://doi.org/10.1177/000312240807300107

Kim, N. (2014). Employee turnover intention among newcomers in travel industry. *International Journal of Tourism Research*, *16*(1), 56–64. https://doi.org/10.1002/jtr.1898

Kinderman, D. (2012). Free us up so we can be responsible!': The co-evolution of corporate social responsibility and neo-liberalism in the UK, 1977-2010. *Socio-Economic Review*, *10*(1), 29–57. https://doi.org/10.1093/ser/mwr028

King, C., Funk, D. C., & Wilkins, H. (2011). Bridging the gap: An examination of the relative alignment of hospitality research and industry priorities. *International Journal of Hospitality Management*, *30*(1), 157–166. https://doi.org/10.1016/j.ijhm.2010.04.009

Knox, A. (2014). Human resource management (HRM) in temporary work agencies: Evidence from the hospitality industry. The Economic and Labour Relations Review, *25*(1), 81–98. https://doi.org/10.1177/1035304613517454

Kouznetsov, A., Dass, M., & Schmidt, P. (2014). Entry mode decisions: The effects of corruption and weak law enforcement on foreign manufacturing SMEs in post-communist Russia. *Baltic Journal of Management*, *9*(3), 277–293. https://doi.org/10.1108/BJM-06-2013-0104

Krippendorff, K. (1980). *Content analysis: An introduction to its methodology.* SAGE.

Kuhlmann, A. (1992). Collaborative research among the Kickapoo tribe of Oklahoma. *Human Organization*, *51*(3), 274–283. https://doi.org/10.17730/humo.51.3.k3n65x64t5nx36x5

Kundu, S. K., & Lahiri, S. (2015). Turning the spotlight on service multinationals: New theoretical insights and empirical evidence. *Journal of International Management*, *21*(3), 215–219. https://doi.org/10.1016/j.intman.2015.05.002

Kusluvan, S., Kusluvan, Z., Ilhan, I., & Buyruk, L. (2010). The human dimension: A review of human resources management issues in the tourism and hospitality industry. *Cornell Hospitality Quarterly*, *51*(2), 171–214. https://doi.org/10.1177/1938965510362871

Lafontaine, F., Perrigot, R., & Wilson, N. E. (2017). The quality of institutions and organizational form decisions: Evidence from within the firm. *Journal of Economics & Management Strategy*, *26*(2), 375–402. https://doi.org/10.1111/jems.12185

León-Darder, F., Villar-García, C., & Pla-Barber, J. (2011). Entry mode choice in the internationalisation of the hotel industry: A holistic approach. *The Service Industries Journal*, *31*(1), 107–122. https://doi.org/10.1080/02642069.2010.485198

Locke, K. (2011). Field research practice in management and organization studies: Reclaiming its tradition of discovery. *Academy of Management Annals*, *5*(1), 613–652. https://doi.org/10.5465/19416520.2011.593319

Lofland, J. (1971). *Analysing social settings.* Wadsworth.

López, J., & Santos, J. (2014). Does corruption have social roots? The role of culture and social capital. *Journal of Business Ethics*, *122*(4), 697–708.

Love, P. (2003). Document analysis. In F. K. Stage & K. Manning (Eds.), *Research in the college context: Approaches and methods* (pp. 83–96). Brunner-Routledge.

Mackenzie, L., Wehner, J., & Correll, S. J. (2019). *Why most performance evaluations are biased, and how to fix them.* Retrieved 11 April 2020, from https://hbr.org/2019/01/why-most-performance-evaluations-are-biased-and-how-to-fix-them

Malina, M. A., Nørreklit, H. S., & Selto, F. H. (2011). Lessons learned: Advantages and disadvantages of mixed method research. *Qualitative Research in Accounting & Management*, *8*(1), 59–71. https://doi.org/10.1108/11766091111124702

Marens, R. (2012). Generous in victory? American managerial autonomy, labour relations and the invention of. *Socio-Economic Review*, *10*(1), 59–84. https://doi.org/10.1093/ser/mwr024

Martorell, O., Mulet, C., & Otero, L. (2013). Choice of market entry mode by Balearic hotel chains in the Caribbean and Gulf of Mexico. *International Journal of Hospitality Management, 32*(1), 217–227. https://doi.org/10.1016/j.ijhm.2012.06.001

McCarthy, D. J., & Puffer, S. M. (2016). Institutional voids in an emerging economy: From problem to opportunity. *Journal of Leadership & Organizational Studies, 23*(2), 208–219. https://doi.org/10.1177/1548051816633070

McNulty, Y., & Brewster, C. (2017). Theorizing the meaning (s) of 'expatriate': Establishing boundary conditions for business expatriates. *The International Journal of Human Resource Management, 28*(1), 27–61. https://doi.org/10.1080/09585192.2016.1243567

McSweeney, B. (2002a). The essentials of scholarship: A reply to Geert Hofstede. *Human Relations, 55*(11), 1363–1372. https://doi.org/10.1177/00187267025511005

McSweeney, B. (2002b). Hofstede's model of national cultural differences and their consequences: A triumph of faith - a failure of analysis. *Human Relations, 55*(1), 89–118. https://doi.org/10.1177/0018726702551004

Meelen, T., Herrmann, A. M., & Faber, J. (2017). Disentangling patterns of economic, technological and innovative specialization of Western economies: An assessment of the Varieties-of-Capitalism theory on comparative institutional advantages. *Research Policy, 46*(3), 667–677. https://doi.org/10.1016/j.respol.2017.01.013

Meyer, K. E., Mudambi, R., & Narula, R. (2011). Multinational enterprises and local contexts: The opportunities and challenges of multiple embeddedness. *Journal of Management Studies, 48*(2), 235–252. https://doi.org/10.1111/j.1467-6486.2010.00968.x

Michailova, S. (2002). When common sense becomes uncommon: Participation and empowerment in Russian companies with Western participation. *Journal of World Business, 37*(3), 180–187. https://doi.org/10.1016/S1090-9516(02)00076-7

Miles, M. B., & Huberman, A. M. (1994). *Qualitative data analysis: An expanded sourcebook*. SAGE.

Miller, D., Lee, J., Chang, S., & Le Breton-Miller, I. (2009). Filling the institutional void: The social behavior and performance of family vs non-family technology firms in emerging markets. *Journal of International Business Studies, 40*(5), 802–817. https://doi.org/10.1057/jibs.2009.11

Minbaeva, D. B., & Muratbekova-Touron, M. (2013). Clanism: Definition and implications for human resource management. *Management International Review, 53*(1), 109–139. https://doi.org/10.1007/s11575-012-0165-9

Minbaeva, D. B., Hutchings, K., & Thompson, S. B. (2007). Hybrid human resource management in post-Soviet Kazakhstan. *European Journal of International Management, 1*(4), 350–371.

Morgan, G. (2012). International business, multinationals and national business systems. In M. Demirbag & G. Wood (Eds.), *Handbook of institutional approaches to international business* (pp. 18–40). Edward Elgar Publishing.

Myloni, B., Harzing, A. K., & Mirza, H. (2004). Host country specific factors and the transfer of human resource management practices in multinational companies. *International Journal of Manpower, 25*(6), 518–534. https://doi.org/10.1108/01437720410560424

Naama, A., Haven-Tang, C., & Jones, E. (2008). Human resource development issues for the hotel sector in Lybia: A government perspective. *International Journal of Tourism Research, 10*(5), 481–492. https://doi.org/10.1002/jtr.683

Niewiadomski, P. (2015). International hotel groups and regional development in Central and Eastern Europe. *Tourism Geographies*, *17*(2), 173–191. https://doi.org/10. 1080/14616688.2014.997278

North, D. C. (1990). *Institutions, institutional change and economic performance: Political economy of institutions and decisions.* Cambridge University Press.

Oyserman, D., Coon, H. M., & Kemmelmeier, M. (2002). Rethinking individualism and collectivism: Evaluation of theoretical assumptions and meta-analyses. *Psychological Bulletin*, *38*(3), 283–309.

Özcan, G. (2016). *Building states and markets: Enterprise development in Central Asia.* Palgrave Macmillan.

Parry, E., Dickmann, M., & Morley, M. (2008). North American MNCs and their HR policies in liberal and coordinated market economies. *The International Journal of Human Resource Management*, *19*(11), 2024–2040. https://doi.org/10.1080/09585190802404262

Patton, M. Q. (2008). *Utilization-focused evaluation.* SAGE.

Patton, M. Q. (2015). *Qualitative research & evaluation methods: Integrating theory and practice* (4th ed.). Thousand Oaks: SAGE.

Pearson, C. M., & Clair, J. A. (1998). Reframing crisis management. *Academy of Management Review*, *23*(1), 59–76. https://doi.org/10.5465/amr.1998.192960

Peltonen, T., & Vaara, E. (2012). Critical approaches to comparative HRM. In C. Brewster & W. Mayrhofer (Eds.), *Handbook of research on comparative human resource management* (pp. 69–89). Edward Elgar Publishing.

Peng, M. W. (2003). Institutional transitions and strategic choices. *Academy of Management Review*, *28*(2), 275–296. https://doi.org/10.5465/amr.2003.9416341

Peretz, H., & Rosenblatt, Z. (2011). The role of societal cultural practices in organizational investment in training: A comparative study in 21 countries. *Journal of Cross-Cultural Psychology*, *42*(5), 817–831. https://doi.org/10.1177/0022022111406786

Perlmutter, H. V. (1969). The tortuous evolution of the multinational corporation. *Columbia Journal of World Business*, *4*(1), 9–18.

Pine, R., Zhang, H. Q., & Qi, P. (2000). The challenges and opportunities of franchising in China's hotel industry. *International Journal of Contemporary Hospitality Management*, *12*(5), 300–307. https://doi.org/10.1108/09596110010339670

Pissarides, F., Singer, M., & Svejnar, J. (2003). Objectives and constraints of entrepreneurs: Evidence from small and medium size enterprises in Russia and Bulgaria. *Journal of Comparative Economics*, *31*(3), 503–531. https://doi.org/10.1016/S0147-5967(03)00054-4

Pomfret, R. (2012). Central Asia after two decades of independence. In G. Roland (Ed.), *Economic transition: The long-run view* (pp. 400–429). Palgrave Macmillan.

Prouska, R., & Psychogios, A. (2018). Do not say a word! Conceptualizing employee silence in a long-term crisis context. *The International Journal of Human Resource Management*, *29*(5), 885–914. https://doi.org/10.1080/09585192.2016.1212913

Psychogios, A. G., Szamosi, L. T., & Wood, G. (2010). Introducing employment relations in South Eastern Europe. *Employee Relations*, *32*(3), 205–211. https://doi.org/10.1108/ 01425451011038753

Psychogios, A., Szamosi, L. T., Prouska, R., & Brewster, C. (2020). Varieties of crisis and working conditions: A comparative study of Greece and Serbia. *European Journal of Industrial Relations*, *26*(1), 91–106. https://doi.org/10.1177/0959680119837101

Pulakos, E. D., & O'Leary, R. S. (2011). Why is performance management broken?. *Industrial and Organizational Psychology*, *4*(2), 146–164. https://doi.org/10.1111/j. 1754-9434.2011.01315.x

Riegel, C. (2011). The causes and consequences of turnover in the hospitality industry. In D. G. Rutherford & M. J. O'Fallon (Eds.), *Hotel management and operations* (pp. 449–454). Wiley.

Ritchie, J., & Lewis, J. (2003). Qualitative research practice. *A guide for social science students and researchers.* SAGE.

Robson, C. (2003). *Real world research.* Blackwell Publishing.

Romani, L. (2004). Culture in management: The measurement of differences. In A.-W. Harzing & J. Van Ruysseveldt (Eds.), *International human resource management* (2nd ed., pp. 141–166). SAGE.

Rosen, C. C., Kacmar, K. M., Harris, K. J., Gavin, M. B., & Hochwarter, W. A. (2017). Workplace politics and performance appraisal: A two-study, multilevel field investigation. *Journal of Leadership & Organizational Studies, 24*(1), 20–38. https://doi.org/10.1177/1548051816661480

Rothbauer, P. M. (2008). Triangulation. In L. Given (Ed.), *The SAGE encyclopaedia of qualitative research methods* (pp. 892–894). SAGE.

Roy, D. (1952). Quota restriction and goldbricking in a machine shop. *American Journal of Sociology, 57*(5), 427–442. https://doi.org/10.1086/221011

Rugman, A. M., & Oh, C. H. (2013). Why the home region matters: Location and regional multinationals. *British Journal of Management, 24*(4), 463–479. https://doi.org/10.1111/j.1467-8551.2012.00817.x

Saunders, M., Lewis, P., & Thornhill, A. (2007). *Research methods for business students.* Pearson Education UK.

Schatz, E. (2004). *Modern clan politics: The power of "blood" in Kazakhstan and beyond.* University of Washington Press.

Serafini, G. O., & Szamosi, L. T. (2015). Five star hotels of a multinational enterprise in countries of the transitional periphery: A case study in human resources management. *International Business Review, 24*(6), 972–983. https://doi.org/10.1016/j.ibusrev.2014.12.001

Serafini, G. O., & Szamosi, L. T. (2018). The application of MNC HR policies and procedures: A case study of the transitional periphery versus developed economies. In G. T. Wood & M. Demirbag (Eds.), *Institutions and the firm in the "Transitional Periphery" – The Post-Soviet economies of the Caucasus and Central Asia* (pp. 173–186). Edward Elgar.

Shenkar, O. (2001). Cultural distance revisited: Towards a more rigorous conceptualization and measurement of cultural differences. *Journal of International Business Studies, 32*(3), 519–535. https://doi.org/10.1057/palgrave.jibs.8490982

Shi, X., & Wang, J. (2011). Interpreting Hofstede model and GLOBE model: Which way to go for cross-cultural research? *International Journal of Business and Management, 6*(5), 93–99. https://doi.org/10.5539/ijbm.v6n5p93

Shinnar, R. S., Young, C. A., & Meana, M. (2004). The motivations for and outcomes of employee referrals. *Journal of Business and Psychology, 19*(2), 271–283. https://doi.org/10.1007/s10869-004-0552-8

Sievers, E. W. (2013). *The post-Soviet decline of Central Asia: Sustainable development and comprehensive capital.* Routledge.

Sims, W. J. (2003). Managing labour turnover in the tourism industry. In S. Kusluvan (Ed.), *Managing employee attitudes and behaviors in the tourism and hospitality industry* (pp. 545–558). Nova Science Publishers.

Sleeman, P. (2002). Archives and statistics. In N. Ó Dochartaigh (Ed.), *The internet research handbook: A practical guide for students and researchers in the social sciences* (pp. 220–227). SAGE.

Smith, P. B. (2006). When elephants fight, the grass gets trampled: The GLOBE and Hofstede projects. *Journal of International Business Studies*, *37*(6), 915–921. https://doi.org/10.1057/palgrave.jibs.8400235

Sorge, A. (2004). Cross-national differences in human resources and organization. In A.-W. Harzing & J. Van Ruysseveldt (Eds.), *International human resource management* (2nd ed., pp. 117–140). SAGE.

Spencer, L., Ritchie, J., Ormston, R., O'Connor, W., & Barnard, M. (2014). Analysis: Principles and processes. In J. Ritchie, J. Lewis, C. M. Nicholls, & R. Ormston (Eds.), *Qualitative research practice: A guide for social science students and researchers* (pp. 269–294). SAGE.

Streeck, W. (2009). *Re-forming capitalism: Institutional change in the German political economy*. Oxford University Press.

Tarique, I., & Schuler, R. S. (2010). Global talent management: Literature review, integrative framework, and suggestions for further research. *Journal of World Business*, *45*(2), 122–133. https://doi.org/10.1016/j.jwb.2009.09.019

Tashakkori, A., & Teddlie, C. (1998). *Mixed methodology: Combining qualitative and quantitative approaches*. SAGE.

Tatoglu, E., Glaister, A. J., & Demirbag, M. (2016). Talent management motives and practices in an emerging market: A comparison between MNEs and local firms. *Journal of World Business*, *51*(2), 278–293. https://doi.org/10.1016/j.jwb.2015.11.001

Temirkoulov, A. (2004). Tribalism, social conflict, and state-building in the Kyrgyz Republic. *Berliner Osteuropa Info*, *21*, 94–100.

Tempel, A., Edwards, T., Ferner, A., Müller-Camen, M., & Wächter, H. (2006). Subsidiary responses to institutional duality: Collective representation practices of US multinationals in Britain and Germany. *Human Relations*, *59*(11), 1543–1570. https://doi.org/10.1177/0018726706072863

Terlutter, R., Diehl, S., & Mueller, B. (2006). The GLOBE study—applicability of a new typology of cultural dimensions for cross-cultural marketing and advertising research. In R. Terlutter, S. Diehl, & B. Mueller (Eds.), *International advertising and communication* (pp. 419–438). Springer.

Topalli, M., & Ivanaj, S. (2016). Mapping the evolution of the impact of economic transition on Central and Eastern European enterprises: A co-word analysis. *Journal of World Business*, *51*(5), 744–759. https://doi.org/10.1016/j.jwb.2016.06.003

Transparency International. (2019). *Corruption perception index 2018*. Retrieved 17 August 2019, from https://www.transparency.org/cpi2018

Trompenaars, F., & Woolliams, P. (2002). A new framework for managing change across cultures. *Journal of Change Management*, *3*(4), 361–375. https://doi.org/10.1080/714023847

Trost, A. (2017). Better alternatives to performance appraisal in an Agile context. In *The end of performance appraisal: A practitioners' guide to alternatives in Agile organisations* (pp. 147–175). Springer.

van Woerkom, M., & de Bruijn, M. (2016). Why performance appraisal does not lead to performance improvement: Excellent performance as a function of uniqueness instead of uniformity. *Industrial and Organizational Psychology*, *9*(2), 275–281. https://doi.org/10.1017/iop.2016.11

Whitley, R. (1999). *Divergent capitalisms: The social structuring and change of business systems*. Oxford University Press.

Wiseman, J. P. (1974). The research web. *Journal of Contemporary Ethnography*, *3*(3), 317–328.

Wolters, A. (2012). The genealogical construction of the Kyrgyz Republic: Kinship, state and "tribalism." *Central Asian Survey*, *31*(4), 469–471. https://doi.org/10.1080/02634937.2012.739294

Wood, G., & Szamosi, L. T. (2016). Recruitment and selection: Debates, controversies and variations in Europe. *International Human Resource Management: Contemporary HR Issues in Europe*, 282–297. https://doi.org/10.4324/9781315773483

Wood, G., & Demirbag, M. (2015). Business and society on the transitional periphery: Comparative perspectives. *International Business Review*, *24*(6), 917–920. https://doi.org/10.1016/j.ibusrev.2015.06.005

Wood, G., Dibben, P., Stride, C., & Webster, E. (2011). HRM in Mozambique: Homogenization, path dependence or segmented business system?. *Journal of World Business*, *46*(1), 31–41. https://doi.org/10.1016/j.jwb.2010.05.015

Woolcock, M., & Narayan, D. (2000). Social capital: Implications for development theory, research, and policy. *The World Bank Research Observer*, *15*(2), 225–249. https://doi.org/10.1093/wbro/15.2.225

Wooldridge, B., & Floyd, S. W. (2017). Some middle managers are more influential than others: An approach for identifying strategic influence. In B. Wooldridge & S. W. Floyd (Eds.), *Handbook of middle management strategy process research* (pp. 56–76). Edward Elgar Publishing.

Yin, R. K. (2009). *Case study research: Design and methods*. SAGE.

Yin, R. K. (2014). *Case study research: Design and methods (Applied social research methods)*. SAGE.

Zhang, M. (2003). Transferring human resource management across national boundaries. *Employee Relations*, *25*(6), 613–626. https://doi.org/10.1108/01425450310501333

Context, governance, associational trust and HRM: diversity and commonalities

Marc Goergen, Salim Chahine, Chris Brewster and Geoffrey Wood

ABSTRACT

This study explores how HRM and trust are inter-related, and what this means for how we understand HRM under different varieties of capitalism. We explore the direct impact of different indicators of societal trust on intra-organisational HRM practice, using large-scale internationally comparative survey evidence. We find that countries with high levels of associational trust, such as the Nordic social democracies, are generally associated with better communication and co-determination over the setting of the employment contract. The converse was true for countries with lower levels of associational trust, such as the liberal market economies. We failed to encounter any significant effects of multi-nationality or country of origin in the case of MNCs; they did not differ significantly from their domestic peers when it came to the relationship between country of domicile levels of associational trust and HRM practice. We draw out the implications for theory and practice.

Introduction

There has been growing interest in the relationship between institutional setting, governance and firm level practice (Bachman & Sidaway, 2016; Hall & Soskice, 2001; Whitley, 1999). It can be argued that the relationship between trust and HRM is a two-way one: systemic trust facilitates high-trust HRM practices in the workplace and, in turn, the latter may help shore up systemic trust. However, the precise nature of this relationship remains uncertain (Guinot & Chiva, 2019; Vanhala & Dietz, 2019). As Zak and Knack (2001) note, there are two different aspects of societal trust relations: 'rights-based trust', which remains the dominant concern of the mainstream economics literature; and 'associational' trust, which forms the dominant strand of the sociological literature. The former affects security in contracting by imparting a predictability to exchange relations. In contrast, sociological approaches that explore associational trust see trust flowing from the operation of groups that inculcate cooperation and altruism amongst members (Knack, 2013). Such relationships tend to be more than a product of one institutional feature. Rather, associational trust concerns the degree of accumulated social capital and other ties between individuals and groups (Lane & Bachmann, 1998).

In a systematic review of the literature on HRM and intra-organisational trust, Guinot and Chiva (2019) found that the literature is 'dispersed' and provides mixed evidence as to whether a link exists at all. In fact, the predominant concern has been with performance outcomes (Guinot & Chiva, 2019; see also Searle, 2018). Other work explores the micro-antecedents of trust and, more specifically, existing propensity to trust management (Shantz et al., 2018), and the relationship between trust and setting at a conceptual level (Hong et al., 2018; c.f. Cooke et al., 2019). In supplementing earlier work, this study seeks to explore the societal trust-based antecedents of HRM practices; in turn, this may help bolster or undermine wider societal trust. Institutional theories hold that micro-level events and institutions are mutually reinforcing (Amable, 2003; Malik et al., 2019). There are two dominant ways of understanding societal trust: associational and rights based. Each assumes institutional features 'work' in a certain way: the former as exerting composite effects on socio-economic ties (Magnin, 2018), and the latter in terms of relative protection of private property (Saravia, 2016). Finally, the literature on HRM in multinational corporations (MNCs suggests both country of origin and domicile effects (c.f. Cooke et al., 2019): hence, we explore whether MNCs differ from their local counterparts when it comes to country of domicile associational trust. The study draws on large-scale comparative survey evidence. We find that in coordinated (and above all, social democratic) markets where there are high levels of associational trust, there is a greater propensity to communicate more widely with employees and to engage in co-determination. However, we encountered no significant differences between MNCs and their local counterparts. The effect of trust on contracting was rather more limited. We draw out the implications for theorising and practice.

The two forms of trust and HRM practice

Associational trust refers to expectations by one party that others will behave reliably and cooperate (Gomez & Rosen, 2001, p. 56). Trust relations are reconstituted through individuals who collect, assess and disseminate supportive information, reducing transaction costs in social interactions (Lapavitsas, 2007, p. 417). Hence, trust relations will be reflected in HRM practices; in turn, low trust HRM practices may reflect a breakdown in systemic trust. This has been a growing topic in HRM and international HRM as a trawl through this journal demonstrates (see e.g. Hong et al., 2019; Hu & Jiang, 2018; Malik et al., 2019). Most of these studies, even when they note the importance of contextual factors, are of HRM in a single country (see e.g. Blunsdon & Reed, 2003; Hu & Jiang, 2018; Iqbal et al., 2019; Tremblay et al., 2010), though more recently there have been cross-country studies. These, however, tend to assign differences to 'culture', even if they do not measure their items against cultures (Iqbal et al., 2019; Iqbal et al., 2019; Jiang et al., 2017). Detailed analyses of national differences in trust and their implications for businesses require a comparison of the value of associational and rights-based trust and their value in explaining trust at the firm level.

Existing theoretical work highlights the linkages between institutions and trust relations, and the likely impact of this on HRM practice. One branch of the institutional literature, that on comparative capitalisms, directly highlights the importance of both formal regulations and informal ties (Cooke et al., 2019; Thelen, 2014). Our paper focuses specifically on associational trust, comparing it with the predictions of rights-based trust theories. Whilst trust may be formed in a variety of ways, societal characteristics broadly guide values, beliefs and choices (Doney et al., 1998, p. 601). In workplaces, associational trust will help firms and individuals feel secure enough to 'expose their vulnerabilities to each other' (Benkert, 1998, p. 285), with the realisation that risk or harm will result if expectations are violated (see also Saunders et al., 2010). In other words, in contexts conducive to promoting associational trust at societal level, firms and workers are more likely to develop open-ended relationships based on give and take, with a greater flow of information and joint decision-making around the employment relationship (Dietz, 2004).

A limitation of the literature on comparative capitalisms is that, although it has been extensively developed over the years to incorporate understanding of systemic change (Amable, 2016), the linkages between societal features, and developments in the workplace are depicted in rather abstract terms; the primary focus is on broad socio-economic features, rather than detailed empirical evidence of firm level practices (Wood et al., 2014). Yet, it has been argued that when there is a shortage of decent and dignified work, underpinned by a basis of trust, this can lead to unpredictable political blowback (Franko & Witko, 2018). This would suggest the need for a much closer understanding of the different types of societal trust, how this relates to HRM policies, and, in turn, the relative propensity of systems to enter sustained crises in the face of unexpected shocks.

The literature on comparative capitalisms (Amable, 2016; 2003; Hall & Soskice, 2001) sees trust as the product of a composite set of institutional features and, hence, institutional effects are best explored through comparing different types of national economy. This approach focuses not only on formal institutions, but also the quality of relationships they sustain; the coordinated markets of the Rhineland and Scandinavia are associated with denser ties between workers, firms and other actors (ibid.). In contrast, a core assumption of rights-based approaches to trust is that one institutional feature (properties rights) is more important than, and moulds, others (Botero et al., 2004; Djankov et al., 2003), thereby impacting on trust in contracting and on firm practices; hence, it is simplest to compare and contrast the direct effects of the single dominant institutional feature on firm practice, rather than bothering with composite effects. In protecting private property, legal tradition matters (Botero et al., 2004): property rights are stronger in common law countries than in civil law ones. Importantly, this approach holds that owner and employee rights under the law are antithetical: where owner rights are strong, employee rights are necessarily weaker and *vice versa* (Botero et al., 2004). This would suggest that in common law countries, firms would be freer to make usage of insecure labour, and adopt harder line HRM policies (Goergen et al., 2010), even if, in legal terms, contracts per se are more robust.

Rather than legal system, Pagano and Volpin (2005) argue that the electoral system is important: there may be greater trust regarding contracting, and property rights are less likely to be challenged, in a 'first past the post' electoral system. The primary concerns of political parties in such systems will be to serve their own narrow constituencies and woo a relatively small pool of swing voters unlikely to be swayed by class loyalties. Such voters are more likely influenced by expensive political campaigns, which property-owning interests are more able to mount. So, in first past the post systems, governments are likely to concentrate on legislation favouring property owners over other stakeholders (Pagano & Volpin, 2005), which encourages high levels of trust in contracting, but lower associational trust. In more proportional electoral systems coalition governments are more likely: the need to accommodate diverse interests encourages governments to enact legislation that secures worker and stakeholder rights, directly impacting on workplace practice.

The property rights approach's dismissal of associational trust as irrelevant or having negative consequences (in contrast to simple trust in contracting) was criticised in Knack and Keefer (1997) argument that associational trust between citizens may substitute for low contractual trust, weak property rights and poor law enforcement. They also predict that higher associational trust societies will have longer investment horizons, rein in opportunism, and incentivise employers' investment in employees for firm-specific skills. Associational trust represents an important component of workplace stability, mutuality and wellbeing (Schindler & Thomas, 1993; Hu & Jiang, 2018). Since no employment contract is ever complete, successful cooperation is contingent on manifestations of trust that go beyond it, facilitating wider ranging mutual understandings and procedural rules (Lorenz, 1999).

Both associational and rights-based forms of trust impact on HRM; yet each may be associated with quite different types of HRM practice which may, in turn, help reconstitute – or potentially erode – societal trust (Hu & Jiang, 2018; Marsden, 1998). Workplace trust may be operationalised in the reciprocal perceptions of individuals and groupings (Mollering et al., 2004), but may also be embodied in workplace practices, with some enhancing and others eroding trust relations (Guinot & Chiva, 2019; Iqbal et al., 2019; Vosse & Aliyu, 2018). Costa et al. (2018) argue that trust at team level is sustained – or eroded – at a range of different levels, with dynamic interaction between them. Looking at the case of disabled workers, Shantz et al. (2018) found that trust in management, and that generated by firm wide HRM policies and practices, both had the effect of reducing employee dissatisfaction (see also Hong et al., 2019). This paper focuses on the potential two-way relationship between broader associational trust and in-firm practices. Firms may adapt practices corresponding to wider societal associational ties, and firm level practices may contribute to deepening solidarities: a relationship of association rather than causality (c.f. Giddens, 1990).

Low trust on entering the organisation may result in low trust relations being perpetuated; in contrast, high initial trust provides 'buffers' against future organisational breaches (Searle, 2018). This may reflect the extent to which, as suggested by the literature on comparative capitalisms, specific practices may be more or less functional in different national settings (Cooke et al., 2019); in some contexts, low trust practices may be a great deal less dysfunctional than in others (Gooderham et al., 2019; Iqbal et al., 2019). Other work has highlighted the importance of both personal and impersonal trust in making specific HRM practices viable, and, in turn, how the latter may help reconstitute them (Vanhala & Ritala, 2016).

Hypotheses: varieties of trust and HRM practice

Here, we identify four hypotheses in order to explore the relationship between associational trust, trust in contracting, and two dimensions of

HRM: the relative flow of information, and formalised mechanisms for employment relationship adjustment.

First, discussing financial and strategic issues is bound up with trust relations (Mayer & Davis, 1999; Redman, 2006). More extensive communication is more common where associational trust is high. Formalised communication systems represent an important structural property (Ahlf et al., 2019), which makes the reconstitution of trust possible (Sydow, 1998, p. 48). Trust is both reflected in and embodied in a willingness to grant 'access to and the sharing of information relating to the organization's operations' (Bratton, 2003, p. 134). Hence, trust relations are acted out through communication and awareness and respect for the other's intentions (Nugent & Abolafia, 2006). Hence, communication represents a central dimension of trustworthy behaviour (Hu & Jiang, 2018). Continually reinforcing their credentials through communication will promote trust relations between individuals (Offe, 1999). Communication is central to associational trust and the degree to which this is possible is bound into wider social realities (Aoki, 2010). As Dodgson (1993) notes, effective interchange of information and associated social ties will promote intra-organisational trust. Such communication facilitates a relationship orientated culture, which promotes and reconstitutes trust relations (Six & Sorge, 2008). In terms of communication with employees, there are two key sub-dimensions. The first is communication around strategy. There is an extensive body of research that confirms that effective strategy implementation depends on good communication with employees (Atkinson, 2006), held up as a hallmark of responsible management (Rasche et al., 2017). Transparency around strategy gives employees time to adjust their activities to shifting needs, making for less disruption (Schnackenberg & Tomlinson, 2016).

Hypothesis 1a: In countries with higher levels of associational trust, there is on average a higher level of communication on strategy within organisations.

However, the need for communication is not the same in all firms. Multinational companies are exposed to greater complexities and sources of uncertainty due to their liability of foreignness (Qian et al., 2013) and are subject to a wider range of expectations than domestic firms (Brewster et al., 2008). Compared to domestic firms, MNCs also deal with diversity and cross-cultural communication barriers due to their presence in countries with different languages and cultures (Maljers, 1992). Lack of proper communication could lead to misunderstandings and conflicts in cross-cultural enterprises (Han et al., 2018). But, what will matter more: country or domicile effects? Within the comparative capitalism literature, the existing body of research points to a mix of country of origin and domicile pressures (Brewster et al., 2008). However, earlier work indicates particularly strong country of origin effects when it comes to information sharing (Lavelle et al., 2010), probably because corporate policy on the latter is likely to be set centrally. Given their complexity, and the diversity of the scale and scope of their operations, it may be important for MNCs to effectively disseminate knowledge and expertise across subsidiary units to strengthen their competitive advantages (Solvell & Zander, 1995). Hence, we expect the impact of associational trust on business strategy briefing to be higher in MNCs than would be the case with domestic firms:

> *Hypothesis 1b: Compared to domestic firms, MNCs are more likely to share business information with their employees than domestic firms.*

The second key sub-dimension of communication is around financial information. The sharing of financial information will impart greater confidence as to an organisation's sustainability and help promote greater trust and sustain mutual commitment (Schnackenberg & Tomlinson, 2016). However, once more, it needs to be systematically shared throughout the organisation to genuinely help sustain organisational level trust. Transparency is sustained through perceptions as to the quality of communication (ibid.), and it could be argued that objective financial information would hold more weight than intrinsically more subjective accounts of managerial strategy.

> *Hypothesis 2a: In countries with higher levels of associational trust, there is on average a higher level of communication on financial matters within organisations.*

As noted above, earlier research indicates a mix of country of origin and domicile effects on HRM practices in the latter (Brewster et al., 2008), but the scale of information sharing is more likely to be set centrally. Indeed, when it comes to financial information sharing, it has been found that home country dynamics play an over-riding role (Aggarwal & Goodell, 2015). As they are likely to be larger, and more visible as 'outsiders' (Eden & Molot, 2002), MNCs may be under greater pressure to share financial information

> *Hypothesis 2b: Compared to domestic firms, MNCs are more likely to share financial information with their employees than domestic firms.*

The classical literature on political economy alerts us to the fact that at the core of modern capitalist production lies the employment contract, whereby a specific amount of labour is exchanged for a cash wage (Hyman, 1995, 1997). The ability for workers to have a formal impact on the setting of both wages and working time is thus of central importance to both the employment contract and, indeed, the wider process of production. Workers may, of course, impact on wage setting and working time in a range of informal ways, from high levels of individual exit, through to individual attempts to push back on the setting of working hours through strategies such as goldbricking (intensive work, hoarding and then releasing production to allow for time off) to unnecessary (in organisational terms) absenteeism. However, such behaviour is, from an organisational perspective, both undesirable and outside of the sphere of workplace regulation and, for the latter reason, falls outside of the scope of this study. When managers accord workers and their representatives a formalised say, through established mechanisms in setting wages and working time, this is a significant shift in the nature of the employment contract and a reduction in managerial power which we call 'co-deterministic employment relationship adjustment mechanisms'. It can be argued that if associational ties are more developed, there are more likely to be ways open to amending the employment relationship on a cooperative basis in the light of events (Whitley, 1999). Hence, we would suggest that the potential impact of variations in associational trust, and countervailing power would equally apply to the ability to adjust the employment contract. Hence:

Hypothesis 3a: Co-deterministic employment relationship adjustment is more common in countries with higher levels of associational trust, property rights, and more proportional electoral systems.

As noted above, MNCs as outsiders, are likely to be more conspicuous in the public eye (Eden & Molot, 2002), and hence under greater pressure to adopt more accommodationist HRM policies. Hence:

Hypothesis 3b: Compared to domestic firms, the positive association between co-deterministic employment relationship adjustment and associational trust, property rights, and proportional electoral systems is higher in MNCs.

Method

Data on HRM practices are taken from the Cranet survey of senior HRM specialists, and which cover Western and Eastern Europe, developed countries such as the USA and Australia and transitional economies such as Serbia. We use data from the six waves of collection extending from 1991 to 2016 and focus on the 37 countries (listed in Table 1) covered by the these Cranet waves, as well as the World Values Survey (WVS) waves and Djankov et al. (2008). The Cranet questionnaire contains mainly closed-ended questions. We aggregate nationally these company level data. The number of organisations covered in each country ranges from 50 in Serbia to 5110 in the UK. The total number of observations across all 37 countries and across time is 31,239 and the average number per country is 844. The survey covers all major sectors within the selected countries and, in all but the largest countries, is a full population survey. With larger economies (e.g. France, Germany, Italy and the UK), random sampling was employed, from publicly available mailing lists, weighted for sector and size. The surveys exclude firms with less than 100 employees. Response rates varied between 10% and 22% according to country, which is considered acceptable for such surveys (Bryman & Bell, 2007, pp. 245–246). Here we have excluded public organisations.

How reliable are the country means? The WVS consists of a common questionnaire administered to almost 100 countries and based on interviews with almost 400,000 respondents. The sample size per country ranges from 33 to 1508 observations. Each country sample is representative of all the people aged 18 and older living in that country, whatever their nationality, citizenship and language. The questionnaire is administered *via* face-to-face interviews or *via* phone for respondents from more remote areas. Following the interviews, the data are subjected to a stringent quality control and cleaning. To test our hypotheses over the six waves, we perform unbalanced panel regressions using country fixed effects, with different numbers of countries in different waves. This gives us 107 observations for managers, professional and clerical employees over the six waves from 1991 to 2016, and 91 observations for manual employees for whom the data is not available in the sixth wave in 2016, and the data remains available upon request. The specific countries, their corresponding waves, number of observations, and trust level are listed in Table 1.

With rights-based trust we use the legal family each country belongs to, which it has been argued is related to trust in contracting (La Porta et al., 1998). We measure associational trust by the proportion of respondents in each country replying that 'most people can be trusted'. For most countries, the measure is taken from the WVS for the corresponding periods of the studied waves.[1] It should be noted that, based on the WVS trust measure, La Porta et al. (1998) find that levels of associational trust are relatively temporally stable. Table 1 shows that trust ranges from 0.028 in the Philippines for 2016–0.795 in Denmark for 2005. Trust levels are highest in the Nordic countries (Netherlands, Finland, Norway and Denmark) ranging from 0.535 to 0.795.

Our studied sample includes companies from various legal regimes (English, French, German and Scandinavian). Table 2 shows that around half of our studied companies are MNCs, that is, firms with their headquarters abroad, with an almost equal distribution of MNCs and

Table 1. Sample distribution.

Wave	Number of observations						Country trust					
	1991	1995	2000	2005	2009	2016	1991	1995	2000	2005	2009	2016
Australia					110	395					0.400	0.544
Austria			230	270	203				0.334	0.444	0.334	
Belgium		314	282	191	240			0.310	0.292	0.331	0.292	
Brazil						354						0.066
Bulgaria			150	157	267				0.268	0.401	0.268	
China						256						0.644
Cyprus					90	87					0.128	0.091
Czech			188	72	54				0.245	0.225	0.245	
Denmark	478	443	520	516	362		0.577	0.621	0.665	0.795	0.665	
Estonia			218	118	74	83			0.235	0.381	0.235	0.396
Finland		276	290	293	136			0.597	0.574	0.629	0.574	
France	990	403	400		157		0.228	0.221	0.213		0.213	
Germany	967	383	503	320	420	278	0.329	0.352	0.375	0.400	0.375	0.424
Greece			136	180	214				0.237	0.205	0.237	
Hungary					139						0.223	
Iceland					138						0.411	
Ireland		139	446					0.415	0.360			
Israel			194	175	114				0.235	0.235	0.235	
Italy	188	59	79		389		0.353	0.340	0.326		0.431	
Lithuania					119						0.259	
Netherlands	223	217	234	397	116	167	0.535	0.568	0.601	0.686	0.601	0.674
Norway	303	358	391	303	98		0.651	0.652	0.653	0.653	0.653	
Philippines					33	138					0.086	0.028
Portugal			169						0.123			
Romania						225						0.071
Russia					56	131					0.240	0.292
Serbia					50						0.118	
Slovakia				259	225					0.185	0.159	
Slovenia			205	161	219	218			0.217	0.250	0.217	0.201
South Africa					192	121					0.131	0.236
Spain	297	250	294			98	0.361	0.310	0.275			0.195
Sweden	295	344	352	383	282	291	0.661	0.662	0.663	0.723	0.663	0.648
Switzerland		187	168		99			0.426	0.370		0.370	
Taiwan					229						0.382	
Turkey		131	258			154		0.100	0.068			0.124
United Kingdom	1508	1178	1091	1115	218		0.437	0.363	0.289	0.384	0.289	
USA					1052	509					0.363	0.382

Notes: The numbers of observations refer to the number of observations from the Cranet surveys six waves from 1991 to 2016. Trust is measured by the proportion of respondents in each country replying that 'most people can be trusted', taken from the World Values Survey waves for the corresponding periods of the studied waves.

domestic firms across the different legal regimes ranging from 44.33% in the French regime to 50.94% in the English regime.

Table 2 provides further descriptive statistics on information sharing within our studied organisations. Panel A shows that virtually all organisations brief their managers about business strategy and financial planning. While a majority of organisations still engage in both of these dimensions of communication with their professional employees, the equivalent proportions of organisations communicating with their clerical and manual employees are much lower. Panels B and C of the table compare the proportion of MNCs with the proportion of domestic firms. Both Panels B and C show that MNCs are significantly more likely to

Table 2. Descriptive statistics.

	Proportion of organizations briefing on							
	Business strategy				Financial planning			
	Management	Professional	Clerical	Manual	Management	Professional	Clerical	Manual
Panel A – Entire sample								
No. of obs.	29,666	28,279	27,633	23,329	29,626	28,504	28,002	23,615
1991	0.938	0.529	0.291	0.232	0.927	0.641	0.486	0.410
1995	0.947	0.652	0.425	0.354	0.919	0.700	0.558	0.472
1999	0.918	0.527	0.335	0.244	0.891	0.609	0.480	0.346
2003	0.995	0.982	0.973	0.968	0.994	0.985	0.982	0.977
2008	0.931	0.693	0.565	0.417	0.920	0.673	0.563	0.417
2016	0.850	0.533	0.353		0.839	0.486	0.343	
Panel B – MNC sub-sample								
No. of obs.	12,705	12,120	11,844	10,311	12,692	12,280	12,100	10,515
1991	0.932	0.514	0.289	0.245	0.929	0.711	0.566	0.499
1995	0.955	0.662	0.436	0.384	0.947	0.766	0.650	0.588
1999	0.939	0.583	0.391	0.303	0.926	0.717	0.596	0.471
2003	1.000	0.998	0.994	0.985	1.000	1.000	0.999	0.995
2008	0.968	0.724	0.612	0.458	0.957	0.729	0.649	0.501
2016	0.941	0.593	0.435		0.928	0.541	0.415	
Total MNC	0.954	0.655	0.478	0.392	0.946	0.746	0.638	0.558
Panel C – Domestic sub-sample								
No. of obs.	15,972	15,239	14,881	12,174	15,944	15,299	14,990	12,260
1991	0.920	0.488	0.278	0.204	0.923	0.638	0.475	0.379
1995	0.950	0.642	0.450	0.356	0.938	0.726	0.586	0.467
1999	0.925	0.535	0.367	0.258	0.900	0.618	0.502	0.356
2003	1.000	0.992	0.982	0.977	0.999	0.994	0.993	0.987
2008	0.946	0.691	0.559	0.423	0.917	0.687	0.536	0.417
2016	0.798	0.497	0.337		0.775	0.441	0.321	
Total domestic	0.925	0.618	0.451	0.364	0.910	0.670	0.541	0.457
Probability *T*-test for diff.	0.000	0.000	0.000	0.000	0.000	0.000	0.000	0.000

Notes: The proportions of firms briefing each of their four categories of employees on business strategy and financial planning. Panel A reports the proportions for the entire sample whereas Panels B and C report the proportions for the sub-sample of MNCs and the sub-sample of domestic firms, respectively. We note that the difference between the total number of observations in Panel A and the sum of observations in Panels B and C is due to missing responses for some firms.

communicate and share information with their employees than domestic firms. The only exception to this pattern is business strategy communicated to clerical and manual employees, where there are no significant differences between MNCs and domestic firms. Similar to Panel A for the entire sample, both Panels B and C confirm that communication is biased towards highly ranked employees in both MNCs and domestic organisations.[2]

In order to test the validity of our hypotheses, we applied OLS regressions, including the level of associational trust on the proportion of organisations briefing managers, professionals, clerical employees and manual workers on business strategy or financial performance using country-level data for the entire sample as well as the sub-samples of domestic firms and MNCs. In further robustness tests, we repeat our tests at the firm-level while controlling for firm characteristics and legal regime. We also examine the effect of country trust, property rights or proportional representation on co-deterministic employment relationship adjustment for the entire sample and separately for the domestic and MNC sub-samples.

Findings

The estimated OLS regressions test the validity of each set of hypotheses and determine whether associational trust or trust in contracting, as measured by the proportional nature of the electoral system or the strength of property rights, best explain access to and sharing of information. Our regressions related to access to and sharing of information are run for the entire sample as well as the sub-samples of MNCs and domestic firms to control for the effect of the international presence of the studied firms.

Organisations briefing employees on business strategy

We tried to explain the proportion of employees that are briefed on business strategy: distinguishing again between (a) managers, (b) professionals, (c) clerical employees and (d) manual workers. Panel A of Table 3 includes the results for the entire sample. The coefficients on country trust in the regressions indicate a growing importance of business briefing from managers to professionals, clerical and then to manual workers. This is consistent with Hypothesis 1a which suggests that businesses sharing organisational strategy with labour are positively related to the level of associational trust.

In detail, columns (1a)–(1c) show the results of the regression of the proportion of organisations briefing their managers on business strategy

Table 3. Business strategy debriefing and associational trust.

		Proportion of organizations briefing		
	Managers $N = 107$	Professional/ employees $N = 107$	Clerical employees $N = 107$	Manual employees $N = 91$
Panel A – The entire sample				
	(1a)	(2a)	(3a)	(4a)
Constant	0.904***	0.595***	0.380***	0.299***
	0.015	*0.035*	*0.032*	*0.039*
Trust	0.067*	0.173**	0.341***	0.384***
	0.038	*0.085*	*0.078*	*0.095*
R^2	0.061	0.048	0.085	0.088
F-statistic	3.150	4.180	18.960	16.380
Prob.	0.079	0.043	0.000	0.000
Panel B – The sub-sample of MNCs				
	(1b)	(2b)	(3b)	(4b)
Constant	0.930***	0.621***	0.391***	0.312***
	0.008	*0.034*	*0.032*	*0.040*
Trust	0.076***	0.201**	0.397***	0.443***
	0.019	*0.082*	*0.078*	*0.097*
R^2	0.125	0.058	0.098	0.106
F-statistic	15.830	5.930	25.820	20.950
Prob.	0.000	0.017	0.000	0.000
Panel C – The sub-sample of domestic firms				
	(1c)	(2c)	(3c)	(4c)
Constant	0.893***	0.567***	0.360***	0.271***
	0.018	*0.037*	*0.033*	*0.039*
Trust	0.086*	0.200**	0.352***	0.404***
	0.045	*0.090*	*0.081*	*0.093*
R^2	0.061	0.053	0.088	0.091
F-statistic	3.630	5.000	18.700	18.680
Prob.	0.060	0.028	0.000	0.000

Tests Hypotheses 1a and 1b on the positive association between associational trust and the proportion of organizations briefing their employees on business strategy, and the differential impact in MNC versus domestic firms.
***, **, * denote significance at the 0.01, 0.05, and 0.10 levels, respectively, using two-tailed tests.
Notes: Unbalanced panel regressions with wave fixed effects. The dependent variable is the proportion of organizations briefing managers in regression (1), the proportion of organizations briefing professional/technical employees in regression (2), the proportion of organizations briefing clerical employees in regression (3) and the proportion of organizations briefing manual employees in regression (4). We repeat our tests in Panels B and C for the sub-samples of MNCs and domestic firms, respectively. Standard errors are in italics.

on the level of associational trust. The coefficient is significant at the 10% level for the entire sample and is significant at the 1% (10%) level for the sub-sample of MNCs (domestic firms). While the *R*-square is relatively low for managers, this is not surprising as most organisations across the 37 countries brief their managers, so there is very little cross-country variation. What matters for organisational level trust, however, is whether information is shared below the management team. Similar results apply for professional, clerical and manual employees, although the significance of the variable has now increased and generally the relationship increases as the data move down the hierarchical scale. This suggests that associational trust in fact has an increasingly positive impact on briefing employees about business strategy through to manual employees. However, we do not find a more significant effect for the sub-sample of MNCs (Panel B) compared to the sub-sample of domestic firms (Panel C). Therefore, Hypothesis 1a is supported, while Hypothesis 1b is rejected.

Organisations briefing employees on financial performance

We then focused on the proportion of organisations briefing staff about financial performance (Table 4). As with strategy, virtually all the organisations from all countries brief their different categories of employees about their financial performance, which is consistent with Hypothesis 2a. The coefficient on the association between associational trust and the proportion of organisations briefing managers on financial performance is positive and significant at the 10% level for the entire sample, and is significant at the 1% (10%) level for the sub-samples of MNCs (domestic firms). As with strategy briefing, the low R-square for managers is related

Table 4. Financial performance debriefing and associational trust – MNCs vs. domestic firms.

	Proportion of organizations briefing			
	Managers	Professional/employees	Clerical employees	Manual employees
Panel A – The entire sample				
	(5a)	(6a)	(7a)	(8a)
Constant	0.886***	0.579***	0.412***	0.320***
	0.018	*0.034*	*0.036*	*0.042*
Trust	0.074*	0.271***	0.425***	0.494***
	0.044	*0.083*	*0.088*	*0.102*
R^2	0.054	0.116	0.161	0.164
F-statistic	2.850	10.750	23.460	23.310
Prob.	0.094	0.001	0.000	0.000
Panel B – The sub-sample of MNCs				
	(5b)	(6b)	(7b)	(8b)
Constant	0.910***	0.617***	0.462***	0.358***
	0.011	*0.036*	*0.039*	*0.045*
Trust	0.085***	0.279***	0.429***	0.551***
	0.026	*0.088*	*0.096*	*0.108*
R^2	0.096	0.112	0.153	0.195
F-statistic	10.480	10.000	19.780	25.890
Prob.	0.002	0.002	0.000	0.000
Panel C – The sub-sample of domestic firms				
	(5c)	(6c)	(7c)	(8c)
Constant	0.876***	0.545***	0.358***	0.258***
	0.021	*0.034*	*0.035*	*0.041*
Trust	0.092*	0.311***	0.489***	0.555***
	0.051	*0.083*	*0.086*	*0.098*
R^2	0.057	0.135	0.187	0.179
F-statistic	3.260	14.150	32.400	32.070
Prob.	0.074	0.000	0.000	0.000

Tests Hypotheses 2a and 2b on the positive association between associational trust and the proportion of organizations briefing their employees on financial performance, and the differential impact in MNC versus domestic firms

***, **, * denote significance at the 0.01, 0.05, and 0.10 levels, respectively, using two-tailed tests.

Notes: Unbalanced panel regressions with wave fixed effects. The dependent variable is the proportion of organizations briefing managers in regression (5), the proportion of organizations briefing professional/technical employees in regression (6), the proportion of organizations briefing clerical employees in regression (7) and the proportion of organizations briefing manual employees in regression (8). We repeat our tests in Panels B and C for the sub-samples of MNC and domestic firms, respectively. Standard errors are in italic.

to little variation between countries at the level of managers. And again, the significance of the variable and the magnitude of the coefficient increase as the data move down the hierarchical scale. This suggests that trust has a greater positive impact on briefing employees about financial performance through to manual employees. The results in Panels B and C are based on MNCs and domestic firms, respectively. We find that the effect of trust on organisations briefing on financial performance is positive and more significant as we move down in the hierarchical scale to manual workers, which supports Hypothesis 2a. However, we do not find that MNCs from high-trust countries are more likely to share financial information with their employees than their domestic counterparts. Hence, Hypothesis 2b is to be rejected.

Co-deterministic employment relationship adjustment

Co-deterministic employment relationship adjustment is measured by three proxies: first, the ability of employees to influence through flexitime aspects their working hours; second, the extent of the resultant delegation of responsibilities through the opportunity to work across a range of projects as and when they arise according to demand and, third, the strength of formal collective employee voice mechanisms, evidenced by relative union penetration (see e.g. Bamber et al., 2016). In other words, co-deterministic employment relationship adjustment can be measured by the extent of the use of flexitime, job rotation and collective representation.

Table 5 reports the empirical results related to the test of our Hypotheses 3a and 3b. In Models 9a–11a of Panel A of Table 5, we find that high-trust contexts are associated with greater use of flexitime ($p = 1\%$) and higher presence of unions ($p = 1\%$), which partially confirms Hypothesis 3a. This suggests that firms in countries with higher trust levels are more likely to have flexitime arrangements, in which they delegate some responsibility to employees in terms of the timing of work. Higher country-level trust is correlated with a greater presence of unions, which voice employees' concerns and maintain a high-trust environment. Our data show similar results for both MNCs and domestic firms, except for job rotation which is negatively associated with the level of trust ($p = 5\%$) in MNCs but not in domestic firms. Although job rotation may indeed involve highly skilled workers changing roles, this could also reflect unskilled workers interchanging basic tasks. This suggests marginal support for Hypothesis 3b. Columns 12a, 13a, and 14a in Panel B show that countries with higher protection rights are associated with lower job rotation ($p = 10\%$). Protection rights are extracted from Djankov et al. (2008). However, the latter may

Table 5. Co-deterministic employment relationship adjustment in the workplace.

	Using the entire sample			Using the sub-sample of MNCs			Using the sub-sample of domestic firms		
	Flexi-time	Rotation	Union	Flexitime	Rotation	Union	Flexitime	Rotation	Union
	(9a)	(10a)	(11a)	(9b)	(10b)	(11b)	(9c)	(10c)	(11c)
Panel A – Co-deterministic employment relationship and country trust									
Constant	2.425***	12.701***	0.621***	2.509***	12.956***	0.607***	2.378***	12.675***	0.620***
	0.263	*1.208*	*0.053*	*0.277*	*1.056*	*0.055*	*0.265*	*1.360*	*0.053*
Trust	2.105***	−4.667	0.347***	1.794***	−5.561**	0.359***	2.284***	−4.320	0.367***
	0.642	*2.954*	*0.132*	*0.678*	*2.582*	*0.136*	*0.647*	*3.324*	*0.133*
No. of obs.	107	107	102	107	107	102	107	107	102
R^2	0.051	0.014	0.073	0.042	0.018	0.078	0.054	0.012	0.076
F-statistic	10.740	2.500	6.860	7.000	4.640	6.950	12.450	1.690	7.600
Prob.	0.001	0.117	0.010	0.010	0.034	0.010	0.001	0.197	0.007
Panel B – Co-deterministic employment relationship and property rights									
	(12a)	(13a)	(14a)	(12b)	(13b)	(14b)	(12c)	(13c)	(14c)
Constant	3.792***	5.368**	0.725***	3.607***	6.673***	0.734***	3.833***	5.208**	0.699***
	0.493	*2.283*	*0.099*	*0.522*	*2.041*	*0.101*	*0.501*	*2.551*	*0.099*
Property rights	−0.108	1.647***	0.012	−0.070	1.238**	0.008	−0.111	1.732**	0.021
	0.136	*0.630*	*0.027*	*0.144*	*0.563*	*0.028*	*0.138*	*0.704*	*0.027*
No. of obs.	96	96	91	96	96	91	96	96	91
R^2	0.001	0.050	0.001	0.000	0.032	0.000	0.001	0.049	0.004
F-statistic	0.630	6.840	0.200	0.240	4.830	0.080	0.650	6.060	0.590
Prob.	0.429	0.011	0.658	0.628	0.031	0.779	0.423	0.016	0.446
Panel C – Co-deterministic employment relationship and proportional representation									
	(15a)	(16a)	(17a)	(15b)	(16b)	(17b)	(15c)	(16c)	(17c)
Constant	3.328***	14.236***	0.667***	3.313***	13.466***	0.641***	3.355***	14.753***	0.686***
	0.312	*1.466*	*0.059*	*0.331*	*1.255*	*0.061*	*0.318*	*1.641*	*0.059*
Proportional representation	0.110	−1.439**	0.053**	0.089	−1.202**	0.062**	0.114	−1.590**	0.047*
	0.127	*0.596*	*0.024*	*0.134*	*0.510*	*0.025*	*0.129*	*0.667*	*0.024*
No. of obs.	90	90	85	90	90	85	90	90	85
R^2	0.010	0.069	0.073	0.007	0.058	0.098	0.010	0.070	0.059
F-statistic	0.75	5.83	4.74	0.44	5.55	6.26	0.77	5.67	3.7
Prob.	0.389	0.018	0.033	0.508	0.021	0.014	0.382	0.020	0.058

***, **, * denote significance at the 0.01, 0.05, and 0.10 levels, respectively, using two-tailed tests.

Notes: Unbalanced panel regressions with wave fixed effects. The dependent variables are the country average flexi-time, staff rotation and employee unions, respectively. All dependent variables are extracted from the Cranet survey. The independent variable is Country Trust in Models (9)–(11), Property Rights in Models (12)–(14), and Proportional Representation in Models (15)–(17). Country Trust is sourced from the World Values Survey corresponding to the studied wave and consists of the percentage of respondents in each country who answer that 'most people can be trusted' to the following question: 'Generally speaking, would you say that most people can be trusted, or that you can't be too careful in dealing with people?', and Property Rights and Proportional Representation are sourced from Djankov et al. (2008). Standard errors are in italic.

also capture insecure gig working, which is increasingly popular in countries where owner rights are strong (Brewster & Holland, 2019; Findlay & Thompson, 2017). Similar to the results in Panel A using the sub-samples of MNCs and domestic firms in Panel B, our findings do not provide support to Hypothesis 3b.

In Panel C, we examine the impact of proportional representation, which is taken from Djankov et al. (2008). The variable equals 3 if all the seats are allocated *via* the proportionality rule, 2 if the majority of seats are allocated *via* this rule, 1 if a minority of seats are allocated proportionally and 0 if no seats are allocated *via* the proportionality rule.[3] Typically, few or no seats in Anglo-Saxon countries are assigned *via* the proportionality rule, whereas in Continental Europe most or all are. Models 15a, 15b and 15c in Panel C show a positive (negative) association between proportional representation and unions (job rotation) ($p = 5\%$). This suggests that countries with political institutions that favour coalitions are more likely to have stronger unions and lower job rotation. The literature on the effects of electoral arrangements on corporate governance suggests that nation-wide coalition-building increases union power – the concerns of collective interests have to be taken seriously. Further, proportional representation is positively (negatively) associated with unions (job rotation) for both domestic firms and MNCs. Hence, the results do not support Hypothesis 3b.

Further robustness checks

In further robustness tests, we repeat our analysis in Tables 3–5 at the firm level using associational trust as well as other control variables used in the literature. This includes firm size, profitability, public listing and a family-controlled dummy. We also control for the legal regime effects (English, French, German and Scandinavian). Although not shown, we find evidence consistent with our previous results, especially for briefing on financial performance. MNCs are more likely to brief lower hierarchal scale employees on their financial performance than domestic firms. We thus confirm our predictions on the positive association between rights-based trust levels and sharing information with employees, and this is more likely to occur in MNCs.

Discussion and conclusion

We begin with a caveat. There are different ways of conceptualising trust and we have chosen a macro national-level measure that is widely reported and used; this is not to deny the validity of other measures, which might yield different results. Again, there are many dimensions to people management, but we focused on information flows and the ability of workers to impact on the employment contract. Communication is central to trust (Patent & Searle, 2019; Schnakenberg & Tomlinson, 2016), whilst at the centre of production lies the employment contract and how its core tenets are amended over time (Hyman, 1975). We found that different types of national institutional order were associated with different forms of trust relations, and that, in turn, associational trust had a strong impact on our selected areas of HRM practice (c.f. Cooke et al., 2019; Gooderham et al., 2019)

We found that trust in contracting – in turn, a feature of stronger private property rights as defined by legal origin – had limited impact. When worker rights under the law were weaker, trust in the employment contract tended to be similarly so, whatever societal measures of trust in contracting (and how well this works for property owners) might suggest. Ironically, where the dominant feature of societal trust relations was in contracting, HRM practices were encountered that might make for lower worker trust around the employment contract. However, we find uneven evidence of a link between institutional features that are likely to directly impact on owner or investor rights, more specifically electoral proportionality, and workplace practices. This may reflect the extent to which there is a difference between formal electoral structures and how they operate. For example, Canada's first past the post system faces strong de facto pressures towards social compromise, so as to accommodate Quebec. The relationship between profit sharing and context was rather more complex, reflecting the very different forms it assumes, and the degree to which differences may supplement, rather than undermine, collective contracts and differences in tax regimes (Poutsma et al., 2005).

A limitation of the literature on intra-organisational trust is that there is sometimes a tendency to focus on personal attributes and associated behavioural outcomes (Guinot & Chiva, 2019; Saunders et al., 2010). However, associational trust is contingent on the development of formal and informal ties, which, at the workplace, is contingent on depth of communication and the exchange of ideas. In turn, the nature and type of exchange is bound up with wider societal features. Indeed, we found a strong relationship between associational trust and communication over both financial issues and strategy (Hypotheses 1a and 2a). Greater and more frequent communication, particularly with manual workers, was significantly more common in coordinated markets (and social democratic Scandinavia in particular), and noticeably weaker in liberal markets. This would confirm the linkage between capitalist institutional archetypes and high-trust HRM practices (Iqbal et al., 2019). Even clearer was the evidence in terms of the hypothesised relationship between

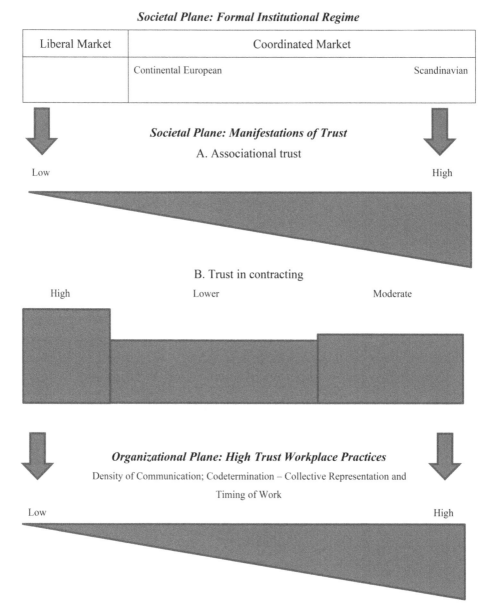

Figure 1. Planes of trust-societal and in HR.

associational trust and such HRM practices: there is support for a relationship between higher levels of the former and the latter (Hypothesis 3a), which was most likely to be the case in coordinated markets. Hence, we found that higher associational trust at societal level is linked to higher trust HRM practices – better communication and co-determination around key dimensions of the employment contract. The key results are summarised in Figure 1.

However, in the case of all three sub-hypotheses (1b, 2b and 3b), we failed to encounter any country of origin or multi-nationality effects: MNCs did not differ significantly from their domestic peers when it came to the impact of country of domicile associational trust on HRM practice. While MNCs are subject to country of origin and domicile pressures (see Cooke et al., 2019; Farndale et al., 2008), this study highlights that, when it comes to trust relations, country of domicile pressures do not have a differential effect. This may be because country of origin pressures cancel out any country of domicile effects; indeed earlier work indicates particularly strong country of origin effects when it comes to information sharing (Lavalle et al., 2010). Again, in terms of the sharing of financial information, Aggarwal and Goodell (2015) found not only strong country of origin effects, but these varied according to where the firm came from: firms from common law countries were less transparent. This may explain why being an MNC per se did not result in particular practice level outcomes.

At an applied level, orthodox rational choice approaches to property rights have been highly influential in the policy community: inter alia, they have informed World Bank reports (Cooney et al., 2011). Yet, our study finds rather more tenuous links between societal level metrics of property rights and contractual trust and actual firm level practice, despite the bold claims of prominent studies (Botero et al., 2004; Djankov et al., 2008). Again, if common law countries are associated with a diminution of worker countervailing power regarding the employment contract, a key element in a neoliberal agenda (Dardot & Laval, 2013), then this would suggest wider-reaching systemic reform is necessary than is currently envisaged, to reduce excessive short-termism that may damage firms and wider national economies.

The relationship between societal level associational ties and better communication at workplace level would reflect how social relations are reconstituted through the choices and decisions of actors (Giddens, 1990; Gooderham et al., 2019; c.f. Cooke et al., 2019). Not only does this mean that certain environments are more conducive to some firm level HRM practices than others, but also potentially that the real decisions made by firms can help support or corrode an existing social order.

What the study highlights is that associational trust at societal level is mirrored by denser ties and relations between employers and employees, encompassing greater information flows and higher levels of communication. We also confirmed that high levels of trust in contracting seem to work well for owners, but less so for employees: the latter was associated with lower trust HRM policies. Indeed, it could be argued that having firm contractual rights may matter less to workers if the wording of the employment contract *per se* makes for insecurity. Different manifestations of trust do different things, but from an employee point of view, associational trust at societal level is mirrored by higher trust HRM practices at the workplace. In turn, the latter might facilitate more cooperative and higher value-added production paradigms. This would challenge the view that trust in contracting is associated with superior institutions, and this will optimize firm level outcomes (c.f. Botero et al., 2004).

As with any research project, this study has a number of limitations. Most importantly, we did not compare the effects of different types of country of origin. Even if, as we found, multi-nationality *per se* did not make for any differences, specific countries of origin might. Again, it was not possible to explore the relationship between high-trust practices at the workplace and objective performance outcomes, owing to the use of an anonymous survey instrument, precluding matching with companies' data. Investigating the impact of country of origin type on the relative incidence of high-trust HRM practices, as well as the relationship between high-trust HRM practices and long and term performance, would constitute fertile paths for future research.

Notes

1. An alternative way of approaching trust would be through comparing differences between countries according to Hofstede's cultural categorisation (Hofstede, 2001). However, a growing body of critical research suggests that none of the dominant cultural metrics devised by Hofstede are sufficiently accurate to be adopted in a large-scale survey study (McSweeney, 2002). However, we do deploy measures of trust which in turn have been shown to depend on cultural factors such as religion and ethnolinguistic diversity (see e.g. Knack & Keefer, 1997; Zak & Knack, 2001). Hence, at least implicitly our result that trust is best at explaining differences across countries implies that culture matters.
2. The correlation matrix is not reported here, but is available on request from the authors.
3. Djankov et al. (2008) source their data from Beck et al. (2001), covering the period from 1975 to 2000.

Disclosure statement

No potential conflict of interest was reported by the authors.

References

Aggarwal, R., & Goodell, J. W. (2015). Governance transparency among the largest multinational corporations: Influence of firm, industry and national factors. *Transnational Corporations, 22*(1), 1–29.

Ahlf, H., Horak, S., Klein, A., & Yoon, S. W. (2019). Demographic homophily, communication and trust in intra-organizational business relationships. *Journal of Business & Industrial Marketing, 34*(2), 474–487.

Amable, B. (2003). *The diversity of modern capitalism.* Oxford University Press.

Amable, B. (2016). Institutional complementarities in the dynamic comparative analysis of capitalism. *Journal of Institutional Economics, 12*(1), 79–103.

Aoki, M. (2010). *Corporations in evolving diversity.* Oxford University Press.

Atkinson, H. (2006). Strategy implementation: A role for the balanced scorecard? *Management Decision, 44*(10), 1441–1460.

Bachmann, R., & Zaheer, A. (Eds.). (2008). *Landmark papers on trust.* Cheltenham.

Bamber, G. J., Lansbury, R. D., Wailes, N., & Wright, C. F. (Eds.). (2016). *International and comparative employment relations* (6th ed.). Allen & Unwin.

Beck, T., Clarke, G., Groff, A., Keefer, P., & Walsh, P. (2001). New tools and new tests in comparative political economy: The database of political institutions. *The World Bank Economic Review, 15*(1), 165–176.

Benkert, G. (1998). Trust, morality, international business. In C. Lane & R. Bachmann (Eds.), *Trust within and between organizations.* Oxford University Press.

Blunsdon, B., & Reed, K. (2003). The effects of technical and social conditions on workplace trust. *International Journal of Human Resource Management, 14*(1), 12–27.

Botero, J. C., Djankov, S., Porta, R. L., Lopez-de-Silanes, F., & Shleifer, A. (2004). The regulation of labor. *Quarterly Journal of Economics, 119*(4), 1339–1382.

Bratton, J. (2003). Work and work organization. In J. Bratton & J. Gold (Eds.), *Human resource management: Theory and practice.* Palgrave.

Brewster, C., & Holland, P. (2019). Work 'or' employment in the 21st century? In A. Wilkinson & M. Barry (Eds.), *Research agenda for the future of work.* Edward Elgar.

Brewster, C., Wood, G. T., & Brookes, M. (2008). Similarity, isomorphism or duality? Recent survey evidence on the human resource management policies of multinational corporations. *British Journal of Management, 19*(4), 320–342.

Bryman, A., & Bell, E. (2007). *Business research methods* (2nd ed.). Oxford University Press.

Cooke, F. L., Wood, G., Wang, M., & Veen, A. (2019). How far has international HRM travelled? A systematic review of literature on multinational corporations (2000–2014). *Human Resource Management Review, 29*(1), 59–75. https://doi.org/10.1016/j.hrmr.2018.05.001

Cooney, S., Gahan, P., & Mitchell, R. (2011). Legal origins, labour law and the regulation of employment relations. In M. Barry & A. Wilkinson (Eds.), *Research handbook of comparative employment relations* (pp. 75–97). Edward Elgar.

Costa, A. C., Fulmer, C. A., & Anderson, N. R. (2018). Trust in work teams: An integrative review, multilevel model, and future directions. *Journal of Organizational Behavior, 39*(2), 169–184.

Dardot, P., & Laval, C. (2013). *The new way of the world: On neo liberal society.* Verso.

Dietz, G. (2004). Partnership and the development of trust in British workplaces. *Human Resource Management Journal, 14*(1), 5–24.

Doney, P., Cannon, J., & Mullen, M. (1998). Understanding the development of national culture on trust. *Academy of Management Review, 23*(3), 601–620.

Djankov, S., Glaeser, E., La Porta, R., Lopez-de-Silanes, F., & Shleifer, A. (2003). The new comparative economics. *Journal of Comparative Economics, 31*(4), 595–619.

Djankov, S., La Porta, R., Lopez-de-Silanes, F., Shleifer, A., & Vishny, R. W. (2008). The law and economics of self-dealing. *Journal of Financial Economics, 88*(3), 430–465.

Dodgson, M. (1993). Learning, trust and technological collaboration. *Human Relations, 46*(1), 77–95. https://doi.org/10.1177/001872679304600106

Eden, L., & Molot, M. A. (2002). Insiders, outsiders and host country bargains. *Journal of International Management, 8*(4), 359–388.

Farndale, E., Brewster, C., & Poutsma, E. (2008). Co-ordinated vs liberal market HRM: The impact of institutionalisation on multinational firms. *International Journal of Human Resource Management, 19*(11), 2004–2023.

Findlay, P., & Thompson, P. (2017). Contemporary work: Its meanings and demands. *Journal of Industrial Relations, 59*(2), 122–138.

Franko, W. W., & Witko, C. (2018). *The new economic populism: How states respond to economic inequality.* Oxford University Press.

Giddens, A. (1990). *The consequences of modernity.* Polity.

Goergen, M., Brewster, C., & Wood, G. (2010). Corporate governance regimes and employment relations in Europe. *Relations Industrielles, 64*(4), 620–640.

Gomez, C., & Rosen, B. (2001). The leader–member exchange as a link between managerial trust and employee empowerment. *Group and Organization Management, 26,* 56–69.

Gooderham, P. N., Mayrhofer, W., & Brewster, C. (2019). A framework for comparative institutional research on HRM. *International Journal of Human Resource Management, 30*(1), 5–30.

Guinot, J., & Chiva, R. (2019). Vertical trust within organizations and performance: A systematic review. *Human Resource Development Review, 18*(2), 196–227.

Hall, P., & Soskice, D. (2001). An introduction to the varieties of capitalism. In P. Hall & D. Soskice (Eds.), *Varieties of capitalism: The institutional basis of competitive advantage.* Oxford University Press.

Han, W., Huang, Y., & Macbeth, D. (2018). Performance measurement of cross-culture supply chain partnership: A case study in the Chinese automotive industry. *International Journal of Production Research, 56*(7), 2437–2451.

Hofstede, G. (2001). Culture's consequences: Comparing *values, behaviours, institutions and organizations across nations* (2nd ed.). Sage.

Hong, J. F., Zhao, X., & Stanley Snell, R. (2019). Collaborative-based HRM practices and open innovation: A conceptual review. *International Journal of Human Resource Management, 30*(1), 31–62.

Hu, X., & Jiang, Z. (2018). Employee-oriented HRM and voice behavior: A moderated mediation model of moral identity and trust in management. *International Journal of Human Resource Management, 29*(5), 746–771.

Hyman, R. (1975). *Industrial relations.* Palgrave Macmillan.

Hyman, R. (1997). The future of employee representation. *British Journal of Industrial Relations, 35*(3), 309–336.

Iqbal, N., Ahmad, M., & Allen, M. M. (2019). Unveiling the relationship between e-HRM, impersonal trust and employee productivity. *Management Research Review, 42*(7), 879–899. https://www.emeraldinsight.com/doi/abs/10.1108/MRR-02-2018-0094

Jiang, Z., Gollan, P. J., & Brooks, G. (2017). Relationships between organizational justice, organizational trust and organizational commitment: A cross-cultural study of China, South Korea and Australia. *International Journal of Human Resource Management, 28*(7), 973–1004.

Knack, S. (2013). Aid and donor trust in recipient country systems. *Journal of Development Economics , 101,* 316–329.

Knack, S., & Keefer, P. (1997). Does social capital have an economic payoff? A cross-country investigation. *Quarterly Journal of Economics*, *112*(4), 1251–1288.

La Porta, R., Lopez-de-Silanes, F., & Shleifer, A. (1999). Corporate ownership around the world. *Journal of Finance*, *54*(2), 471–517.

La Porta, R., Lopez-de-Silanes, F., Shleifer, A., & Vishny, R. W. (1998). Law and finance. *Journal of Political Economy*, *106*(6), 1113–1155.

Lane, C., & Bachmann, R. (1998). *Trust within and between organizations*. Oxford University Press.

Lapavitsas, C. (2007). Information and trust as social aspects of credit. *Economy and Society*, *36*(3), 416–436.

Lavelle, J., Gunnigle, P., & McDonnell, A. (2010). Patterning employee voice in multi-national companies. *Human Relations*, *63*(3), 395–418.

Lorenz, E. (1999). Trust, contract and economic cooperation. *Cambridge Journal of Economics*, *23*(3), 301–315.

Magnin, E. (2018). Varieties of capitalism and sustainable development: Institutional complementarity dynamics or radical change in the hierarchy of institutions? *Journal of Economic Issues*, *52*(4), 1143–1158. https://doi.org/10.1080/00213624.2018.1536017

Malik, A., Pereira, V., & Tarba, S. (2019). The role of HRM practices in product development: Contextual ambidexterity in a US MNC's subsidiary in India. *International Journal of Human Resource Management*, *30*(4), 536–564.

Maljers, F. (1992). Inside unilever: The evolving transnational corporation. *Harvard Business Review*, (September–October), 46–51.

Marsden, D. (1998). Understanding the role of inter-firm institutions in sustaining trust in the employment relationship. In C. Lane & R. Bachmann (Eds.), *Trust within and between organizations*. Oxford University Press.

Mayer, R. C., & Davis, J. H. (1999). The effect of the performance appraisal system on trust for management: A field quasi-experiment. *Journal of Applied Psychology*, *84*(1), 123–136.

McSweeney, B. (2002). Hofstede's model of national cultural differences and their consequences: A triumph of faith – A failure of analysis. *Human Relations*, *55*(1), 89–117.

Mollering, G., Bachmann, R., & Lee, S. H. (2004). Introduction: Understanding organizational trust – foundations, constellations and operationalization. *Journal of Managerial Psychology*, *19*, 556–570.

Nugent, P., & Abolafia, M. (2006). The creation of trust through interaction and exchange. *Group and Organization Management*, *31*(6), 628–650.

Offe, C. (1999). How can we trust our fellow citizens? In M. E. Warren (Ed.), *Democracy and trust*. Cambridge University Press.

Pagano, M., & Volpin, P. (2005). The political economy of corporate governance. *American Economic Review*, *95*(4), 1005–1030.

Patent, V., & Searle, R. H. (2019). Qualitative meta-analysis of propensity to trust measurement. *Journal of Trust Research*, *9* (2), 136–128.

Poutsma, E., Ligthart, P. E. M., & Schouteten, R. (2005). Employee share schemes in Europe. The influence of US multinationals. *Management Revue*, *16*(1), 99–122.

Qian, G., Li, L., & Rugman, A. (2013). Liability of country foreignness and liability of regional foreignness: Their effect on geographic diversification and firm performance. *Journal of International Business Studies*, *44*(6), 635–647.

Rasche, A., Morsing, M., & Moon, J. (Eds.). (2017). *Corporate social responsibility: Strategy, communication, governance*. Cambridge University Press.

Redman, T. (2006). Performance appraisal. In T. Redman & A. Wilkinson (Eds.), *Contemporary human resource management* (2nd ed.). Prentice-Hall Financial Times.

Saravia, A. (2016). Institutions of economic freedom and generalized trust: Evidence from the Eurobarometer surveys. *European Societies, 18*(1), 5–24.

Saunders, M., Skinner, D., Dietz, G., Gillespie, N., & Lewicki, R. J. (Eds.). (2010). *Organizational trust: A cultural perspective.* Cambridge University Press.

Schindler, P. L., & Thomas, C. C. (1993). The structure of interpersonal trust in the workplace. *Psychological Reports, 73*(2), 563–573. https://doi.org/10.2466/pr0.1993.73.2.563

Schnackenberg, A. K., & Tomlinson, E. C. (2016). Organizational transparency: A new perspective on managing trust in organization–stakeholder relationships. *Journal of Management, 42*(7), 1784–1810.

Searle, R. H. (2018). Trust and HRM. In R. Searle, A.-M. Nienaber, & S. Sitkin (Eds.), *The Routledge companion to trust* (pp. 483–505). Routledge.

Shantz, A., Wang, J., & Malik, A. (2018). Disability status, individual variable pay, and pay satisfaction: Does relational and institutional trust make a difference? *Human Resource Management, 57*(1), 365–380. https://doi.org/10.1002/hrm.21845

Six, F., & Sorge, A. (2008). Creating a high-trust organization: An exploration into organizational policies that stimulate interpersonal trust building. *Journal of Management Studies, 45*(5), 857–884.

Solvell, O., & Zander, I. (1995). Organization of the dynamic multinational enterprise: The home-based and the heterarchical MNE. *International Studies of Management, 25*(1–2), 17–38.

Sydow, J. (1998). Understanding the constitution of inter-organizational trust. In C. Lane & R. Bachmann (Eds.), *Trust within and between organizations.* Oxford University Press.

Thelen, K. (2014). *Varieties of liberalization and the new politics of social solidarity.* Cambridge University Press.

Tremblay, M., Cloutier, J., Simard, G., Chênevert, S., & Vandenberghe, C. (2010). The role of HRM practices, procedural justice, organizational support and trust in organizational commitment and in-role and extra-role performance. *International Journal of Human Resource Management, 21*(3), 405–433.

Vanhala, M., & Dietz, G. (2019). How trust in one's employer moderates the relationship between HRM and engagement related performance. *International Studies of Management & Organization, 49*(1), 23–42.

Vanhala, M., & Ritala, P. (2016). HRM practices, impersonal trust and organizational innovativeness. *Journal of Managerial Psychology, 31*(1), 95–10.

Vosse, B. J. F., & Aliyu, O. A. (2018). Determinants of employee trust during organisational change in higher institutions. *Journal of Organizational Change Management, 31*(5), 1105–1118.

Whitley, R. (1999). *Divergent capitalisms.* Oxford University Press.

Wood, G., Dibben, P., & Ogden, S. (2014). Comparative capitalism without capitalism, and production without workers: The limits and possibilities of contemporary institutional analysis. *International Journal of Management Reviews, 16*(4), 384–396.

Zak, P. J., & Knack, S. (2001). Trust and growth. *The Economic Journal, 111*(470), 295–321.

Human resource capabilities in uncertain environments

Misagh Tasavori ⬡, Nayereh Eftekhar ⬡, Ghanbar Mohammadi Elyasi
and Reza Zaefarian

ABSTRACT

Increasingly, multinational companies (MNCs) are entering less explored markets with highly uncertain environments. In such an environment, MNCs must develop new solutions to tackle unpredictable changes. While there are some studies focusing on firm strategies in turbulent environments, there is a scant understanding of how the human resource strategies of MNCs should change in precarious environments. Thus, built upon the dynamic capability perspective, we focus on the human resource capabilities that MNCs develop in an uncertain emerging economy. In this research, we carried out a multiple case study and interviewed six MNCs' subsidiaries operating in the Islamic Republic of Iran. Our findings demonstrate that in an uncertain environment, human resource managers should be able to develop flexible cost management, adapt compensation packages, employ frequent and transparent communication, ensure retention of their top-quality managers, develop long-term oriented team-based and quick decision-making, and have the autonomy from MNC headquarters to enact these initiatives.

1. Introduction

With increasingly saturated markets and fierce competition in developed countries, some multinational companies (MNCs) are targeting fewer but untapped markets in emerging economies (Ghauri et al., 2014; Tasavori et al., 2015) where they might be faced with highly uncertain environments. Unpredictable changes from war, terrorism, sanctions, economic crises, or political changes in these environments create uncertainty and a more challenging situation for MNCs (Wood et al., 2018). Such environmental conditions also make it difficult for businesses to apply their standardised practices and become successful (Mellahi et al., 2013). To overcome this, MNCs have to develop new strategies, not for improving their performance, but sometimes with the aim of survival (Nijssen & Paauwe, 2012).

In an uncertain environment, employees are also affected. In such an environment, because of the possibility of fluctuations in firm revenues, companies may consider downsizing (Sahdev et al., 1999; Schenkel & Teigland, 2017). Employees' bargaining power is also impacted (Wilkinson & Wood, 2017) and they might experience a reduction in their benefits and wages (Streeck, 2009). In addition, employees might feel more vulnerable and less rational in their decision-making (Weick, 1993) with the resultant threats to their job security (Shoss, 2017; Streeck, 2009). The possibility of all these potential changes might also lead to the development of negative emotions such as fear, worry, anxiety (Lerner & Keltner, 2001), and stress (Subramaniam, 2018).

Considering the impact of the uncertain environment on employees is particularly crucial as the development of solutions to best utilise human assets (Björkman et al., 2007) can be a source of competitive advantage for the firm (Barney, 1991; Collings & Mellahi, 2009; Pfeffer, 1994) in an unpredictable environment. With volatile environmental conditions impacting not only the firm but also its employees, human resource (HR) departments have to be proactive and take measures to prevent any potential disruptions in the workplace (Mirza, 2018). Despite the prominence of human resource management (HRM), there is little understanding of HRM-related strategic changes that MNCs must deploy in turbulent environments (Bader et al., 2015; Nijssen & Paauwe, 2012; Oh & Oetzel, 2011; Wood et al., 2018). Therefore, the first objective of this research is to bridge this gap and shed light on how HRM practices should be amended in a precarious environment.

To answer this question, we adopt a dynamic capability perspective. Dynamic capability scholars suggest that in a rapidly changing environment, in addition to possession of distinctive resources, MNCs should also be able to develop capabilities to adapt to environmental changes (Ambrosini et al., 2009; Eisenhardt & Martin, 2000). Capabilities are defined as capacities and processes that enable the firm to renew, rebuild, and reconfigure its resources to meet the changing environment (Teece, 2007; Teece et al., 1997). Therefore, we investigate if, and if so how, HRM-related dynamic capabilities can enable a firm to adapt to a highly uncertain environment.

As an uncertain environment, we have selected the Islamic Republic of Iran (IRI). The IRI has a population of approximately 82.5 million (WorldoMeters, 2019) and is the second biggest economy in the Middle

East and North Africa (MENA) (World Bank, 2018b). Despite its large market size, the country has faced several political and economic challenges over the past few decades, which makes it an uncertain environment for MNCs to invest in (Wilkinson & Wood, 2017; Wood et al., 2018). According to the World Bank (2018a), there are two main sources of uncertainty in the IRI: first, from the *external* point of view, the IRI's nuclear programme and the related sanctions on the country have created enormous uncertainties. Second, from the *domestic* viewpoint, the government has to respond to these political and economic pressures by changing its policies, rules, and regulations continuously, which contributes to the environmental uncertainty in the country (Segal, 2018).

In the context of the IRI, we selected six subsidiaries of MNCs and carried out interviews with their top managers to shed light on specific capabilities and practices that are developed by MNCs' subsidiary HR departments.

Our study aims to offer several contributions. First, while there is a plethora of research about the HR strategies that MNCs adopt in stable environments (e.g. Laine et al., 2009; Sahdev et al., 1999; Stavrou et al., 2010), there is not much known about the successful human resource practices in highly uncertain environments (Bader et al., 2015; Wood et al., 2018). Thus, our research aims to complement the existing understandings in the field of HRM. Second, we contribute to the dynamic capability perspective (Teece, 2007; Teece & Pisano, 1994) and extend it to the context of international HRM and an uncertain emerging economy. Our findings reveal specific HR capabilities that are crucial in a precarious environment and examine the applicability of this theoretical perspective in such an environment. Finally, our research has been conducted in the IRI, an emerging market that has been relatively less studied. Prior studies have highlighted the scant knowledge about the Middle East and have called for the conduction of further research in this region, particularly in the field of HRM (Budhwar & Mellahi, 2007; Soltani & Wilkinson, 2011).

2. The context of the IRI

The IRI has a population of approximately 82.5 million, which ranks it 18th, globally (WorldoMeters, 2019). The country is the second-biggest economy in MENA (World Bank, 2018b) with a GDP per capita of $5,415 in 2017 (World Bank, 2017). The IRI benefits from one of the biggest natural resources in the world. According to the statistics published by the BP Statistical Review of World Energy 2018, the IRI is ranked fourth in oil reserves and second in natural gas reserves

(Paraskova, 2018); as a result, crude oil sales are the primary source of its foreign income (Trading Economics, 2019).

The country has faced an uncertain environment in the past few decades. In 1979, the country experienced a revolution (BBC., 2018). In 1980, the IRI-Iraq war started, which continued for around eight years. In 1995, the United States (US) imposed oil and trade sanctions, accusing the IRI of sponsoring terrorism and engaging in the pursuit of nuclear arms (BBC., 2018). Since 1995, several economic sanctions have been imposed against the country, although there have been periods when the sanctions were suspended.

Over the years, the IRI has attempted to develop its nuclear programme for peaceful purposes, which has nevertheless created concerns globally. After several years of negotiation between the IRI and P5 + 1 countries (China, France, Russia, the United Kingdom, and the US, plus Germany) over the country's nuclear programme, the IRI agreed to sign the Joint Comprehensive Plan of Action (JCPOA) in 2015 which led to the lifting of financial and economic sanctions (BBC., 2018). However, in spring 2018, the US president announced that the US was planning to withdraw from the JCPOA (The White House, 2018b). As a result, on the 8th of May 2018, President Trump announced that all sanctions that were waived or lifted as a result of JCPOA would be re-imposed within six months (The White House, 2018a). The US sanctions against the IRI included economic, trade (including selling oil), scientific and military (US Department of State, 2019). In May 2018, the European Commission (EC) announced that they would continue to implement JOCPA and attempt to nullify the US sanctions against the IRI, and support European companies to operate in the IRI (Deutsche, 2018; Strupczewski, 2018).

According to Segal (2018), US sanctions impacted the IRI's economy through declining oil production, the collapse of GDP growth, the weakening of the IRI's currency, and increasing rates of inflation. Following the imposition of sanctions, many MNCs also decided to exit the country or postpone any new investments to avoid risking their relationship with the US (Segal, 2018).

3. Literature review

3.1. Undertaking business in uncertain environments

With the presence of uncertain environments in the world, an important issue is how companies carry out business in such an environment (Bruton et al., 2018; Julio & Yook, 2012; McCarthy & Puffer, 2002; Rodgers et al., 2019). In this section, we provide a brief overview of some of the findings of these studies. Some scholars, for example, have pointed to the emergence of institutional voids, 'situations where institutional arrangements that support markets are absent, weak, or fail to accomplish the role expected of them'(Mair & Marti, 2009, p. 419), and highlighted the importance of the development of entrepreneurial orientation when dysfunctional competition exists. McCarthy and Puffer (2002) explain how environmental changes made the Soviet Union restructure corporate governance. In the face of political uncertainty such as an election period, Julio and Yook (2012) found that organizations adopt strategies that reduce their investment and risk. Rodgers et al. (2019) elaborate on how service MNCs in the turbulent institutional environment of Ukraine developed non-market strategies to survive. Despite the existence of some literature shedding light on how companies operate in a precarious environment, there is limited research investigating how firms should also develop strategies to cope with the effects of uncertainty inside their firms, especially in managing their employees (Wood et al., 2018). Below, we point to some of these HR-related findings.

In highly uncertain environments, cost reduction is a common strategy that also impacts HR departments. Prior studies have shown that when faced with a crisis, companies may decide to change employees' compensation packages (Dewatripont & Roland, 1995), lay them off (Luan et al., 2013), or reduce their wages, actions which are usually perceived as a breach of the psychological contract between the employer and employees (Chambel & Fortuna, 2015) and which lead to employee dissatisfaction (Robinson & Rousseau, 1994). Moreover, in turbulent environments, more flexible, extemporaneous decisions may be needed to respond quickly which can change the previous decision-making procedures of some MNCs to more distributed, localized ones (Williams et al., 2017; Wood et al., 2018) that is built upon the "rare Knowledge" acquired in such environments (Suder et al., 2019). The decision-making processes of managers will also be affected (Drabek, 1986; Pearson & Clair, 1998; Williams et al., 2017). MNC managers will have to accelerate the speed of their decision-making under limited time pressure which requires having managers with better cognitive ability (Pearson & Clair, 1998).

Some scholars have also pointed out the role of communication with employees about both the uncertain environment and the strategies that the company is going to pursue to create a shared understanding among employees (Dyer & Shafer, 2003; Nijssen & Paauwe, 2012; Pearson & Clair, 1998). Prior research has also corroborated that in precarious environments, subsidiaries may need to have a higher level of control over HRM practices to conform to the local conditions (Mellahi et al., 2013).

Finally, in the face of unstable environmental conditions, some scholars have highlighted the importance of the development of resilience in employees (Coutu, 2002; Luthans, 2002). Resilience has been found to be a critical factor that supports employees in managing work-related stress and coping with challenging environmental conditions.

Considering the uncertain environment of the IRI, in the next section, we review some of the prior findings about the HRM practices in this country.

3.2. HRM in the IRI

There is very limited research about *international* HRM in the context of the IRI (Soltani, 2010; Soltani & Liao, 2010), particularly considering the impact of the uncertain environment on HRM. Prior studies conducted on local Iranian firms have revealed the prominence of flexibility in Iran. Feiz and Golshahi (2017), for example, argue that in an uncertain environment, strategic flexibility allows Iranian companies to respond to environmental changes more quickly and better utilise their resources which can improve their firm performance.

Aezami Nejad (2014), a board member of Iran's Human Resource Management Society, highlights the importance of communication with employees in an uncertain environment. He explains that when the environment is changing rapidly if managers do not communicate with their employees frequently, employees may start creating rumours or assume that their managers are incapable of managing the new situation. Similarly, Jalalkamali et al. (2016) found that communication satisfaction (relational and informational) of employees can positively affect the job performance of employees working in international joint ventures operating in Iran.

The research of Gholipor and Eftekhar (2017) on talent management of telecom companies in the IRI's uncertain environment illustrates that their current approach could not only retain and develop talent in turbulent times but could also lead to the loss of their talent or their disengagement. Talented employees are particularly important in uncertain environments to come up with innovative solutions to address potential challenges (Holland & Scullion, 2019; Scullion et al., 2010; e.g. Zhang et al., 2015).

Latifi (1997) refers to the impact of Islam's values and Iran's national culture on managers' values. She sheds light on some of the work-related values of Iranians such as behaving kindly towards employees and involving employees in decision-making. By contrast, Tayeb (2001) indicates that decision-making in Iranian companies is usually centralised as employees (particularly at lower and middle levels) are not committed to the organisation and are reluctant to contribute to the decision-making.

Similarly, Balali et al. (2009) conducted research on the Iranian managerial decision-making style. They found that Iranian managers make decisions individually, and do not change their decisions based on certain cultural norms; in fact, they may ask others for suggestions but there is no participatory method of decision-making in Iranian companies.

MNCs' HR managers might also be faced with the dilemma of pursuing standardised headquarter HR practices or adapting HR policies to suit the environmental conditions of the IRI. According to Tayeb (1998), international companies can have enterprise-wide policies, but to meet the local circumstances of the IRI, they have to adapt their HR practices. Similarly, Soltani and Wilkinson (2011) shed light on how managers assigned to subsidiary MNCs in the IRI are under pressure to find a balance between orders from their headquarters and the environmental uncertainty in the country.

3.3. Dynamic capability perspective

To examine specific HR practices of MNCs in the uncertain environment of the IRI, we have adopted a dynamic capability perspective which is built upon the resource-based view (RBV) of the firm. According to the RBV, it is the possession of valuable, rare, inimitable, and non-substitutable (VRIN) resources that support firms to gain a competitive advantage and enhance their performance (Barney, 1991, 2001). However, dynamic capability scholars argue that the sole possession of VRIN resources would only create a competitive advantage in stable environments (Ambrosini et al., 2009), and in volatile environmental conditions, companies should develop dynamic capabilities to adapt to complex or changing environments (Nelson, 1991; Teece & Pisano, 1994). According to them, in a precarious environment, dynamic capabilities are required to enable firms to transform their existing resources and create a new bundle of resources to achieve the firms' strategic objectives (Ambrosini & Bowman, 2009; Helfat & Peteraf, 2009). Teece (2007) explains that the development of capabilities allows firms to better sense the opportunities in a changing environment and seize them, which can then enhance firm performance. Dynamic capabilities are defined as "the firm's ability to integrate, build, and reconfigure internal and external competencies to address rapidly changing environments" (Teece et al., 1997, p.516). They are considered as latent capacities that cannot be detected directly but can be identified through observable routines and their outcomes (Di Stefano et al., 2014).

Capabilities are built upon the organisational and managerial processes of a firm (Amit & Zott, 2001; Dosi et al., 2008). Managers employ these processes to transform their resources into new useful assets that enable the firm to conform to environmental changes (Colbert, 2004). Wang et al. (2012) found that to retain dynamic capabilities, firms should work on their human capital to realise maximum productivity, and engage them in leveraging the core competencies of the company; these competencies then become the differentiating factor of the organisation and can be adjusted to the new and future needs of the environment.

4. Research method

4.1. Research design

To understand how environmental uncertainty impacts employees and the way that MNCs' subsidiaries' HR departments design HR capabilities to be agile and respond to uncertainties, we conducted qualitative exploratory research (Saunders et al., 2016). The qualitative approach allows a deep understanding of the phenomenon in its context (Bryman, 2015) and facilitates the development of new insights (Yin, 2014). A multiple case-study approach was employed as this supports replication logic and enabled us to identify the similar capabilities that were developed and employed by different MNCs' subsidiaries' HR departments (Eisenhardt & Graebner, 2007; Yin, 2014).

4.2. Case selection

In this research, HR departments of subsidiaries of six MNCs in the IRI were selected. Case selections were based on two approaches: *purposive* sampling, based on the information we received from a person working in a governmental organisation supporting MNCs' operations in the IRI, and *convenience* sampling. Convenience sampling (Saunders et al., 2016) is a common practice in emerging markets (Zaefarian, Eng, and Tasavori et al., 2016) as gaining access to top managers of these companies is quite difficult, particularly when they are dealing with many challenges as a result of uncertainties in the environment. When deciding on which companies to interview, we endeavoured to select MNCs' subsidiaries operating in different industries and from different countries of origin. Heterogeneity of cases allowed us to compare the findings in different industries and facilitated generalisation (Schuster & Holtbrügge, 2012; Tasavori et al., 2014). An overview of company cases, number of years of operation in the IRI, their industry, and the continent of origin is provided in Table 1. To respect the anonymity and confidentiality of interviewees and the interviewed companies, a pseudonym is given to MNCs' subsidiaries.

Table 1. Overview of interviewed MNCs.

No.	Name of the company	Industry	Number of employees	Years of operation in Iran	Origin
1	ComCo.	High Tech	>1000	10	A developing country
2	Medicine Co.	Pharmaceutical and biopharmaceutical industry	400- 500	>20	A developed country
3	FoodCo.	Food manufacturing	400- 500	>40	A developed country
4	Chain Store	Retail	> 1000	<10	A developing country
5	Consumer Goods	Chemical and consumer goods company	400-500	>40	A developed country
6	Herbal Med.	Pharmaceutical industry	<100	<5	A developed country

Table 2. Overview of interviewees.

No.	Name of the company	Number of interviews	Position of interviewees
1	ComCo.	4	HR Vice President; HR manager, HR experts
2	Medicine Co.	1	HR Senior Manager
3	FoodCo.	1	HR Manager
4	Chain Store	2	HR Manager, HR Expert
5	Consumer Goods	2	HR Vice President, CEO Vice President
6	Herbal Med	4	CEO, Marketing and HR Manager, Financial Manager

4.3. Data Collection

Data for this research were collected from multiple sources. Primary data were collected by interviewing top managers and employees of MNCs' subsidiaries in the IRI. Overall, 14 interviews were conducted (see Table 2 for an overview of interviewees) between August 2018 and February 2019. Before the interview date, an explanation of the research project and the list of interview questions were sent to the interviewees and they were invited to participate in the research. After their initial consent, an interview was arranged.

Interviews lasted between 30 and 90 minutes, with an average duration of about 60 minutes. Interviewees included HR managers, HR employees, technical managers, project managers, marketing managers, and vice presidents. Other managers were also interviewed for triangulation purposes (Stake, 2010) and to obtain a more comprehensive picture. After conducting the first interview in each company, snowball sampling (Bryman, 2015; Kuzel, 1992) was employed to interview the second informant in the firm. Interviewing several people in a company allowed us to achieve a more comprehensive understanding (Golden-Biddle & Locke, 2007) of the impact of uncertainties on employees, and how HR departments were addressing them. We also interviewed some of the employees of these companies for triangulation purposes (Ghauri & Firth, 2009; Perry, 2000). Before each interview, we confirmed the anonymity and confidentiality of the data and obtained the permission of interviewees to record the interviews. Interviews were then transcribed to facilitate data analysis (Bryman, 2015). Except for two interviews that were conducted in English, the rest were carried out in Persian.

Based on the reviewed literature, we designed an interview guideline (King & Horrocks, 2010) and constructed semi-structured and open-ended questions. The interviewees were asked to provide some information about the background of the company, their position and experience of working in the firm, the environmental uncertainties impacting the firm, and how the HR department was developing new capabilities in the face of these uncertainties.

Secondary data were also collected by reading different supporting documents, reports, journal articles, news, company websites, and brochures. Secondary data can be helpful in providing a comprehensive picture and corroborating the primary data (Yin, 2014).

4.4. Data analysis

We first developed a story of each company case based on the number of interviews that we had conducted. Interviews were analysed and coded by employing a thematic analysis approach to identify emerging themes (Braun & Clarke, 2006; Gaur & Kumar, 2018; Ghauri & Gronhaug, 2010; Miles & Huberman, 1994). Thematic analysis was used because it enables the summarising of critical aspects of a large body of data, facilitates the highlighting of similarities and differences, and allows the acquisition of unpredicted insights from the dataset (Braun & Clarke, 2006). Consistent with prior studies, codes were both theory and data-driven (Sinkovics et al., 2005). In the coding process, we identified the textual data of each interview corresponding to the code. Subsequently, we subsumed codes under broader categories wherever possible. We then carried out a within-case analysis to identify more detailed emergent patterns (Miles & Huberman, 1994). When following this process, we allowed the emergence of the patterns of each case before a cross-case generalisation. To ensure the reliability of coding (Bryman, 2015), each author coded the interviews independently; the codes were then compared with each other to identify and achieve consensus on any potential discrepancies. Such an approach also helps to improve data analysis and extend insight into the data (Koen et al., 2014, pp. 185–186). Following the suggestion of some researchers (Ghauri & Gronhaug, 2010; Miles & Huberman, 1994; Yin, 2014), we then pursued pattern matching and compared and contrasted the identified themes and patterns across cases. We employed MAXQDA12 software in the process of data coding and analysis as it supports the analysis of data from multiple sources and facilitates coding, segmenting, classifying, and analysing interviews (Gibbs, 2002).

5. Findings

In our interviews, we endeavoured to examine capabilities that MNCs' subsidiaries' HR departments developed in highly uncertain environments that enabled them to adapt to environmental changes.

5.1. Impact of uncertainties on employees and the aim of development of capabilities

The key uncertainties that were highlighted in our interviews were related to sanctions and consequently high exchange rates, high inflation rates and changes of government rules and regulations in response to sanctions. In line with the existing literature (e.g. Weick, 1993; Wilkinson & Wood, 2017), we also found that highly uncertain environments not only had impacted MNCs' subsidiaries but also their employees. Between February 2018 and November 2018 when the country was facing the possibility of more sanctions, the exchange rate and inflation rate surged considerably (Segal, 2018). These sudden changes in the environment made people very anxious about the future of the country,the continuity of the operations of MNCs in the IRI, and the likelihood that they would lose their jobs. As suggested in the literature (Halkos & Bousinakis, 2010), the managers we interviewed also pointed out that in such environmental conditions, the efficiency of employees dropped and they were not as focused on their jobs as they should be. For example, an HR Senior Manager of ComCo. commented:

> "I really do not want to follow the news, but all my colleagues are talking about the situation and what they should do. They do not concentrate on their job, and they are just searching for solutions to maintain their standard of living [because of the rise in the inflation rate and the exchange rate]."

Figure 1 demonstrates an overview of the sources of uncertainties and their impact on employees working in MNCs' subsidiaries in the IRI.

Our interviews highlighted that the HR departments attempted to develop new capabilities in the face of environmental uncertainties. Specifically, they explained that they were developing capabilities with the hope of reducing the anxiety of employees about the future, enhancing their concentration and efficiency, ensuring their job security, enhancing employees' purchasing power, and improving the resilience and morale of employees. In the next section, we explain specific capabilities that were developed in these subsidiaries to achieve these goals.

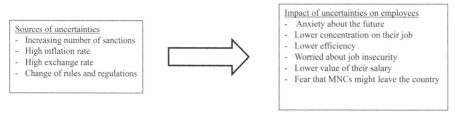

Figure 1. Uncertainties and their impact on employees.

5.2. HR capabilities developed in the uncertain environment

5.2.1. Flexible cost management of HR operations

Interviewees indicated that in the face of an unpredictable future and to run the business for a longer period, they had to develop new cost management capability. Specifically, from the HR point of view, they attempted to reduce unnecessary HR costs and redesign training strategies. These initiatives are explained below.

Managing unnecessary HR costs. Most of the interviewed companies emphasised that they decided to prioritise saving more jobs in an uncertain environment by reducing the overall HR costs. The HR manager of Consumer Goods, for example, explained that every year they funded extravagant celebrations for the New Year. However, this year, to reduce costs they decided not to organise such an expensive event; instead, they decided to allocate part of this money to the benefits that they were going to pay to employees. According to her,

> "Every year, we had a very big and costly ceremony for Iranian New Year, which is the best practice here, but because of the economic situation, we found out that it is not necessary to have it like other years; we are also reducing other costs so we could pay more money to our employees."

Based on our interviews, this strategy was both accepted and welcomed by employees as it ensured the continuation of the company over a longer period.

Another type of cost reduction strategy employed by HR departments was restricting unnecessary overtime working and consequently reducing HR overall costs (e.g. in the case of ComCo.).

Flexible training and development processes. In the uncertain environment, interviewees revealed that they had to adapt previous standards of training provided by their headquarters. In agreement with their headquarters, they decided to reduce or postpone unnecessary training and wherever possible, reduce the cost of training. For example, they indicated that they decided to reduce the number of offshore training programmes. Due to the increase in the exchange rate, they found it too expensive to travel overseas and pay for hotels and workshop registration fees, among other outgoings. Nevertheless, to cover headquarters' training standards, subsidiaries' HR managers had to find new ways of covering the training needs of their staff. For example, they attempted to identify local institutions to offer the required training (e.g. in the case of ComCo.) or offer internal training (e.g. in the case of FoodCo. and Herbal Med.). The HR manager of FoodCo. elaborated:

> "We check if someone else in the company has received this training before; we then ask him/her to train others in the company to reduce our costs in this environmental condition".

5.2.2. Adapting compensation packages

Interviewed companies also asserted that in the face of uncertain economic conditions, they decided to redesign their compensation package by focusing more on the primary and basic needs of their employees. The HR Vice President of the ComCo., for example, indicated,

> "We have many incentive packages like travel, sport, etc. We found out, in this difficult economic situation, our employees are in desperate need of cash so we are no longer offering any of these: instead, we are giving them gift cards so they can spend them on their more urgent needs."

Similarly, the HR manager of the Medicine Co. spoke about small changes they made to help their employees feel better in the face of uncertainty within the external environment:

> "We cannot do significant work financially, but we do small things to increase the welfare of the employee in the office, like having breakfast or snacks or changing the compensation package".

Another interesting initiative was offering extensive medical check-ups because of the higher stress levels among employees. One of the HR managers postulated that people may pay less attention to their health during tough economic conditions; therefore, they decided to provide this benefit for their employees. In the words of this manager,

> "We had some health check-ups every year, but this year, we had them done more comprehensively, and I think it has had a very positive effect. Before that, we had just blood, eye and ear tests but this year we have added heart tests and some internal organs' tests for men and women." (Consumer Good HR Vice President)

Another interviewee, the HR manager of FoodCo, explained that to enhance the resilience of their employees, they are now offering more stress management workshops to reduce the stress of employees to support them during uncertain environmental situations. Specifically, she said,

"Look, we provide some crisis management training for our staff, so our people know how to manage their stress in critical situations and help our team to be one step ahead."

5.2.3. Frequent and transparent communication with employees

The interviewees pointed out that the volatile environmental situations had impacted their employees by reducing their morale and efficiency as they were worried about losing their jobs and anxious about their prospects. To reduce this problem, HR managers found it critical to develop the capability of more frequent and transparent communication with their employees. Almost all interviewee managers highlighted that they were arranging more frequent and transparent meetings with their employees, emphasising that they were not planning to leave the country or that making employees redundant was not on their agenda. The Chain Store HR manager said,

"We have told our employees that the last MNC to leave the country would be us!"

In their communication, managers also attempted to enhance the resilience of their employees by asserting:

"Do not worry, this [referring to the sanctions and related uncertainties] will also pass." (HR manager of the Chain Store)

One of the HR senior experts of ComCo. said:

"There was a time when everyone was stressfully following news and the exchange rate, it was an overall panic, but through indirect communication, we showed that although our business is very dependent on the rate, we are doing our business and we will survive in Iran; so anxiety reduced little by little".

Another advantage of frequent and transparent communication was to give the employees the impression that if the company could not continue working in the IRI, their managers would inform them so they would have enough time to plan. The Vice President of the Consumer Goods Company, for example, commented:

"We have been very honest with our employees, and we inform them of any changes in advance, so they have enough time to plan what to do".

5.2.4. Talent retention

To be able to adapt to environmental conditions quickly, most of the interviewees also acknowledged the importance of retention of their key capable top managers. While most of the company cases asserted that they had developed loyal and committed managers over the years, some revealed that because of the high inflation rate and high exchange rate, the company had decided to develop specific strategies to retain their key managers. Some of the companies (e.g. Chain Store and Medicine Co.) explained that they even decided to improve the key managers' compensation packages to ensure that these managers did not leave their companies.

The importance of employing capable managers in the interviewed cases was emphasised by almost all managers. Even though most of them had decided not to recruit new employees in the uncertain environment, they were attempting to collect information about potential top candidates who had lost their jobs (because of the turbulent environment), so as to recruit them as soon as the economic conditions improved.

5.2.5. Long-term-oriented, team-based, and accelerated decision-making of top managing teams

Interviewed subsidiaries said that, in order to adapt to environmental changes, they found it critical to focus on the long-term operations of their business in the IRI as the environment would not always be volatile. For example, the Chain Store HR manager mentioned that the IRI had quite a large middle-class population and, in the long term, it was quite profitable. However, not every MNC, particularly those from developed countries that were not used to uncertain environments, could continue doing business in those conditions. Similarly, the HR managers of Consumer Goods and FoodCo. said they had been operating in the IRI for a long time (over 40 years) and were not planning to leave the country, a fact which was taken into account when they were making decisions during times of turbulence.

Interviewed managers also highlighted the necessity of developing more team-based decisions and involving HR departments even more (e.g. Consumer Goods, ComCo., FoodCo.). Also, team-based decision-making allowed companies to reduce risks and undertake a more comprehensive analysis of the situation. For example, the HR Vice President of the Consumer Goods said,

> "When we encounter a crisis, we develop a crisis management team; we choose a team from different departments to work on finding solutions for the crisis. We arrange the team in a way that we have a comprehensive view of the problem".

Interviewees also indicated that, when faced with environmental changes, they found it crucial to make quick decisions at the firm level. As these decisions also required some changes at the HR level and support of HR managers in aligning their strategies with the firm's responses, managers said they also had to make HR-related decisions quicker than would normally be the case.

5.2.6. Delegation of autonomy to subsidiaries' HR departments

In line with the previous capability, we also found that quick adaptation of MNCs' subsidiaries would not have been possible without the trust and support of the company headquarters. Specifically, we noticed that some of these MNCs' subsidiaries' HR departments could be agile in the context of the IRI because of the autonomy that was given to them by their headquarters. Although the headquarters wanted to be informed about the decisions being made, over the years of operation in the country, they had learnt to trust the analysis and solutions proposed by top managers of their subsidiaries. For example, the HR manager of FoodCo. said that,

> "We have specific guidelines for the number of training hours that our employees should attend in a foreign country, but we convinced our headquarters to change this practice and offered this training locally".

Similarly, the HR Vice President of the Consumer Goods elaborated that,

> "Over the years, they [the headquarters] accepted our understanding of the environment; of course, they still expect us to inform them about any challenges that we face. However, they ask *us* to offer at least three solutions and they will pick one".

It should be mentioned that delegation of autonomy would not have been possible if the company did not have highly qualified top managers, almost all of whom were Iranian (except in the case of Chain Store and one manager in Consumer Goods). The need to know the culture and contexts in decision-making was indicated by all our interviewees. For example, the marketing manager of Herbal Med Co. stated,

> "We proved ourselves to our headquarters by having a breakthrough from the beginning. Therefore, they did not feel that this subsidiary needs to have an expatriate to run and develop the business".

An overview of our findings is presented in Figure 2.

6. Discussion and conclusion

In this research, we set out to examine how MNCs' HR departments can be agile and overcome highly uncertain environmental conditions by shedding light on specific HR-related capabilities that they develop to adapt to precarious environments. Our findings reveal that HR departments of MNCs operating in the IRI developed six capabilities: these are

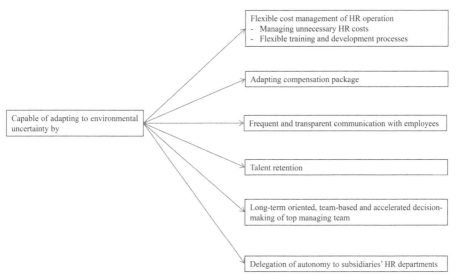

Figure 2. Summary of capabilities developed by HR in highly uncertain environments.

(i) flexible cost management of HR operations, (ii) adapting compensation packages, (iii) frequent and transparent communication, (iv) talent retention, (v) long-term oriented, team-based and accelerated decision-making of top management teams, and (vi) delegation of autonomy to subsidiaries' HR departments. Our research also highlights that the immediate aim of developing these capabilities was to support employees to adapt to environmental changes and consequently support the firm to have congruence with the precarious environment. Figure 3 presents a summary of our findings.

Our research offers several contributions. First, it adds to the international HRM literature by exploring HRM in highly uncertain environments, which has rarely been studied (Wood et al., 2018). We extend this body of literature by employing the dynamic capability perspective and illuminating several key HR capabilities that should be developed to enable MNCs to adapt to turbulent economic environments.

The first capability that we found was related to the flexible cost management of HR operations. While the prior literature points out to downsizing as a dominant strategy in times of economic downturn (Luan et al., 2013; Schenkel & Teigland, 2017), our research suggests that because of the high level of uncertainty, interviewed MNCs preferred to postpone any more severe actions such as laying off employees for as long as possible. Instead, they started with reducing unnecessary HR-related costs, and pursuing flexible training, supporting previous studies that have highlighted the importance of flexibility in the context of the IRI (Feiz & Golshahi, 2017). While the dominant HRM literature suggests that these types of reductions lead to decreased satisfaction of

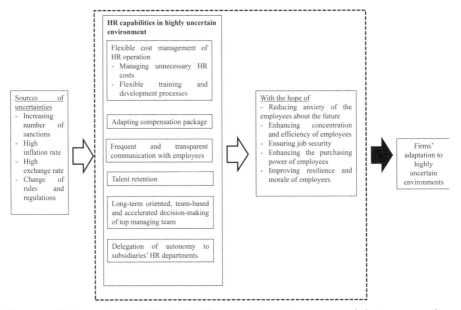

Figure 3. HR dynamic capabilities in highly uncertain environments and their outcome Data Availability Statement.

employees (Robinson & Rousseau, 1994), our findings provide a different perspective. Specifically, we found that in a highly uncertain economic environment, employees are willing to sacrifice a portion of their benefits to support the company to adapt to environmental changes and to reduce the risk of imminent job loss.

In line with previous studies (Dewatripont & Roland, 1995), our research also illustrates the necessity of adapting compensation packages in the face of highly uncertain environments and economic crises. As revealed by some scholars (Kautt, 2018; Sadri & Bowen, 2011), we also found out that in turbulent environments, companies decided to change how they remunerated their employees by focusing on their critical needs and expectations

In congruence with other studies (Aezami Nejad, 2014; Dyer & Shafer, 2003; Jalalkamali et al., 2016; Nijssen & Paauwe, 2012; Pearson & Clair, 1998), the necessity of frequent and transparent communication in a highly uncertain environment was indicated as another critical capability to be pursued by HR managers. Transparent and honest communications have been found to reduce employees' stress (Subramaniam, 2018) and enhance their job performance (Jalalkamali et al., 2016). Sharing information about the uncertain environment and coping strategies of the firm also enables employees to rebuild their shattered assumptions and reduce feelings of vulnerability (Pearson & Clair, 1998).

Based on our research results, one of the main activities of the HR department of the MNCs working in the IRI is focusing on top talent retention. This is supported by the overall talent management literature: that retaining 'star' or A-players is the most important strategy among the talent management activities (e.g. Zhang & Stewart, 2017). Talent retention is even more critical in the context of the IRI as prior studies have revealed that Iranian managers may not be very successful at retaining their talented staff (Gholipor & Eftekhar, 2017).

The fourth capability that we found was related to the decision-making process of the management team. Our research highlighted three key characteristics of top management decisions in a highly uncertain environment. First, in the context of the IRI, managers preferred to consider the long-term future of their business in the country rather than focusing on short-term volatile environments. This corroborates prior studies pinpointing the necessity of the pursuit of long-term orientation in large-sized markets where operations might be challenging (Ghauri et al., 2014; Tasavori et al., 2016). Second, all our company cases were inclined towards team-based decision-making by involving all top managers to ensure a more comprehensive analysis of the situation and the related solutions. Although some scholars have pointed out that Iranian managers may prefer centralised decision-making (Balali et al., 2009; Tayeb, 2001), our research illustrates that when faced with unpredictable changes, Iranian managers working in MNCs prefer to adopt more team-based decision-making. It might be because this type of decision-making can facilitate the development of more creative solutions (Sommer & Pearson, 2007) which is essential in a dynamic environment (Mirza, 2018). Finally, managers have to make much quicker decisions to respond in a timely fashion to opportunities and threats in a dynamic environment, as previously reported (Drabek, 1986; Pearson & Clair, 1998; Williams et al., 2017).

The last capability that we found critical in the context of high uncertainty was related to delegating decision-making to local managers. Prior research has also emphasised that in a precarious environment, subsidiaries may need to have higher levels of control of HRM practices to conform to the local conditions (Mellahi et al., 2013; Suder et al., 2019). Our interviewed MNCs had decided to develop this capability because of the importance of quick decision making, and because their managers had a good understanding of the context of the IRI. This confirms prior literature highlighting the necessity of local responsiveness and decentralised decision-making in such an environment (Soltani & Wilkinson, 2011; Williams et al., 2017; Wood et al., 2018).

Our research also contributes to the dynamic capability literature (Teece, 2007; Teece & Pisano, 1994). First, prior research has referred to dynamic capabilities as factors that enable firms to sense and seize opportunities in turbulent environments (e.g. Teece, 2007), but the role of HRM has been relatively ignored in this process, particularly in highly uncertain economic environments (Wood et al., 2018). Our study illustrates that in such an environment, not only the firm but also its employees are impacted, and it is crucial to support employees' ability to carry out their jobs. Our research reveals that in order to adapt to the uncertain environment, MNCs should first develop HR-specific capabilities to tackle the negative impacts of uncertain environments on their employees. This is vital, as prior research has indicated that employees with anxiety or stress will not be able to work productively (Anderson, 1976).

Finally, this research was conducted in the IRI which has had relatively little research focused on international business and international HRM (Soltani, 2010; Soltani & Liao, 2010). However, for the purpose of this research, this context offered a unique insight as it was undertaken at a time when the country and MNCs' subsidiaries were experiencing one of the most uncertain environmental situations (i.e. sanctions imposed by the US).

Managerially, our findings offer several implications to HRM managers working in highly uncertain environments. First, our research suggests that in a volatile economic environment, not only the firm but also the employees suffer, and this should be considered when designing HRM policies and practices. Employees might also feel fear, anxiety, and stress etc. which can directly impact their performance. Therefore, in such environmental conditions, HR departments should develop capabilities to adapt to environmental changes by reducing the negative consequences of uncertain environments on their employees and improving their employees' morale and resilience.

Our findings also illustrate that adaptation with highly uncertain environments requires the development of specific capabilities. First, our research suggests that generic MNC HR practices may not necessarily work in a precarious environment, and HR managers may benefit from redesigning HR-related activities and focussing on more essential programmes to save money and be able to continue their business for a longer period. Being flexible in training was specifically highlighted as an area which can help HR managers to save money.

Second, in a highly uncertain situation, it is particularly important to be flexible in designing employees' compensation packages. In fact, according to our findings, managers might have to focus on more primary needs, particularly if there is a significant economic downturn. Third, our findings suggest that in a continuously changing environment, frequent and transparent communication is necessary between managers and employees about environmental changes and how the company is going to tackle these volatile situations.

In a turbulent environment, managers may have to make many quick decisions in response to environmental changes. As a result, as is corroborated by our research, it is especially important that MNCs' subsidiaries attempt to retain their talented staff even if it means payment of higher compensation packages. In addition, employing team-based managerial decision-making in an unpredictable environment allows managers to develop a more comprehensive analysis of the situation and make better decisions within a short period of time. Moreover, it is vital for HR managers working in volatile situations to have a long-term view and see beyond those uncertainties when designing their strategies.

Finally, our research advises that, in highly uncertain environments, subsidiary HR managers should be authorised to make quick decisions if necessary. This also emphasises the significance of recruiting and developing qualified local managers.

This study is not without limitations. First, this research was conducted over a short period of time, and future studies can add to our findings by employing a longitudinal approach and by investigating the potential capabilities that should be developed and how MNCs' subsidiaries might have to adapt them over time. In our research, we only focused on one country and specific uncertainties, which limits the generalizability of our findings. Future researchers can add to our study by addressing this shortcoming. Our research was also qualitative and limited to very few cases. The international HRM literature could benefit from studies that test our findings on a larger scale. Finally, we only interviewed the MNCs' subsidiaries' top managers. Future studies could expand our findings by exploring views on this topic from MNCs' headquarters.

Disclosure statement

No potential conflict of interest was reported by the authors.

ORCID

Misagh Tasavori (iD) http://orcid.org/0000-0003-3714-4238
Nayereh Eftekhar (iD) http://orcid.org/0000-0002-3364-6460

Data Availability Statement

The data that support the findings of this study are available on request from the corresponding author. The data are not publicly available because they contain information that could compromise the privacy of research participants.

References

Aezami Nejad, M. (2014). *Communication tools in organizational uncertainity*. https://khabarfarsi.com/u/68721#redirect.

Ambrosini, V., & Bowman, C. (2009). What are dynamic capabilities and are they a useful construct in strategic management? *International Journal of Management Reviews*, *11*(1), 29–49. https://doi.org/10.1111/j.1468-2370.2008.00251.x

Ambrosini, V., Bowman, C., & Collier, N. (2009). Dynamic capabilities: An exploration of how firms renew their resource base. *British Journal of Management*, *20*(S1), S9–S24. https://doi.org/10.1111/j.1467-8551.2008.00610.x

Amit, R., & Zott, C. (2001). Value creation in e-business. *Strategic Management Journal*, *22*(6–7), 493–520. https://doi.org/10.1002/smj.187

Anderson, C. R. (1976). Coping behaviors as intervening mechanisms in the inverted-U stress-performance relationship. *The Journal of Applied Psychology*, *61*(7), 30–34. https://doi.org/10.1037/0021-9010.61.1.30

Bader, B., Schuster, T., & Dickmann, M. (2015). Danger and risk as challenges for HRM: How to manage people in hostile environments. *The International Journal of Human Resource Management*, *26*(15), 2015–2017. https://doi.org/10.1080/09585192.2015.1038116

Balali, M., Ahmadi, S. B., Javadin, S. R. S., & Farhangi, A. (2009). Decision making model and behavior of Iranian top managers. *Iranian Journal of Management Studies*, *3*(3), 75–89.

Barney, J. B. (1991). Firm resources and sustained competitive advantage. *Journal of Management*, *17*(1), 99–120. https://doi.org/10.1177/014920639101700108

Barney, J. B. (2001). Is the resource-based "view" a useful perspective for strategic management research? Yes,' *Academy of Management Review*, *26*(1), 41–56.

BBC. (2018). *Iran profile - timeline*. https://www.bbc.co.uk/news/world-middle-east-14542438

Björkman, I., Fey, C. F., & Park, H. J. (2007). Institutional theory and MNC subsidiary HRM practices: Evidence from a three-country study. *Journal of International Business Studies*, *38*(3), 430–446. https://doi.org/10.1057/palgrave.jibs.8400267

Braun, V., & Clarke, V. (2006). Using thematic analysis in psychology. *Qualitative Research in Psychology*, *3*(2), 77–101. https://doi.org/10.1191/1478088706qp063oa

Bruton, G. D., Su, Z., & Filatotchev, I. (2018). New venture performance in transition economies from different institutional perspectives. *Journal of Small Business Management*, *56*(3), 374–391. https://doi.org/10.1111/jsbm.12266

Bryman, A. (2015). *Social research methods*. Oxford University Press.

Budhwar, P., & Mellahi, K. (2007). Introduction: Human resource management in the Middle East. *The International Journal of Human Resource Management*, *18*(1), 2–10. https://doi.org/10.1080/09585190601068227

Chambel, M. J., & Fortuna, R. (2015). Wage reduction of Portuguese civil servants and their attitudes: The psychological contract perspective. *The International Journal of Human Resource Management*, *26*(22), 2853–2871. https://doi.org/10.1080/09585192.2015.1004099

Colbert, B. A. (2004). The complex resource-based view: Implications for theory and practice in strategic human resource management. *Academy of Management Review*, *29*(3), 341–358. https://doi.org/10.5465/amr.2004.13670987

Collings, D. G., & Mellahi, K. (2009). Strategic talent management: A review and research agenda. *Human Resource Management Review*, *19*(4), 304–313. https://doi.org/10.1016/j.hrmr.2009.04.001

Coutu, D. L. (2002). How resilience works. *Harvard Business Review, 80*(5), 46–55.

Deutsche, W. (2018). *EU to reactivate 'blocking statute' against us sanctions on Iran for European Firms*. https://www.dw.com/en/eu-to-reactivate-blocking-statute-against-us-sanctions-on-iran-for-european-firms/a-43826992

Dewatripont, M., & Roland, G. (1995). The design of reform packages under uncertainty. *The American Economic Review, 85*(5), 1207–1223.

Di Stefano, G., Peteraf, M., & Verona, G. (2014). The organizational drivetrain: A road to integration of dynamic capabilities research. *Academy of Management Perspectives, 28*(4), 307–327. https://doi.org/10.5465/amp.2013.0100

Dosi, G., Faillo, M., & Marengo, L. (2008). Organizational capabilities, patterns of knowledge accumulation and governance structures in business firms: An introduction. *Organization Studies, 29*(8-9), 1165–1185. https://doi.org/10.1177/0170840608094775

Drabek, T. E. (1986). *Human system responses to disaster-an inventory of sociological findings*. Springer-Verlag.

Dyer, L., & Shafer, R. (2003). Dynamic organizations: Achieving marketplace and organizational agility with people. In R. S. Peterson & E. A. Mannix (Eds.), *Leading and managing people in the dynamic organization*. Lawrence Erlbaum7-38.

Eisenhardt, K. M., & Graebner, M. E. (2007). Theory buidling from cases: Opportunities and challenges. *Academy of Management Journal, 50*(1), 25–32. https://doi.org/10.5465/amj.2007.24160888

Eisenhardt, K. M., & Martin, J. A. (2000). Dynamic capabilities: What are they? *Strategic Management Journal, 21*(10–11), 1105–111121. https://doi.org/10.1002/1097-0266(200010/11)21:10/11<1105::AID-SMJ133>3.0.CO;2-E

Feiz, D., & Golshahi, B. (2017). Identifying networking human resource practices effecs on firm performance based on a combinotrial approach: Analyzing the role of strategic flexibility and environmental uncertainty. *Management Research in Iran, 21*(3), 193–215.

Kautt, G. (2018). Needs-based' pay policy: Use Maslow's hierarchy of needs to help set your firm's compensation approach and prompt growth. *Financial Planning, 48*(4), 26–28.

Gaur, A., & Kumar, M. (2018). A systematic approach to conducting review studies: An assessment of content analysis in 25 years of IB research. *Journal of World Business, 53*(2), 280–289. https://doi.org/10.1016/j.jwb.2017.11.003

Ghauri, P. N., & Firth, R. (2009). The formalization of case study research in international business. *Der Markt, 48*(1–2), 29–40. https://doi.org/10.1007/s12642-009-0003-1

Ghauri, P. N., & Gronhaug, K. (2010). *Research methods in business studies: A practical guide*. Financial Times/Prentice Hall.

Ghauri, P., Tasavori, M., & Zaefarian, R. (2014). Internationalisation of service firms through corporate social entrepreneurship and networking. *International Marketing Review, 31*(6), 576–600. https://doi.org/10.1108/IMR-09-2013-0196

Gholipor, A., & Eftekhar, N. (2017). Introducing a talent management model based on grounded theory (case study: telecom operator) (Published in Persian). *Public Management Researches, 9*(34), 59–90.

Gibbs, G. R. (2002). *Qualitative data analysis: Explorations with nvivo*. Open University.

Golden-Biddle, K., & Locke, K. (2007). *Composing qualitative research*. Sage.

Sadri, G., & Bowen, C. R. (2011). Meeting employee requirements: Maslow's hierarchy of needs is still a reliable guide to motivating staff. *Industrial Engineer: IE, 43*(10), 44–48.

Halkos, G., & Bousinakis, D. (2010). The effect of stress and satisfaction on productivity. *International Journal of Productivity and Performance Management, 59*(5), 415–431. https://doi.org/10.1108/17410401011052869

Helfat, C. E., & Peteraf, M. A. (2009). Understanding dynamic capabilities: Progress along a developmental path. *Strategic Organization, 7*(1), 91–102. https://doi.org/10.1177/1476127008100133

Holland, D., & Scullion, H. (2019). Towards a talent retention model: Mapping the building blocks of the psychological contract to the three stages of the acquisition process. *The International Journal of Human Resource Management,* 1–46. https://doi.org/10.1080/09585192.2019.1569546

Jalalkamali, M., Ali, A. J., Hyun, S. S., & Nikbin, D. (2016). Relationships between work values, communication satisfaction, and employee job performance: The case of international joint ventures in Iran. *Management Decision, 54*(4), 796–814. https://doi.org/10.1108/MD-01-2015-0003

Julio, B., & Yook, Y. (2012). Political uncertainty and corporate investment cycles. *The Journal of Finance, 67*(1), 45–83. https://doi.org/10.1111/j.1540-6261.2011.01707.x

King, N., & Horrocks, C. (2010). *Interviews in qualitative research.* Sage.

Koen, M. P., Du Plessis, E., & Koen, V. (2014). Data analysis: The world café. In M. D. Chesnay (Ed.), *Nursing research using data analysis: Qualitative designs and methods in nursing.* Springer Publishing Company.

Kuzel, A. J. (1992). Sampling in qualitative inquiry. In B. Crabtree and W. L. Miller (Eds.), *Doing qualitative research* (pp. 31–44). SAGE Publications, Inc.

Laine, M., van der Heijden, B. I. J. M., Wickström, G., Hasselhorn, H.-M., & Tackenberg, P. (2009). Job insecurity and intent to leave the nursing profession in Europe. *The International Journal of Human Resource Management, 20*(2), 420–438. https://doi.org/10.1080/09585190802673486

Latifi, F. (1997). *Management learning in national context an extension of Mintzberg's theory of managerial roles, and a survey of management learning needs in Iran.* Brunel University.

Lerner, J. S., & Keltner, D. (2001). Fear, anger, and risk. *Journal of Personality and Social Psychology, 81*(1), 146–159. https://doi.org/10.1037/0022-3514.81.1.146

Luan, C.-J., Tien, C., & Chi, Y.-C. (2013). Downsizing to the wrong size? A study of the impact of downsizing on firm performance during an economic downturn. *The International Journal of Human Resource Management, 24*(7), 1519–1535. https://doi.org/10.1080/09585192.2012.725073

Luthans, F. (2002). The need for and meaning of positive organization behavior. *Journal of Organizational Behavior, 23*(6), 695–706. https://doi.org/10.1002/job.165

Mair, J., & Marti, I. (2009). Entrepreneurship in and around institutional voids: A case study from Bangladesh. *Journal of Business Venturing, 24*(5), 419–435. https://doi.org/10.1016/j.jbusvent.2008.04.006

McCarthy, D., & Puffer, S. (2002). Corporate governance in Russia: Towards a European. *European Management Journal, 20*(6), 630–640. https://doi.org/10.1016/S0263-2373(02)00114-7

Mellahi, K., Demirbag, M., Collings, D. G., Tatoglu, E., & Hughes, M. (2013). Similarly different: A comparison of HRM practices in mne subsidiaries and local firms in Turkey. *The International Journal of Human Resource Management, 24*(12), 2339–2368. https://doi.org/10.1080/09585192.2013.781434

Miles, M. B., & Huberman, A. M. (1994). *An expanded source book qualitative data analysis.* Sage Publications.

Mirza, M. S. (2018). *How agile is your HR function? Score yourself on the HR agility scale.* https://www.insidehr.com.au/how-agile-is-your-hr-function-score-yourself-on-the-hr-agility-scale/

Nelson, R. R. (1991). Why do firms differ, and how does it matter. *Strategic Management Journal, 12*(S2), 61–74. https://doi.org/10.1002/smj.4250121006

Nijssen, M., & Paauwe, J. (2012). HRM in turbulent times: How to achieve organizational agility? *The International Journal of Human Resource Management, 23*(16), 3315–3335. https://doi.org/10.1080/09585192.2012.689160

Oh, C. H., & Oetzel, J. (2011). Multinationals' response to major disasters: How does subsidiary investment vary in response to the type of disaster and the quality of country governance? *Strategic Management Journal, 32*(6), 658–681. https://doi.org/10.1002/smj.904

Paraskova, T. (2018). *Iran claims it holds the most oil, gas reserves in the world.* https://oilprice.com/Energy/Energy-General/Iran-Claims-Its-Holds-Most-Oil-Gas-Reserves-In-The-World.html

Pearson, C. M., & Clair, J. A. (1998). Reframing crisis management. *The Academy of Management Review, 23*(1), 59–76. https://doi.org/10.2307/259099

Perry, C. (2000). Case research in marketing. *The Marketing Review, 1*(3), 303–323. https://doi.org/10.1362/1469347002530790

Pfeffer, J. (1994). *Competitive advantage through people: Unleashing the power of the work force.* Harvard Business Press.

Robinson, S. L., & Rousseau, D. M. (1994). Violating the psychological contract: Not the exception but the norm. *Journal of Organizational Behavior, 15*(3), 245–259. https://doi.org/10.1002/job.4030150306

Rodgers, P., Stokes, P., Tarba, S., & Khan, Z. (2019). The role of non-market strategies in establishing legitimacy: The case of service MNEs in emerging economies. *Management International Review,), 59*(4), 515–540. https://doi.org/10.1007/s11575-019-00385-8

Sahdev, K., Vinnicombe, S., & Tyson, S. (1999). Downsizing and the changing role of HR. *The International Journal of Human Resource Management, 10*(5), 906–923. https://doi.org/10.1080/095851999340224

Saunders, M., Lewis, P., & Thornhill, A. (2016). *Research methods for business students.* Pearson Education.

Schenkel, A., & Teigland, R. (2017). Why doesn't downsizing deliver? A multi-level model integrating downsizing, social capital, dynamic capabilities, and firm performance. *The International Journal of Human Resource Management, 28*(7), 1065–1107. https://doi.org/10.1080/09585192.2015.1130734

Schuster, T., & Holtbrügge, D. (2012). Market entry of multinational companies in markets at the bottom of the pyramid: A learning perspective. *International Business Review, 21*(5), 817–830. https://doi.org/10.1016/j.ibusrev.2011.09.007

Scullion, H., Collings, D., & Caligiuri, P. (2010). *Global Talent Management (Global HRM).* Routledge.

Segal, S. (2018). *The economic impact of Iran sanctions.* https://www.csis.org/analysis/economic-impact-iran-sanctions

Shoss, M. K. (2017). Job insecurity: An integrative review and agenda for future research. *Journal of Management, 43*(6), 1911–1939. https://doi.org/10.1177/0149206317691574

Sinkovics, R. R., Elfriede, P., & Ghauri, P. N. (2005). Analysing textual data in international marketing research. *Qualitative Market Research: An International Journal, 8*(1), 9–38. https://doi.org/10.1108/13522750510575426

Soltani, E. (2010). The overlooked variable in managing human resources of Iranian organizations: Workforce diversity – some evidence. *The International Journal of Human Resource
Management, 21*(1), 84–108. https://doi.org/10.1080/09585190903466871

Soltani, E., & Liao, Y. (2010). Training interventions fulfilling managerial ends or prolif-
erating invaluable means for employees: Some evidence from Iran. *European Business
Review, 22*(2), 128–152. https://doi.org/10.1108/09555341011023498

Soltani, E., & Wilkinson, A. (2011). The Razor's edge: Managing MNC affiliates in Iran.
Journal of World Business, 46(4), 462–475. https://doi.org/10.1016/j.jwb.2010.10.007

Sommer, A., & Pearson, C. M. (2007). Antecedents of creative decision making in
organizational crisis: A team-based simulation. *Technological Forecasting and Social
Change, 74*(8), 1234–1251. https://doi.org/10.1016/j.techfore.2006.10.006

Stake, R. E. (2010). *Qualitative research: Studying how things work*. The Guilford Press.

Stavrou, E. T., Brewster, C., & Charalambous, C. (2010). Human resource management
and firm performance in Europe through the lens of business systems: Best fit, best
practice or both? *The International Journal of Human Resource Management, 21*(7),
933–962. https://doi.org/10.1080/09585191003783371

Streeck, W. (2009). *Reforming capitalism: Institutional change in the German political
economy*. Oxford University Press.

Strupczewski. (2018, January). *Eu to Start Iran Sanctions Blocking Law Process on
Friday*. https://www.reuters.com/article/iran-nuclear-eu-response/eu-to-start-iran-sanc-
tions-blocking-law-process-on-friday-idUSL5N1SO4W2.

Subramaniam, K. G. (2018). *Strategies for reducing employee stress and increasing
employee engagement*. Walden University.

Suder, G., Reade, C., Riviere, M., Birnik, A., & Nielsen, N. (2019). Mind the gap: The
role of HRM in creating, capturing and leveraging rare knowledge in hostile environments. *The International Journal of Human Resource Management, 30*(11), 1794–1821.
https://doi.org/10.1080/09585192.2017.1351462

Tasavori, M., Ghauri, P. N., & Zaefarian, R. (2016). Entering the base of the pyramid
market in India: A corporate social entrepreneurship perspective. *International
Marketing Review, 33*(4), 555–579. https://doi.org/10.1108/IMR-03-2014-0085

Tasavori, M., Ghauri, P. N., & Zaefarian, R. (2014). Entry of multinational companies to
the base of the pyramid: Network perspective. In C. Jones & Y. Temouri (Eds.),
International business, institutions and performance after the financial crisis (pp.
39–52). Palgrave Macmillan.

Tasavori, M., Zaefarian, R., & Ghauri, P. N. (2015). The creation view of opportunities
at the base of the pyramid. *Entrepreneurship & Regional Development, 27*(1–2),
106–126. https://doi.org/10.1080/08985626.2014.1002538

Tayeb, M. (1998). Transfer of HRM practices across cultures: An American Company in
Scotland. *The International Journal of Human Resource Management, 9*(2), 332–358.
https://doi.org/10.1080/095851998341125

Tayeb, M. (2001). Human Resource Management in Iran. In P. S. Budhwar & Y. A.
Debrah (Eds.), *Human resource management in developing countries* (pp. 121–134).
Routledge.

Teece, D. J. (2007). Explicating dynamic capabilities: The nature and microfoundations
of (sustainable) enterprise performance. *Strategic Management Journal, 28*(13),
1319–1350. https://doi.org/10.1002/smj.640

Teece, D. J., & Pisano, G. (1994). The dynamic capabilities of firms: An introduction.
Industrial and Corporate Change, 3(3), 537–556. https://doi.org/10.1093/icc/3.3.537-a

Teece, D. J., Pisano, G., & Shuen, A. (1997). Dynamic capabilities and strategic management. *Strategic Management Journal*, *18*(7), 509–533. https://doi.org/10.1002/(SICI)1097-0266(199708)18:7<509::AID-SMJ882>3.0.CO;2-Z

The White House. (2018a). Executive order reimposing certain sanctions with respect to Iran. https://www.whitehouse.gov/presidential-actions/executive-order-reimposing-certain-sanctions-respect-iran/

The White House. (2018b). *Remarks by President Trump on the joint comprehensive plan of action*. https://www.whitehouse.gov/briefings-statements/remarks-president-trump-joint-comprehensive-plan-action/

Trading Economics. (2019). *Iran exports by category*. https://tradingeconomics.com/iran/exports-by-category

US Department of State. (2019). *Iran sanctions*. https://www.state.gov/e/eb/tfs/spi/iran/index.htm

Wang, C. Y.-P., Jaw, B.-S., & Tsai, C. H.-C. (2012). Building dynamic strategic capabilities: A human capital perspective. *The International Journal of Human Resource Management*, *23*(6), 1129–1157. https://doi.org/10.1080/09585192.2011.561234

Weick, K. E. (1993). The collapse of sensemaking in organizations: The Mann Gulch disaster. *Administrative Science Quarterly*, *38*(4), 628–652. https://doi.org/10.2307/2393339

Wilkinson, A., & Wood, G. (2017). Global trends and crises, comparative capitalism and HRM. *The International Journal of Human Resource Management*, *28*(18), 2503–2518. https://doi.org/10.1080/09585192.2017.1331624

Williams, T. A., Gruber, D. A., Sutcliffe, K. M., Shepherd, D. A., & Zhao, E. Y. (2017). Organizational response to adversity: Fusing crisis management and resilience research streams. *Academy of Management Annals*, *11*(2), 733–769. https://doi.org/10.5465/annals.2015.0134

Wood, G., Cooke, F. L., Demirbag, M., & Kwong, C. (2018). International human resource management in contexts of high uncertainties. *The International Journal of Human Resource Management*, *29*(7), 1365–1373. https://doi.org/10.1080/09585192.2018.1477547

World Bank. (2017). *Gdp Per capita*. https://data.worldbank.org/indicator/NY.GDP.PCAP.CD

World Bank. (2018a). *Iran's Economic Outlook - October 2018*. https://www.worldbank.org/en/country/iran/publication/economic-outlook-october-2018

World Bank. (2018b). *Islamic Republic of Iran*. https://www.worldbank.org/en/country/iran

WorldoMeters. (2019). *Iran population*. https://www.worldometers.info/world-population/iran-population/

Yin, R. K. (2014). *Case study research: Design and methods*. Sage Publications, Inc.

Zaefarian, R., Eng, T. Y., & Tasavori, M. (2016). An exploratory study of international opportunity identification among family firms. *International Business Review*, *25*(1), 333–345. https://doi.org/10.1016/j.ibusrev.2015.06.002

Zhang, J., Ahammad, M. F., Tarba, S., Cooper, C. L., Glaister, K. W., & Wang, J. (2015). The effect of leadership style on talent retention during merger and acquisition integration: Evidence from China. *The International Journal of Human Resource Management*, *26*(7), 1021–1050. https://doi.org/10.1080/09585192.2014.908316

Zhang, C., & Stewart, J. (2017). Talent management and retention. In H. W. Goldstein, E. D. Pulakos, J. Passmore, & C. Semedo (Eds.), *The wiley blackwell handbook of the psychology of recruitment, selection and employee retention*. Wiley Blackwell, 473–493.

Idiosyncratic deals in less competitive labor markets: testing career i-deals in the Greek context of high uncertainties

Anastasia A. Katou, Pawan S. Budhwar and Charmi Patel

ABSTRACT

This study investigates the impact of pre-hiring (ex-ante) and after-hiring (ex-post) negotiation on organizational citizen behavior (OCB), through three serially connected relationships: (1) between the timing of negotiation and career i-deals (idiosyncratic deals), moderated by feelings of self-worth; (2) between career i-deals and OCB, mediated by psychological contract fulfillment, and employee organizational commitment; and (3) between employer and employee psychological contract fulfillment, mediated by employee organizational commitment. To do so, it utilizes the social exchange theory, and a sample of 1768 employees working within 162 private organizations in the current context of high economic and financial uncertainties in Greece. Using a comprehensive framework tested by structural equation multilevel modeling, the study conclusions imply that in the less-competitive labor market of Greece, (a) core self-evaluation (CSE), which reflect individual differences, do not moderate the relationship between timing of negotiation and career i-deals, but independently predicts career i-deals; (b) career i-deals influence psychological contract expressed in promises fulfillment (PF); employee organizational commitment constitutes the binding epicenter of the relationships between employer and employees PF and between career i-deals and OCB. Based on these findings, the study has several theoretical and practical implications for high uncertainty contexts.

Introduction

Research on business and human resource management (HRM) in contexts of high uncertainties although is fragmented among many disciplines, there has been a great growth in recent years. For example, studies investigate the influence of turbulent times on HRM (e.g. Nijssen & Paauwe, 2012), voice and silence (e.g. Prouska & Psychogios, 2018a, 2018b; Schlosser & Zolin, 2012), adverse working conditions (e.g. Psychogios et al., 2019); and recessionary bundles (e.g. Teague & Roche, 2014). However, research on the influence of high uncertainty contexts on i-deals remains scarce. Questions focusing on changes of the bargaining power between employers and employees, during uncertain situations created by economic and financial crisis, are still unanswered. In particular, the influence of these changes in the bargaining power of employers and employees on HR outcomes has not been fully examined (Wood et al., 2018).

This study seeks to recognize the impact of changes in the bargaining power between employers and employees, expressed by i-deals negotiations, on employee attitudes and behaviors in a representative environment of high uncertainties like that of Greece. Considering that 'high uncertainly contexts do not affect different sectors uniformly' (Wood et al., 2018, p. 1370), the research framework is tested using data from a large national sample of Greece, covering private organizations in three sectors: manufacturing (e.g. home commodities production, food processing, electricity, mining); services (e.g. tourism, hotel and hospitality, health, education, banking); and trade (e.g. super markets, multi stores, distributive trades). Additionally, taking into consideration that individuals follow different paths in managing i-deals negotiations, our study covers individuals with different characteristics (e.g. related to demography and personality) and different psychological tendencies (e.g. psychological contract) in coping successfully responsibilities in turbulent situations (Wood et al., 2018, p. 1367). Overall, the current study investigates the serially mediating process of i-deals content and psychological contract (PC), in the relationship between the timing of i-deals negotiation and HR outcomes in periods of high uncertainty.

Specifically, since the influential study by Rousseau (2005), investigations (e.g. Anand et al., 2010; Ho & Kong, 2015; Hornung et al., 2009, 2014; Liu et al., 2013) have verified that i-deals are arranged in organizations to improve attitudinal (e.g. motivation, organizational commitment) and behavioral (e.g. work engagement, and organizational citizenship behavior – OCB) employee outcomes. I-deals refer to particular employment arrangements that are adapted to the personal preferences and requirements of employees (Ng & Feldman, 2015). Considering that i-deals content refers to the particular resources they include (Rousseau et al., 2006), it has been supported that the content of i-deals may differ. Accordingly, a typology for i-deals content has been proposed indicating *task i-deals* (i.e. the customized arrangements individual employees bargain to make their job content more inspiring and pleasant), *career i-deals* (i.e. the customized arrangements individual employees negotiate for advancing professional careers), and *flexibility i-deals* (i.e. the personalized arrangements individual employees negotiate for achieving time working schedules that better fit their requirements and preferences) (Hornung et al., 2014). Later, this typology has been extended including *location i-deals* (i.e. unique job arrangements that permit staff to get involved with the work in geographical places far from the office) (Ho & Kong, 2015; Liao et al., 2016) and *financial i-deals* (i.e. the payment arrangements that fit personal requests) (Rosen et al., 2013).

In spite of the development of i-deals literature, three important gaps still remain. First, although the structure of the connection between timing of negotiation and i-deals content is important for attracting and retaining talent, it may vary substantially due to differences in the national context of labor markets where negotiation is taking place (Rousseau et al., 2009). In particular, few studies have investigated this connection in less competitive labor markets experiencing severe economic and financial crisis and immense economic uncertainties (like Greece, amongst many others). Less competitive labor markets refer to the national contexts where the bargaining power in the negotiating process leans in favor of employers. In most cases, i-deals research has been focused within the context of competitive labor markets, such as Germany (e.g. Hornung et al., 2008, 2009), the USA (e.g. Lai et al., 2009; Ng & Feldman, 2010) and the UK (e.g. Coyle-Shapiro & Conway, 2005), where the bargaining power in the negotiating process leans in favor of employees. However, the 2008 global economic crisis produced high unemployment in many countries and people had to adapt to new economic realities (Bal & Dorenbosch, 2015). In these cases, where unemployment is high, and the labor market is accordingly considered to be less competitive, the bargaining power in the negotiating process leans in favor of employers. Thus, in stressful economic times of high uncertainties, it's an opportunity to examine the influence of the timing of i-deals negotiation and their content on employee outcomes.

Accordingly, the purpose of this research is to examine the relationship between i-deals and employee outcomes in the unique context of Greece, which being under severe economic and financial crises, with high unemployment, is categorized as a less competitive labor market (CIPD, 2016). This study focuses only on career i-deals, because we argue that in turbulent times, individuals put more emphasis on work safety which is reflected more by careers development than by other types of i-deals. In other words, employers grand career i-deals to those individuals who are valuable and trustworthy, and as such they support them and plan to keep them for longer periods in the organization (Rousseau, 2005). Individuals feel this practice of the organizations as a message that they are here to stay, thus reflecting job security in an adverse environment (Liao et al., 2016). Accordingly, the boundary conditions of our study distinguish between competitive and less competitive labor markets and the boundary conditions function refers to the accuracy of the predictions in the context of the less competitive labor markets (Busse et al., 2017).

Second, although i-deals are distinct from psychological contracts (Liao et al., 2016), and despite the increasing amount of research about both i-deals and psychological contracts (PCs) in describing the employment relationship (e.g. Kasekende et al., 2015; Lee & Hui, 2011), few studies have treated i-deals to be among the antecedents of PCs (Sturges et al., 2005). On the contrary, most studies were treating HRM policies to be the major predictors of PCs (Suazo et al., 2009). This is unexpected, taking into consideration the high increase in concern for outcomes from i-deals negotiation (Bal & Dorenbosch, 2015) and the fact that employees start developing their PCs about an organization even prior to hiring, and that this is further developed after hiring (Rousseau, 2005). Psychological contract is defined as 'an individual's system of belief, shaped by the organization, regarding terms of an exchange agreement between him/herself and the organization' (Rousseau & Greller, 1994, p. 385). As such, it is argued that PC is appropriate to separate labor market, reflecting the tendency of individuals to pursue i-deals from their employers. However, considering that i-deals content expresses the interests of both parties in negotiation, we argue that the content of i-deals constitutes the core mechanism that connects i-deals negotiation and PC. This is because i-deals content is the result of i-deals negotiation, which in turn establishes the quality of the employment relations reflected in the PC. Empirically, we may say that this is expressed in the objective nature of i-deals content constructs and in the subjective nature of PC constructs. Accordingly, we address this gap by investigating whether career i-deals mediate the timing of i-deals negotiation – PC relationship (Lee & Hui, 2011).

Third, research till now supports the view that the effects of i-deals on employee outcomes depend on their content (Hornung et al., 2008). Although, relatively few studies have been recently conducted in less developed countries such as the Philippines (Las Heras et al., 2017a, 2017b) and in under studied contexts such as Italy (Ng & Lucianetti, 2016), it is usually supported that in cases where employees are granted i-deals that meet their prospects they will respond positively (Ng &

Feldman, 2010; Sturges, 2012). Additionally, although i-deals are accepted to be a win-win case for both employers and employees (Rousseau, 2005), it is argued that this process depends upon the complexity of the environmental work context and the specific costs attached to it (Vidyarthi et al., 2014). Further, based on the social exchange expectation (Blau, 1964) between the employee and the employer, a number of the individual level employee outcomes attributed to i-deals are also credited to PCs (Rosen et al., 2013). Nevertheless, relatively little is known about why and how employees improve their outcomes as a reaction to getting i-deals (Ng & Feldman, 2015). However, the strength of this response may depend on the characteristics of the individuals to whom i-deals have been granted (Ng & Feldman, 2010). This may be true, and we argue that the characteristics of the individuals, such as gender, age, education, hierarchical position and personality, may be also important during i-deals negotiation. For example, apart from the type of the labor market, the feelings of self-worth may play a major role in how individuals conduct their i-deals negotiation. For that reason, we consider the state of self-worth as another boundary condition between negotiation and career i-deals (Busse et al., 2017) in periods of economic uncertainty.

Taking into consideration the above and based on the social exchange theory (SET) and the norm of reciprocity (Blau, 1964), this study investigates three serially connected relationships. First, between the timing of negotiation and career i-deals, moderated by feelings of self-worth (Ng & Feldman, 2010). We believe that self-worth illuminates this relationship because most studies that use CSE are focused on the 'one-step-later' relationship, between i-deals content and employee attitudes and behavior, bypassing the influence of CSE between the initiating influence of timing of negotiation on career i-deals (Ng & Feldman, 2010). Second, between career i-deals and OCB, mediated by psychological contract fulfillment (Bal et al., 2012), and employee organizational commitment. We consider that this angle of looking at things is important because most studies have investigated the direct influence of career i-deals on OCB (e.g. Liao et al., 2016), without offering new insights into this relationship. Third, employer and employee psychological contract fulfillment, mediated by employee organizational commitment (Katou & Budhwar, 2012). The rationale for the choice of the specific constructs and the proposed relationships is detailed in the next section. Thus, while scholars are more likely to examine how PC (and often its breach) leads to an employee negotiating i-deals (Ng & Feldman, 2012), we investigate the opposite, considering it is rather difficult for this sequence of events to take place in a less competitive labor market with high unemployment, produced by economic and financial crisis, and as such, we exclude the possibility of reverse causality. Finally, these serially connected processes are tested in the current context of high economic and financial uncertainties in Greece, using multilevel structural equation analyses due to the nested nature of data (Muthen & Muthen, 2014).

Research framework and hypotheses

The Greek context

Greece although is a member-state of the European Union, it has been seriously affected by the 2008 economic and financial crises. Large fiscal and current account deficits have been running for many years and inefficacy and corruption in most aspects of public administration has resulted in inefficient organizations. A total of 244,712 firms have been closed in the period 2008–2015, with a loss of 842,670 jobs in that period. The decrease in the number of businesses comes from bankruptcies or closure of businesses as well as from companies that have moved their operations abroad (for details see Bellos, 2017).

In this bleak picture, Greek firms are trying to avoid closure and employees are struggling to stay in employment. Many small and medium enterprises (SME) ignore labor law legislations and compensate employees to lower levels than the current labor laws indicate (Wood et al., 2016). Greece, being a member-state of the Euro-zone, and having agreed on a Memorandum of Economic and Financial Practices with the three institutions (i.e. EC, IMF, and ECB), had to implement policies to reinforce market assurance and make the economy more competitive. In this respect, the working conditions changed by relaxing the standard level of the weekly eight hours, cutting reward rates, extending the working week time, and intensifying work conditions (Wood et al., 2016). In general, the worker rights seemed to be more precarious in Greek SME than in other countries (Psychogios & Wood, 2010).

Nevertheless, the extent to which employment terms and conditions are negotiable in Greece may depend on its labor market characteristics. Greece is considered to belong to a low degree zone of negotiability, which refers 'to the conditions of employment available for negotiation by workers and their employer' (Rousseau, 2001, p. 264). This is because most employment conditions are pre-specified by the Eurozone central directives. But, considering the high level of unemployment in Greece (about 25 percent), the bargaining power of individuals (employed or unemployed) is rather weak, reflecting a less competitive labor market.

The timing of negotiation and career i-deals

I-deals can be negotiated either before hiring (ex-ante), or after hire (ex-post) or both prior and during employment (Rousseau, 2005). In general, it is argued that people usually tend to negotiate ex-post i-deals more often than ex-ante i-deals (Rousseau et al., 2006). This is because ex-ante negotiation is taking place only at a limited time, for example before hiring period, may be considered to be a static phenomenon. In contrast, ex-post negotiation may be considered to be dynamic because it is taking part during the on-going employment relationship between an employer and employees (Chand et al., 2017). However, negotiation of i-deals is linked with the individual differences which are usually reflected in self-worth (e.g. core self-evaluations) and demographics (e.g. age, gender, education) (Ng & Feldman, 2010), along with the power of the two parties (i.e. the employee and the employer) involved in negotiation which is usually based on the characteristics of the labor market (e.g. more or less competitive) (Rousseau et al., 2006).

Core self-evaluations (CSE) refer to the basic properties people hold about themselves (Judge et al., 1997). Four specific traits indicate CSE. *Self-esteem* indicates the extent to which individuals believe that they are people of worth. *Self-efficacy* indicates the extent to which individuals believe that they are able to efficiently perform tasks. *Emotional stability* is the extent to which individuals believe that they are mentally healthy and useful. *Locus of control* is the extent to which individuals believe that they can control their own future. In general, individuals who believe to have high assessments about these four CES traits are considered to have high self-evaluation (Ng & Feldman, 2010).

The construct of CSE has been used in earlier research mostly as an independent variable that influences employee outcomes (Judge et al., 1998). In later research, studies tried to investigate the moderating effect of CES in various employee relationships and the independent variable effects on i-deals (Chand et al., 2017). It is argued that individuals with feelings of high self-evaluation negotiate strongly both ex-ante and ex-post i-deals believing that they are entitled to these i-deals. On the contrary, individuals with feelings of low self-evaluation negotiate weak ex-ante or ex-post ideals, and if taken together, these i-deals will feel much obligated and as such they will try strongly to reciprocate (Ng & Feldman, 2010).

In competitive labor markets (with low unemployment rates), where the supply of certain skills and abilities is lower than demand, the power is more on the side of highly marketable employees (Rousseau, 2001). This is because employers trying to attract talent are likely to grant ex-ante i-deals to important human resources according to their knowledge, skills and abilities (KSAs), reflecting their market value (Rousseau et al., 2006). Additionally, in such markets employers in trying to retain productive employees usually grant ex-post i-deals to employees after they have proven to be honest and important (Rousseau, 2005). Thus, employers being afraid of losing employees that have proven to be good and are difficult to replace, put more emphasis on ex-post i-deals than on ex-ante i-deals. Accordingly, in such a context, it is usually assumed that the degree of ex-post i-deals is higher than the degree of ex-ante i-deals (Rousseau et al., 2009).

On the contrary, in less competitive labor markets such as those existing over the last 10 years in Greece due to economic crisis (e.g. financial crises, deep recession), the power is more on the side of the employer. This is because in such markets the supply of certain skills is higher than demand, resulting in high unemployment and low wages and salaries. Thus, candidates or existing employees may feel weak in negotiating either ex-ante or ex-post i-deals. For example, candidates before hire may think that they may not get the job by pushing negotiation too hard, otherwise another candidate with similar qualifications may be chosen. Similarly, workers in jobs may fear being substituted by others from the unemployed candidate pool if they push negotiation too hard for their demands. Accordingly, the power of negotiation is with employers in such markets.

It is further argued that negotiation in terms of timing and i-deals with respect to content are interdependent (Rousseau et al., 2009). Research referring to the timing of negotiation and i-deals usually considers that the employment relationship takes place in a competitive labor market context. In this context, employees during ex-ante negotiation are usually concentrating on getting tangible i-deals such as payment and work schedules. On the contrary, employees during ex-post negotiation is likely to concentrate on getting intangible i-deals such as mentoring and work promotion paths (Rousseau et al., 2009). However, in less-competitive labor markets this may not be true as individuals may feel weak in negotiating either ex-ante or ex-post i-deals. Therefore, we argue that the employment relationship is quasi-symmetric between employed and unemployed individuals in markets with high unemployment.

All types of i-deals content (i.e. task, career, flexibility, location, and financial i-deals) are usually granted in competitive labor markets (Ho & Kong, 2015; Hornung et al., 2014; Liao et al., 2016; Rosen et al., 2013). However, in less competitive labor markets this may not hold. In particular, in less competitive labor markets, such as Greece, unemployed people trying to find a job do not have the power to enter negotiation.

They just want to get the job. This is because under the austerity conditions that usually prevail in these markets, individuals believe that they do not have the luxury to ask for work that fits their personal strengths (i.e. task i-deals) or work that is customized to their needs (i.e. flexibility i-deals). Individuals with high self-evaluation may accept temporarily any ex-ante i-deal, or employed people being scared of losing their job may accept any ex-post i-deal postponing temporarily career opportunities. This is because individuals try to reconcile future career targets with current other i-deals priorities (King, 2004). Individuals do not have the privilege to ask for location i-deals because they also know that employers, especially in SMEs such as those of Greece, do not value location i-deals. This is based on the supposition that employers tend to identify location i-deals with low efficient activities when people work within the family context (Las Heras et al., 2017a). Individuals do not have the authority to request for financial i-deals because they know that other people from the unemployment pool are ready to accept smaller wages (Kousta & Stamati, 2012). Generally, people are less likely to talk about and seek for financial i-deals in such settings because of secrecy surrounding them and people do not often like to talk about rewards and compensation (Marescaux et al., 2019).

In summary, taking into consideration that in both competitive and less competitive labor markets with high uncertainties 'individuals are becoming increasingly responsible for managing their own careers (Briscoe & Hall, 2006)' (cited in Ng & Feldman, 2010, p. 419), and that seek to find jobs or keep their jobs that prescribe future safety. This study concentrates on career i-deals for both theoretical and practical reasons because it is not possible to include other types of i-deals in one paper. This is because career i-deals by referring to personal goals, development opportunities and professional advancement (Schaufeli et al., 2002) make them to feel more secure. Additionally, when individuals develop in the organization the employer has more information about them (and presumably have invested more in the employee) than when the individual is new to the organization. Thus, the extent of the static phenomenon of ex-ante negotiation is less than the extent of the dynamic ex-post negotiation. Nevertheless, the relationship between ex-ante or ex-post negotiation and career i-deals may be moderated by CSE. Thus, taking into account that a small number of studies have investigated career i-deals with respect to the timing of negotiation (Hornung et al., 2010; Liao et al., 2016), we hypothesize that:

Hypothesis 1: *(a) CSE moderates the relationship between ex-ante negotiation and career i-deals, and (b) CSE moderates the relationship between ex-post negotiation and career i-deals, such that the relationships are stronger for individuals high on CSE.*

Career i-deals, organizational commitment and psychological contract

Although i-deals are related to psychological contracts (Lee & Hui, 2011), the two concepts are undoubtedly different (Hornung et al., 2014). After successful negotiation, i-deals constitute specific and official arrangements that enable employees to acquire things that their peers did not get (Guerrero et al., 2014). In contrast, the PC represents an individual's beliefs regarding employee and employer obligations, which refer to the terms and conditions that constitute the employment relationship (Robinson & Rousseau, 1994). In particular, the PC of an employee refers to his/hers beliefs about the obligations of the employer to him/her (also called inducements) and his/hers obligations to the employer (also called contributions) (Bordia et al., 2017). PCs are considered to be subjective to a great extent (McDonald & Makin, 2000). However, despite this subjectivity there are many common features that usually classify PCs into two categories. The first category is called *transactional contracts* and it includes features such as performance-based pay and competitive wage rates, which have the characteristics of being specific, short-term, and monetary-in-nature beliefs. This second category is called *relational contracts* and it includes features such as career development, job security commitment, trust, and loyalty, which have the characteristics of being less specific, long-term and monetary and non-monetary-in-nature beliefs (Rousseau, 1995).

Despite the economic turbulence and high unemployment in less competitive labor markets, talent remains a fundamental source of competiveness for companies across industries. Strategic HRM has become increasingly important means for realizing the value that exists in employees. Scholars (e.g. Kroon et al., 2015) position i-deals as a strategic choice within strategic HRM and introduce i-deals as part of HRM policies in the organization. They argue that strategic HRM combines standardized HRM practices and i- deals as part of the process of managing human capital. As such, taking into consideration that PCs are important predictors of employee outcomes most studies support that strategic HRM practices are major predictors of PCs (Suazo et al., 2009). In particular, Guest (2004) supports the view that PCs are influenced over time by i-deals. In practice, employees negotiate i-deals to adjust their jobs to better suit their personal circumstances and thus shape the employer-employee relationship reflected in their PC (Meijerink, 2014). In simple words, career i-deals influence employer and employee promises fulfillment because employers having granted career i-deals try to keep their promises, and employees having got career i-deals try to reciprocate by also keeping their promises. In this study, we focus on the employer promises fulfillment as perceived by employees, who are likely to reciprocate by fulfilling their own promises (Conway & Briner, 2005; De Jong et al., 2009; Katou & Budhwar, 2012).

This is due to the fact that the outcomes of the psychological contract are more strongly related to the fulfillment of promises than to promises per se (Lambert et al., 2003; Katou & Budhwar, 2012).

Considering that i-deals constitute a dimension of the strategic HRM process of managing human capital and that PCs can be considered as obligations that gush from the achievement of i-deals (Lee et al., 2011), we argue that career i-deals positively influence organizational commitment both directly and indirectly through PCs. Meyer and Allen (1991) describe organizational commitment with respect to the extent an individual is attached to the organization and 'has at least three separable components reflecting: (a) a desire (affective commitment), (b) a need (continuance commitment), and (c) an obligation (normative commitment) to maintain employment in an organization' (p. 61). Career i-deals directly influence organizational commitment, because 'perceptions of idiosyncratic deals may increase employees' trust in their employers and cement their bonds with them (Rousseau, 2005)' (Ng & Feldman, 2010, p. 420). They will indirectly influence organizational commitment through PCs because 'the state of the psychological contract in terms of fulfillment or breach will result in positive or negative employee attitudes, respectively, which in turn will have an impact on employees in fulfilling their promises' (Katou & Budhwar, 2012, p. 796). Thus, we argue that organizational commitment is the heart that joins career i-deals and psychological contract. Accordingly, we hypothesize that:

Hypothesis 2: (a) Career i-deals are positively related to organizational commitment and employer and employee promises fulfillment, and (b) organizational commitment will mediate the relationship between employer and employee promises fulfillment.

Organizational commitment, psychological contract and OCB

It is generally accepted that those employees who will get i-deals may feel obliged to their employer and in return they will react positively (Anand et al., 2010). Although there are many types of employee outcomes considered individually in studies, we focus on the attitudinal outcome of organizational commitment and the behavioral outcome of OCB. *OCB* refers to work behavior that exceeds what is dictated by the job description (Organ, 1988), and usually is described with the five dimensions of *altruism* (i.e. behaving in a way that demonstrates selflessness and concern for the welfare of others), *courtesy* (i.e. taking actions that help prevent problems of occurring, or taking advance actions to mitigate a problem), *sportsmanship* (i.e. choosing not to complaint or act in negative ways), conscientiousness (i.e. exhibiting commitment to high levels of work quality and completion), and *civic virtue* (i.e. adopting a posture of responsible, constructive involvement in the political or governance process of the organization) (Somech & Drach-Zahavy, 2018, p. 529).

I-deals are known to influence PCs, however, most studies have focused on the implications of their breach or violation instead of their fulfillment (Nelson & Tonks, 2007). This study focuses on the fulfillment of PCs in terms of both the employer and the employee fulfillment (De Jong et al., 2009). This is because the fulfillment of promises influences more heavily PC outcomes than promises as such (Lambert et al., 2003). In particular, based on the SET, it is argued that fulfillment of the PC positively influences employee outcomes (Gardner et al., 2015), because this fulfillment is reciprocated by employee motivation, commitment, satisfaction and OCB (Agarwal, 2014; Coyle-Shapiro & Kessler, 2000). 'Nearly all conceptualizations of the psychological contract emphasize two elements of the employee psychological contract: the 'taking' of employer inducements obligates the employee to 'give' in terms of contributions' (Bordia et al., 2017, p. 3). In particular, in less competitive labor markets, employees are strongly interested in engaging more to relational than to transactional psychological contracts, inferring that the type of the employer-employee relationship is of social exchange nature (Lee & Hui, 2011; Rousseau et al., 2009).

We argued previously that career i-deals directly influence organizational commitment (Ng & Feldman, 2010). However, taking into consideration that attitudinal outcomes predict behavioural outcomes (Guest, 1997), we argue that organizational commitment predicts OCB. Combining these two relationships we argue that organizational commitment mediates the relationship between career i-deals and OCB. Accordingly, we hypothesize that:

> **Hypothesis 3:** *(a) Organizational citizen behavior is positively related to employer and employee promises fulfillment, and (b) organizational commitment will mediate the relationship between career i-deals and organizational citizen behavior.*

Based on the above-presentation, Figure 1 presents our conceptual and hypothesized model.

Method

Sample and procedure

Survey data were collected between October and December 2015 from 400 private firms with more than 20 employees operating in three Greek sectors (manufacturing, services, and trade). For increasing the reliability of measures (Gerhart et al., 2000) and the generalization of conclusions (Hochwarter,

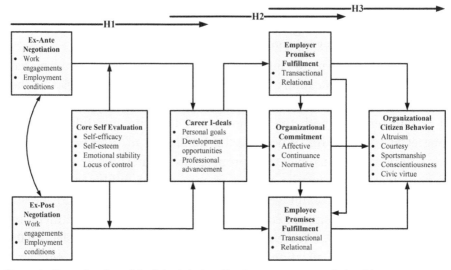

Figure 1. Operational model of the i-deals – Employee outcomes relationship.

2014), we collected at least 10 responses from three actors within each firm (senior managers, middle managers, low level employees). We managed to get 1768 questionnaires from 162 firms, resulting in 40.50 percent firm level response rate and 44.2 percent employee level response rate.

The distribution of the 162 sample organizations is as follows: 75.9 percent had 20 to 100 employees, 14.2 percent had 101 to 200 employees, and 9.9 percent had more than 200 employees; 18.5 percent were manufacturing firms, 35.8 percent services firms, and 45.7 percent trade firms. The characteristics of the 1768 sample respondents are as follows: 54.3 percent were male, and 45.7 percent female; 2.1 percent had elementary education, 31.2 percent high school/lyceum education, and 66.7 percent had college/university degree. The average age of respondents was 37.22 (±9.81) years old, and the average seniority was 8.61 (±7.58) years. 84.0 percent had full-time contract and 16.0 percent had part-time contract. Finally, 19.2 percent were senior managers, 20.4 percent were middle managers, and 60.5 percent were lower level employees.

Measures

Unless otherwise indicated, we used a five-level Likert scale and/or a five-point ordinal scale.

I-deals timing: We followed Rousseau et al. (2009) for measuring ex-ante (Cronbach's $\alpha = 0.915$) and ex-post ($\alpha = 0.896$) negotiation. Each dimension had two items.

I-deals content: We followed Hornung et al. (2014) for measuring career support ($\alpha = 0.894$).

Psychological contract: This scale was developed following the CIPD (2012) fact sheet. In particular, the employer promises fulfillment (PF) construct ($\alpha = 0.806$) comprised of transactional ($\alpha = 0.878$) and relational ($\alpha = 0.922$) PF, and the employee promises fulfillment construct ($\alpha = 0.763$) comprised of transactional ($\alpha = 0.767$) and relational ($\alpha = 0.864$) PF.

Attitudinal employee outcomes: The organizational commitment scale ($\alpha = 0.754$) developed by Allen and Meyer (1990), has three sub-scales – affective commitment ($\alpha = 0.918$), continuance commitment ($\alpha = 0.714$), and normative commitment ($\alpha = 0.706$).

Behavioral employee outcomes: The OCB scale ($\alpha = 0.795$) developed by Niehoff and Moorman (1993), has the five sub-scales of altruism ($\alpha = 0.868$), courtesy ($\alpha = 0.799$), sportsmanship ($\alpha = 0.806$), conscientiousness ($\alpha = 0.771$), and civic virtue ($\alpha = 0.854$).

Many controls influence the i-deals – outcomes relationship (Ng & Feldman, 2010). These controls are usually classified between *organizational controls* (e.g. sector, size), *personal controls* (e.g. gender, age, education), and *employment individual controls* (e.g. tenure, seniority, hierarchy).

Data properties and statistical analysis

All Cronbach alphas reported previously are higher than 0.70, indicating construct internal consistency. In Table 1, the values of the average variances extracted (AVE) obtained by confirmatory factor analysis (CFA) are presented. All these values are higher than 0.50, indicating that the instrument construct validity is acceptable (Hair et al., 2008). Additionally, in Table 1 the composite reliability scores are reported. Considering that these scores are very close to 0.90, they indicate that construct composite reliability is adequate (Pavlou & Gefen, 2005). Finally, the correlation coefficients between all constructs used in the study are also reported in Table 1. All these coefficients are smaller than the square root of the corresponding AVE, ensuring that the constructs are separate (Hair et al., 2008).

Considering the hierarchical nature of our data, with employees nested within organizations, we adopted multilevel structural equation modeling (MSEM) *via* Mplus (Muthen & Muthen, 2014) in testing our multilevel model (MLM).

Results

The measurement model

While testing the hypothesized structure, the analyses showed acceptable fit (Chi-Square = 1332.584 df = 404, $p = 0.000$, Normed-Chi-Square =

Table 1. Means, standard deviations, reliability indices, and correlation coefficients of the constructs used in the study.

Constructs	Means (standard deviations)	Construct composite reliability	Correlation coefficients						
			Ex-ante negotiation	Ex-post negotiation	Career i-deals	Employer promises fulfillment	Employee promises fulfillment	Organizational commitment	OCB
Ex-ante negotiation	2.618 (0.801)	0.971	[0.943]*						
Ex-post negotiation	2.874 (0.713)	0.961	0.730	[0.925]					
Career i-deals	3.512 (0.931)	0.934	0.382	0.364	[0.863]				
Employer promises fulfillment	3.696 (0.840)	0.918	0.343	0.295	0.516	[0.752]			
Employee promises fulfillment	4.034 (0.613)	0.896	0.151	0.123	0.326	0.549	[0.673]		
Organizational commitment	3.841 (0.660)	0.859	0.204	0.165	0.461	0.593	0.524	[0.669]	
OCB	4.123 (0.537)	0.863	0.110	0.110	0.366	0.514	0.615	0.586	[0.503]

Notes: All correlation coefficients are significant at $p < 0.01$.
*Average Variance Extracted (AVE).

3.298, RMSEA = 0.036, CFI = 0.947, TLI = 0.934, SRMR-within = 0.039, SRMR-between = 0.120). Further, we examined all factor loadings and their squares for evaluating indicator reliability and we conclude that all measures are meaningfully related to their proposed latent dimensions. Next, we compared the fit of the proposed measurement model to an alternative less restrictive model, with all items loading on a single factor. This model was found to fit worse than the hypothesized model (Chi-Square = 8825.286 df = 460, $p = 0.000$, Normed-Chi-Square = 19.185, RMSEA = 0.101, CFI = 0.523, TLI = 0.475, SRMR-within = 0.128, SRMR-between = 0.499), supporting the proposed factor structure of the constructs used in this study. Additionally, comparing the results of these two MCFA (i.e. Δchi-square = 7492.702, Δdf = 56, Δratio = Δchi-square/Δdf = 133.798), we conclude that the latent factors represent distinct constructs and that common method bias is limited because the Δratio = 133.798 is much larger that the critical value of 3.84 per degree of freedom (see Brown, 2015).

Structural model

Before estimating the operational model, we investigated the necessary conditions justifying multilevel analysis. The intra-correlation coefficients ICC1 found to range between 0.128 (for self-esteem) and 0.249 (for affective commitment). Because these values are larger than 0.10, there is sufficient between-unit variation to justify multilevel analysis. The intra-correlation coefficients ICC2 found to range between 0.784 (for altruism) and 0.986 (for civic virtue). Because these values are larger than 0.50, the constructs ensure that there is sufficient within-unit agreement to justify aggregation. Similarly, the inter-rater agreement measures $r_{wg}(j)$ found to range between 0.786 (for employer promises fulfillment) and 0.967 (for OCB). As these values are larger than 0.70, the constructs ensure that there is also sufficient within-unit agreement to justify aggregation (see Kozlowski & Klein, 2000).

In estimating the operational model of the study, we estimated two MLM: a CSE moderating model, as it is presented in Figure 1, and a mediating model treating CSE as an independent construct. With respect to the moderating model, the fit indices were very poor (Chi-Square = 16072.752, df = 548, $p = 0.000$, Normed Chi-Square = 29.330, RMSEA = 0.127, CFI = 0.563, TLI = 0.505, SRMR-within = 0.212, SRMR-between = 0.237) and the interaction terms of CSE$\times$(Ex-ante negotiation) and CSE$\times$(Ex-post negotiation) were not significant. Thus, we turned to the mediating model. Figures 2 and 3 present the MLM estimation results for the within and the between dimensions of the

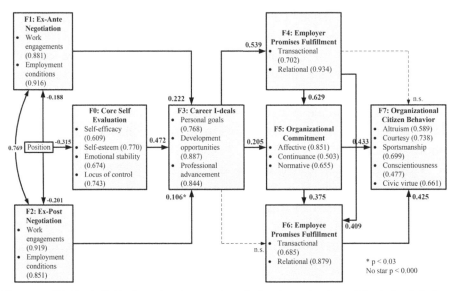

Figure 2. Within individuals estimation results of the Operational model of the i-deals – Employee outcomes relationship.

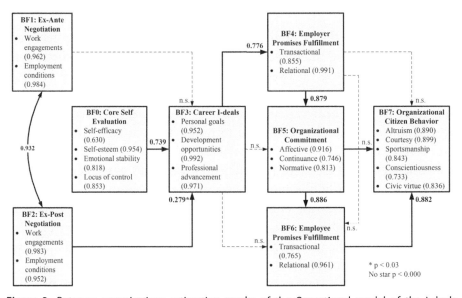

Figure 3. Between organizations estimation results of the Operational model of the i-deals – Employee outcomes relationship.

mediating operational model respectively, where all the variables included were significant. Given the fit indices (Chi-Square = 1902.685, df = 460, $p=0.000$, Normed Chi-Square = 4.136, RMSEA = 0.042, CFI = 0.919, TLI = 0.907, SRMR-within = 0.086, SRMR-between = 0.163), the variety of information and the sensibility of estimates, we can accept the model as a plausible representation of the data.

Testing the hypotheses

The results reported in Figure 2 (within) indicate that both ex-ante and ex-post negotiation predict career i-deals, and in Figure 3 (between) ex-post negotiation predicts career i-deals. However, hypothesis 1 is not supported, as we previously mentioned, the interaction effects between CSE and ex-ante or ex-post constructs were not significant. On the contrary, CSE as an independent construct strongly predicts career i-deals. Thus, we may say that this result verifies the view of existing research (e.g. Judge et al., 1998) that CES independently influences employee outcomes. Moreover, utilizing a paired t-test between the means presented in Table 1, we see that the extent of ex-post negotiation (mean 2.874 ± 0.713) is significantly larger than the extent of ex-ante negotiation (mean 2.618 ± 0.801). This means that this finding, which holds for completive labor markets (Rousseau et al., 2009) is also true for less competitive labor markets. This is perhaps due to the dynamic on-going nature of ex-post negotiation compared to the static nature of ex-ante negotiation. Additionally, we see that employment conditions constitute the prevailing factor in ex-ante negotiation whilst work arrangements constitute the prevailing factor in ex-post negotiation, self-esteem is the prevailing factor in CSE, and development opportunities is prevailing factor in career i-deals.

Results reported in Figure 2 indicate that career i-deals are positively related to organizational commitment and employer promises fulfillment, whilst results in Figure 3 indicate that career i-deals positively predict only employer promises fulfillment. Thus, hypothesis 2(a) is partially supported. In terms of the structure of PC, we see that both in Figures 2 and 3 organizational commitments mediate the relationship between employer and employee promises fulfillment, supporting thus hypothesis 2(b). In particular, considering Figure 2, we see that organizational commitment partially mediates the relationship between employer and employee promises fulfillment (total $= 0.645$, total indirect $= 0.236$, $p = 0.000$), and employer promises fulfillment partially mediates the relationship between career-ideals and organizational commitment (total $= 0.544$, total indirect $= 0.339$, $p = 0.000$). Considering Figure 2, we see that organizational commitment fully mediates the relationship between employer and employee promises fulfillment (total $= 0.779$, total indirect $= 0.779$, $p = 0.000$), and employer promises fulfillment fully mediates the relationship between career-ideals and organizational commitment (total $= 0.682$, total indirect $= 0.682$, $p = 0.000$). Additionally, we see that affective commitment constitutes the prevailing factor in organizational commitment, and relational PC constitutes the prevailing factor in both employer and employee promises fulfillment.

Results reported in Figures 2 and 3 indicate that OCB is positively and directly related to employee promises fulfillment only, thus, partially supporting hypothesis 3(a). Additionally, taking into consideration the 'small picture' of the mediation mechanism, we see that organizational commitment mediates the relationship between career i-deals and OCB according to the results in Figure 2, and it is not mediating this relationship according to the results of Figure 3. However, taking into consideration the 'large picture' of the mediation mechanism, we see that in both Figures 2 and 3 results, organizational commitment mediates the relationship between career i-deals and OCB. This is because for Figure 2 we get a significant serially mediating mechanism (total $= 0.416$, total indirect $= 0.416$, $p = 0.000$), and a similar mediating mechanism for Figure 3 (total $= 0.533$, total indirect $= 0.533$, $p = 0.000$). Therefore, hypothesis 3(b) is supported. Additionally, we see that courtesy constitutes the prevailing factor in OCB.

Finally, considering the controls used in the study, the significant results derived are those presented in Figure 2 and refer to the position of the individual. From these results we see that negotiation is weaker for non-managerial employees, and non-managerial employees seem to have lower self-evaluation.

Discussion

Grounded in the social exchange theory, the purpose of this study is to investigate the relationship between the timing of i-deals negotiation and OCB, for understanding the employment relationship in Greece, which is under severe economic and financial crises. Completeness is the major asset of this study since it incorporates in the proposed model: (1) timing of i-deals expressed by both ex-ante and ex-post negotiations; (2) content of i-deals referring to career i-deals; (3) CSE as a possible moderating factor when negotiating career i-deals; (4) both employer and employee perspectives of PC fulfillment; (5) employee attitudinal mediating outcomes such as organizational commitment, and (6) employee behavioral ultimate outcomes, such as OCB. Therefore, this study augments the relevant literature and offers a number of both theoretical and practical implications.

Theoretical implications

Considering that the literature is limited in relating i-deals to PC (Liao et al., 2016), our study advances the debate by arguing that i-deals influence the formation of psychological contracts in less competitive labor markets due to economic and financial crises and the resultant high uncertainties. Rousseau and Greller (1994) argue that PCs constitute a system of individual's beliefs with respect to the terms and conditions of an exchange agreement between the individual and the organization. This system is subjective, and it is shaped by the general practices the organization is advancing aiming at all individuals. In our study we argue that it is not only the general practices the organization is advancing aiming at all individuals, but it is also the specific practices reflected in i-deals that the organization advances aiming at specific individuals. Thus, we argue that PCs have two dimensions based on the initiating factors that shape them: the general (as a result of the practices aiming at all individuals) and the specific (as a result of i-deals aiming at specific individuals). In our study, we have concentrated on the career i-deals specific dimension of PCs. It would be interesting for future research to investigate and compare the effects of these two dimensions of PCs.

It is usually argued that the reactions of individuals to events are influenced by how worthy they view themselves (Chang et al., 2012). In this study we found that although CSE is not moderating the relationship between timing of negotiation and career i-deals, when CSE, and especially self-esteem of individuals is improving then they achieve better career i-deals, and especially development opportunities. Thus, we suggest that future research should investigate the moderating – mediating alternatives in the relationship between timing of negotiation and career or other i-deals.

Responding to calls for more studies investigating the effects of i-deals on the employment relationship (e.g. Liao et al., 2016), we included in our investigation two relevant mediating relationships: the career i-deals and OCB relationship through organizational commitment; and the employer employee promises fulfillment relationship through organizational commitment. We found that career i-deals create a work environment that brings out bonds between PC and attitudinal and behavioural outcomes. In particular, bearing in mind that career i-deals influence PCs, we argue that not only the results of PCs are based in social exchange theory but also the results of both career i-deals and PCs are based in this theory. This is reflected in the finding that organizational commitment constitutes the 'heart mediating bond' of two distinct relationships: the first is between employer and employee promises fulfillment, and the other is between career i-deals and OCB. Thus, future research would benefit from examining this 'heart mediating bond'.

However, we further argue that 'social' exchange is framed within the 'social context' where i-deals and PCs refer. In other words, we agree with the extant literature that in competitive labor markets (like those of the western economies) at the time of ex-ante negotiation individuals are more likely to engage in transactional PCs and at the time of ex- post negotiation individuals are more likely to engage in relational PC (Rousseau et al., 2009). In contrast, we argue that this picture is reversed when we refer to the Greek context. This is because in its labor market, where unemployment is high, individuals are looking for i-deals, such as career i-deals, that will ensure security (e.g. tenure) for the rest of their working life. This means that individuals are more engaged in relational than in transactional PCs. This is also evident from our findings, which indicate that PCs are more influenced by ex-ante negotiation (when referring to within individuals estimation), and more influenced by ex-post negotiation (when referring to between organizations estimation). Accordingly, we believe that we have provided evidence that in contexts of high uncertainties the influence of ex-ante and ex-post negotiation on transactional and relational PC is reversed in comparison with their influence in competitive labor markets. In other words, crises change the psychological state of people, who in turbulent times chose more security than money.

Managerial implications

Based on the findings that apart of ex-ante and ex-post negotiation, CSE constitutes a largely significant personality factor in shaping career i-deals, and that career i-deals create a work environment that ties together PC and attitudinal and behavioural outcomes, the role of man-agers is very important in translating negotiation into obtainment (Rofcanin et al., 2017), in contexts with high uncertainties such as Greece. First, managers having granted career i-deals should fulfill their promises, because this fulfillment will activate employee organizational commitment, that in turn, will push employees also to fulfill their prom-ises (Katou & Budhwar, 2012). Second, considering that in turbulent times, employee work safety *via* career development i-deals is of high importance to employees, managers should support the building of rela-tional PCs, since these contracts by producing a feeling of security to employees makes them to reciprocate accordingly. Third, considering that 'workers are more likely to attribute their ex-post i-deals to the qual-ity of their relationship with their employers' (Rousseau et al., 2006, p. 983), managers should enhance this attribute by trying to improve the employment relationship. Fourth, although employees asking for ex-ante career i-deals are in a weak negotiating position when unemployment is high, managers should try professionally to ascertain the positive charac-teristics of the prospective employees.

Limitations

This study has a number of limitations. First, the cross-sectional nature of the data could imply a contrary sequence of events and accordingly it is very difficult to support dynamic causal inferences. Therefore, future studies should focus on longitudinal data, which give the opportunity to investigate the lagged effects of i-deals negotiation on employee attitudinal and behavioral outcomes through PCs that in turn improve organizational performance. Second, although the estimation methodology followed is based on MLM, the use of self-reporting multiple respondents within senior managers, middle managers, and other employees in each firm may have not eliminated common method bias. Third, following Schaufeli (2015), in estimation we allowed correlations between pairs of associated errors of constructs (e.g. ex-ante and ex-post negotiation), taking into consideration that there is possibly no clear-cut between some latent constructs. Fourth, all variables were reported in retrospect, raising measurement concerns (especially for the ex-ante negotiation) about recall bias (Lippman & Mackenzie, 1985). Finally, in generalizing the results of this study, future research should be directed to countries that experience similar economic and financial crises or economic depression.

Conclusion

In an effort to uncover the positive impact of i-deals on organizational performance, previous research has provided wide-ranging empirical evidence of i-deals on employee outcomes. The current study is to some extent analogous with Rousseau et al. (2009), who examined the influence of timing of negotiation on social and economic exchange, through the mediating influence of work hour and development i-deals, and Lee and Hui (2011), who examined the influence of employee characteristics on employer and employee PCs, through the mediating influence of timing and content of i-deals. As indicated above, our model is comprehensive since it integrates important and related sets of constructs. Although the data used is from the Greek context, which is experiencing high unemployment and 'other work anomalies, such as the widespread underpayment of high performers relative to low performers' (Rousseau, 2005 cited in Anand et al., 2010) due to a severe economic and financial crisis, the model connecting career i-deals with attitudinal and behavioral employee outcomes seemed to work rather well in this less competitive labor market, supporting that 'i-deals are not limited to workers in competitive markets' (Hornung et al., 2008, p. 661). In particular, taking into consideration the purpose of the study, we believe that career i-deals content, which is objective in nature, and employer and employee PC fulfillment, which is subjective in nature, constitute the mediating epicenter of the timing of negotiation and employee outcomes relationship. Moreover, the study supports the view that context constitutes a critical factor in studying i-deals. In other words, competitive versus less competitive labor markets due to various forms of crisis where organizations are operating should be considered when studying i-deals.

Disclosure statement

No potential conflict of interest was reported by the authors.

References

Agarwal, U. A. (2014). Linking justice, trust and innovative work behaviour to work engagement. *Personnel Review, 43*, 1, 41–73.

Allen, N. J., & Meyer, J. P. (1990). The measurement and antecedents of affective, continuance, and normative commitment to the organization. *Journal of Occupational Psychology, 63*(1), 1–18. https://doi.org/10.1111/j.2044-8325.1990.tb00506.x

Anand, S., Vidyarthi, P. R., Liden, R. C., & Rousseau, D. M. (2010). Good citizens in poor-quality relationships: Idiosyncratic deals as a substitute for relationship quality. *Academy of Management Journal, 53*(5), 970–988. https://doi.org/10.5465/amj.2010.54533176

Bal, P. M., De Jong, S. B., Jansen, P. G. W., & Bakker, A. B. (2012). Motivating employees to work beyond retirement: A multi-level study of the role of i-deals and unit climate. *Journal of Management Studies, 49*(2), 306–331. https://doi.org/10.1111/j.1467-6486.2011.01026.x

Bal, P. M., & Dorenbosch, L. (2015). Age-related differences in the relations between individualised HRM and organisational performance: A large-scale employer survey. *Human Resource Management Journal, 25*(1), 41–61. https://doi.org/10.1111/1748-8583.12058

Bellos, I. (2017). Business sector in Greece shrank by over 244,000 firms in just seven years. *ekathimerini.com,* May 11. www.ekathimerini.com/208159/article/

Blau, P. (1964). *Exchange and power in social life.* Wiley.

Bordia, P., Restubog, S. L. D., Bordia, R. L., & Tang, R. L. (2017). Effects of resource availability on social exchange relationships: The case of employee psychological contract obligations. *Journal of Management, 43*(5), 1447–1471. https://doi.org/10.1177/0149206314556317

Briscoe, J. P., & Hall, D. T. (2006). The interplay of boundaryless and protean careers: Combinations and implications. *Journal of Vocational Behavior, 69*(1), 4–18. https://doi.org/10.1016/j.jvb.2005.09.002

Brown, T. A. (2015). *Confirmatory factor analysis for applied research* (2nd ed.). The Guilford Press.

Busse, C., Kach, A. P., & Wagner, S. M. (2017). Boundary conditions: What they are, how to explore them, why we need them, and when to consider them. *Organizational Research Methods, 20*(4), 574–609.

Chand, M. D., Budhwar, P. S., & Katou, A. A. (2017). Investigating idiosyncratic deals in the Indian hospitality industry. In M. D. Chand (Ed.), *Opportunities and Challenges for Tourism and Hospitality in the BRIC Nations* (pp. 221–238). IGI-Global.

Chang, C.-H., Ferris, D. L., Johnson, R. E., Rosen, C. C., & Tan, J. A. (2012). Core self-evaluations: A review and evaluation of the literature. *Journal of Management*, 38(1), 81–128. https://doi.org/10.1177/0149206311419661

CIPD. (2012). *The psychological contract*. Chartered Institute of Personnel and Development.

CIPD. (2016). *Understanding the economy and labour market*. Chartered Institute of Personnel and Development.

Conway, N., & Briner, R. B. (2005). *Understanding psychological contracts at work*. Oxford University Press.

Coyle-Shapiro, J. A.-M., & Conway, N. (2005). Exchange relationships: Examining psychological contracts and perceived organizational support. *Journal of Applied Psychology*, 90(4), 774–781. https://doi.org/10.1037/0021-9010.90.4.774

Coyle-Shapiro, J. A.-M., & Kessler, I. (2000). Consequences of the psychological contract for the employment relationship: A large scale survey. *Journal of Management Studies*, 37(7), 903–930. https://doi.org/10.1111/1467-6486.00210

De Jong, J., Schalk, R., & de Cuyper, N. (2009). Balanced versus unbalanced psychological contracts in temporary and permanent employment: associations with employee attitudes. *Management and Organization Review*, 5(3), 329–351. https://doi.org/10.1111/j.1740-8784.2009.00156.x

Gardner, D. G., Huang, G.-H., Niu, X., Pierce, J. L., & Lee, C. (2015). Organization-based self-esteem, psychological contract fulfillment, and perceived employment opportunities: A test of self-regulatory theory. *Human Resource Management*, 54(6), 933–953. https://doi.org/10.1002/hrm.21648

Gerhart, B., Wright, P. M., Mahan, G. C., & Snell, S. A. (2000). Measurement error in research on human resources and firm performance: How much error is there and how does it influence effect size estimates? *Personnel Psychology*, 53(4), 803–834. https://doi.org/10.1111/j.1744-6570.2000.tb02418.x

Guerrero, S., Bentein, K., & Lapalme, M.-E. (2014). Idiosyncratic deals and high performers' organizational commitment. *Journal of Business and Psychology*, 29(2), 323–334. https://doi.org/10.1007/s10869-013-9316-7

Guest, D. (1997). Human resource management and performance: A review and research agenda. *The International Journal of Human Resource Management*, 8(3), 263–276. https://doi.org/10.1080/095851997341630

Guest, D. E. (2004). The psychology of the employment relationship: An analysis based on the psychological contract. *Applied Psychology*, 53(4), 541–555. https://doi.org/10.1111/j.1464-0597.2004.00187.x

Hair, F., Anderson, R., Tatham, R., & Black, W. (2008). *Multivariate data analysis with readings*. Prentice-Hall.

Ho, V. T., & Kong, D. T. (2015). Exploring the signaling function of idiosyncratic deals and their interaction. *Organizational Behavior and Human Decision Processes*, 131, 149–161. https://doi.org/10.1016/j.obhdp.2015.08.002

Hochwarter, W. (2014). On the merits of student-recruited sampling: Opinions a decade in the making. *Journal of Occupational and Organizational Psychology*, 87(1), 27–33. https://doi.org/10.1111/joop.12043

Hornung, S., Rousseau, D. M., & Glaser, J. (2008). Creating flexible work arrangements through idiosyncratic deals. *Journal of Applied Psychology*, *93*(3), 655–664. https://doi.org/10.1037/0021-9010.93.3.655

Hornung, S., Rousseau, D. M., & Glaser, J. (2009). Why supervisors make idiosyncratic deals: Antecedents and outcomes of I-Deals from a managerial perspective. *Journal of Managerial Psychology*, *24*(8), 738–764. https://doi.org/10.1108/02683940910996770

Hornung, S., Rousseau, D. M., Glaser, J., Angerer, P., & Weigl, M. (2010). Beyond top-down and bottom-up work redesign: Customizing job content through idiosyncratic deals. *Journal of Organizational Behavior*, *31*(2–3), 187–215. https://doi.org/10.1002/job.625

Hornung, S., Rousseau, D. M., Weigl, M., Muller, A., & Glaser, J. (2014). Redesigning work through idiosyncratic deals. *European Journal of Work and Organizational Psychology*, *23*(4), 608–626. https://doi.org/10.1080/1359432X.2012.740171

Judge, T. A., Locke, E. A., & Durham, C. C. (1997). The dispositional causes of job satisfaction: A core evaluations approach. *Research in Organizational Behavior*, *19*, 151–188.

Judge, T. A., Locke, E. A., Durham, C. C., & Kluger, A. N. (1998). Dispositional effects on job and life satisfaction: The role of core evaluations. *Journal of Applied Psychology*, *83*(1), 17–34. https://doi.org/10.1037/0021-9010.83.1.17

Kasekende, F., Munene, J. C., Ntayi, J. M., & Ahiauzu, A. (2015). The interaction effect of social exchanges on the relationship between organizational climate and psychological contract. *Leadership & Organization Development Journal*, *36*(7), 833–848. https://doi.org/10.1108/LODJ-01-2014-0007

Katou, A. A., & Budhwar, P. S. (2012). The link between HR practices, psychological contract fulfilment and organizational performance: The case of the Greek services sector. *Thunderbird International Business Review*, *54*(6), 793–809. https://doi.org/10.1002/tie.21504

King, Z. (2004). *Career management: A CIPD guide*. Chartered Institute of Personnel and Development.

Kousta, E., & Stamati, A. (2012). The impact on labor relations under the threat of unemployment during the recession and the crisis. *Greek Labor Institute*, *36*, 87–155.

Kozlowski, S. W., & Klein, K. J. (2000). A multilevel approach to theory and research in organizations: Contextual, temporal, and emergent processes. In K. J. Klein & S. W. J. Kozlowski (Eds.), *multilevel theory, research, and methods in organizations: Foundations, extensions, and new directions* (pp. 3–90). Jossey-Bass.

Kroon, B., Freese, C., & Schalk, R. (2015). A strategic HRM perspective on I-deals. In P. M. Bal & D. M. Rousseau (Eds.), *Idiosyncratic deals between employees and organizations: Conceptual issues, applications, and the role of coworkers* (pp. 92–106). Psychology Press.

Lai, L., Rousseau, D. M., & Chang, K. T. T. (2009). Idiosyncratic deals: Coworkers as interested third parties. *Journal of Applied Psychology*, *94*(2), 547–556. https://doi.org/10.1037/a0013506

Lambert, L. S., Edwards, J. R., & Cable, D. M. (2003). Breach and fulfilment of the psychological contract: A comparison of traditional and expanded views. *Personnel Psychology*, *56*(4), 895–934. https://doi.org/10.1111/j.1744-6570.2003.tb00244.x

Las Heras, M., Rofcanin, Y., Bal, M. B., & Stollberger, J. (2017a). How do flexibility I-deals relate to work performance? Exploring the roles of family performance and organizational context. *Journal of Organizational Behavior*, *38*(8), 1280–1294. https://doi.org/10.1002/job.2203

Las Heras, M., van der Heijden, B., de Jong, J., & Rofcanin, Y. (2017b). Handle with care: The mediating role of I-Deals in the relationship between supervisors' care-giving responsibilities and employee outcomes. *Human Resource Management Journal*, *27*(3), 335–349. https://doi.org/10.1111/1748-8583.12160

Lee, C., & Hui, C. (2011). Antecedents and consequences of idiosyncratic deals: A frame of resource exchange. *Frontiers of Business Research*, 5, 3, 380–401.

Lee, C., Liu, J., Rousseau, D. M., Hui, C., & Chen, Z. X. (2011). Inducements, contributions, and fulfillment in new employee psychological contracts. *Human Resource Management*, *50*(2), 201–226. https://doi.org/10.1002/hrm.20415

Liao, C., Wayne, S. J., & Rousseau, D. M. (2016). idiosyncratic deals in contemporary organizations: A qualitative and meta-analytical review. *Journal of Organizational Behavior*, *37*, S9–S29. https://doi.org/10.1002/job.1959

Lippman, A., & Mackenzie, S. G. (1985). What is "recall bias" and does it exist? In M. Marois (Ed.), *Prevention of physical and mental congenital defects: Part c. Basic and medical science, education, and future strategies* (pp. 205–209). Alan R. Riss.

Liu, J., Lee, C., Hui, C., Kwan, H. K., & Wu, L.-Z. (2013). Idiosyncratic deals and employee outcomes: The mediating roles of social exchange and self-enhancement and the moderating role of individualism. *Journal of Applied Psychology*, *98*(5), 832–840. https://doi.org/10.1037/a0032571

Marescaux, E., De Winne, S., & Sels, L. (2019). Idiosyncratic deals from a distributive justice perspective: Examining co-workers' voice behavior. *Journal of Business Ethics*, *154*(1), 263–281. https://doi.org/10.1007/s10551-016-3400-7

McDonald, D. J., & Makin, P. J. (2000). The psychological contract, organizational commitment and job satisfaction of temporary staff. *Leadership & Organization Development Journal*, *21*(2), 84–91. https://doi.org/10.1108/01437730010318174

Meijerink, J. (2014). Practicing social innovation: Enactment of the employee-organisation relationship by employees. In T. Bondarouk and M. R. Olivas-Lujian (Eds.), *Human resource management, social innovation and technology* (pp. 135–153). Emerald Group Publishing Limited.

Meyer, J. P., & Allen, N. J. (1991). A three-component conceptualization of organizational commitment. *Human Resource Management Review*, *1*(1), 61–89. https://doi.org/10.1016/1053-4822(91)90011-Z

Muthen, L. K., & Muthen, B. O. (2014). *Mplus computer software*. Muthen & Muthen.

Nelson, L., & Tonks, G. (2007). Violations of the psychological contract: Experiences of a group of causal workers. *Research and Practice in Human Resource Management*, *15*(1), 22–36.

Ng, T. W. H., & Feldman, D. C. (2010). Idiosyncratic deals and organizational commitment. *Journal of Vocational Behavior*, *76*(3), 419–427. https://doi.org/10.1016/j.jvb.2009.10.006

Ng, T. W. H., & Feldman, D. C. (2012). Breaches of past promises, current job alternatives, and promises of future idiosyncratic deals: Three-way interaction effects on organizational commitment. *Human Relations*, *65*(11), 1463–1486. https://doi.org/10.1177/0018726712453472

Ng, T. W. H., & Feldman, D. C. (2015). Idiosyncratic deals and voice behavior. *Journal of Management*, *41*(3), 893–928. https://doi.org/10.1177/0149206312457824

Ng, T. W. H., & Lucianetti, L. (2016). Goal striving, idiosyncratic deals, and job behavior. *Journal of Organizational Behavior*, *37*(1), 41–60. https://doi.org/10.1002/job.2023

Nijssen, M., & Paauwe, J. (2012). HRM in turbulent times: How to achieve organizational agility? *The International Journal of Human Resource Management*, *23*(16), 3315–3335. https://doi.org/10.1080/09585192.2012.689160

Niehoff, B. P., & Moorman, R. H. (1993). Justice as a mediator of the relationship between methods of monitoring and organizational citizen behaviour. *Academy of Management Journal, 36*(3), 527–556. https://doi.org/10.2307/256591

Organ, D. W. (1988). *Organizational citizenship behaviour: The good solider syndrome.* Lexington Books.

Pavlou, P. A., & Gefen, D. (2005). Psychological contract violation in online marketplaces: Antecedents, consequences, and moderating role. *Information Systems Research, 16*(4), 372–399. https://doi.org/10.1287/isre.1050.0065

Prouska, R., & Psychogios, A. G. (2018a). Do not say a word! Conceptualizing employee silence in a long-term crisis context. *The International Journal of Human Resource Management, 29*(5), 885–914. https://doi.org/10.1080/09585192.2016.1212913

Prouska, R., & Psychogios, A. G. (2018b). Should i say something? A framework for understanding silence from a line manager's perspective during an economic crisis. *Economic and Industrial Democracy, 40*(3), 611–635. https://doi.org/10.1177/0143831X17752869

Psychogios, A., Nyfoudi, M., Theodorakopoulos, N., Szamosi, L. T., & Prouska, R. (2019). Many hands lighter work? Deciphering the relationship between adverse working conditions and organization citizenship behaviours in small and medium-sized enterprises during a severe economic crisis. *British Journal of Management, 30*(3), 519–537. https://doi.org/10.1111/1467-8551.12245

Psychogios, A., & Wood, G. (2010). Human resource management in Greece in comparative perspective: Alternative institutionalist perspectives and empirical realities. *The International Journal of Human Resource Management, 21*(14), 2614–2630. https://doi.org/10.1080/09585192.2010.523578

Robinson, S. L., & Rousseau, D. M. (1994). Violating the psychological contract: Not the exception but the norm. *Journal of Organizational Behavior, 15*(3), 245–259. https://doi.org/10.1002/job.4030150306

Rofcanin, Y., Kiefer, T., & Strauss, K. (2017). What seals the I-deal? Exploring the role of employees' behaviours and managers' emotions. *Journal of Occupational and Organizational Psychology, 90*(2), 203–224. https://doi.org/10.1111/joop.12168

Rosen, C. C., Slater, D. J., Chang, C.-H., & Johnson, R. E. (2013). Let's make a deal: Development and validation of the ex post I-deals scale. *Journal of Management, 39*(3), 709–742. https://doi.org/10.1177/0149206310394865

Rousseau, D. M. (1995). *Psychological contracts in organisations: Understanding the written and unwritten agreements.* Sage.

Rousseau, D. M. (2001). The idiosyncratic deal: Flexibility versus fairness? *Organizational Dynamics, 29*(4), 260–273. https://doi.org/10.1016/S0090-2616(01)00032-8

Rousseau, D. M. (2005). *I-Deals: Idiosyncratic deals employees bargain for themselves.* M.E. Sharpe.

Rousseau, D. M., & Greller, M. M. (1994). Human resource practices: Administrative contract makers. *Human Resource Management, 33*(3), 385–401. https://doi.org/10.1002/hrm.3930330308

Rousseau, D. M., Ho, V. T., & Greenberg, J. (2006). I-deals: Idiosyncratic terms in employment relationships. *Academy of Management Review, 31*(4), 977–994. https://doi.org/10.5465/amr.2006.22527470

Rousseau, D. M., Hornun, S., & Kim, T. G. (2009). Idiosyncratic deals: Testing propositions on timing, content, and the employment relationship. *Journal of Vocational Behavior, 74*(3), 338–348. https://doi.org/10.1016/j.jvb.2009.02.004

Schaufeli, W. B. (2015). Engaging leadership in the job demands-resources model. *Career Development International*, *20*(5), 446–463. https://doi.org/10.1108/CDI-02-2015-0025

Schaufeli, W. B., Salanova, M., Gonzalez-Roma, V., & Bakker, A. B. (2002). The measurement of engagement and burnout: A two sample confirmatory factor analytic approach. *Journal of Happiness Studies*, *3*(1), 71–92.

Schlosser, F., & Zolin, R. (2012). Hearing voice and silence during stressful economic times. *Employee Relations*, *34*(5), 555–573. https://doi.org/10.1108/01425451211248569

Somech, A., & Drach-Zahavy, A. (2018). Rethinking organizational citizenship behavior in service organizations: Its nature and conceptualization. In P. M. Podsakoff, S. B. Mackenzie, and N. P. Podsakoff (Eds.), *The Oxford handbook of organizational citizenship behavior* (pp. 527–542). Oxford University Press.

Sturges, J. (2012). Crafting a Balance between work and home. *Human Relations*, *65*(12), 1539–1559. https://doi.org/10.1177/0018726712457435

Sturges, J., Conway, N., Guest, D., & Liefooghe, A. (2005). Managing the career deal: The psychological contract as a framework for understanding career management, organizational commitment and work behavior. *Journal of Organizational Behavior*, *26*(7), 821–838. https://doi.org/10.1002/job.341

Suazo, M. M., Martinez, P. G., & Sandoval, R. (2009). Creating psychological and legal contracts through human resource practices: A signaling theory perspective. *Human Resource Management Review*, *19*(2), 154–166. https://doi.org/10.1016/j.hrmr.2008.11.002

Teague, P., & Roche, W. K. (2014). Recessionary bundles: HR practices in the Irish economic crisis. *Human Resource Management Journal*, *24*(2), 176–192. https://doi.org/10.1111/1748-8583.12019

Wood, G., Cooke, F. L., Demirbag, M., & Kwong, C. (2018). International Journal of Human Resource Management (IJHRM) special issue on: International human resource management in contexts of high uncertainties. *The International Journal of Human Resource Management*, *29*(7), 1365–1373. https://doi.org/10.1080/09585192.2018.1477547

Wood, G., Szamosi, L. T., Psychogios, A., Sarvanidis, S., & Fotopoulou, D. (2016). Rethinking Greek capitalism through the lens of industrial relations reform: A view until the 2015 referendum. *Relations Industrielles*, *70*(4), 698–717. https://doi.org/10.7202/1034900ar

Vidyarthi, P. R., Chaudhry, A., Anand, S., & Liden, R. C. (2014). Flexibility I-Deals: How much is ideal? *Journal of Managerial Psychology*, *29*(3), 246–265. https://doi.org/10.1108/JMP-07-2012-0225

Afterword
Researching IHRM in an uncertain world: methodological challenges and solutions

Geoffrey Wood, Mehmet Demirbag, Caleb Kwong and Fang Lee Cooke

The early 2020s has been marked by high levels of uncertainties in the international business contexts characterised by the persisting momentum of the global pandemic and growing regional tensions in many parts of the world. These events have led to volatile situations, such as the breaking down of the global supply chains, large numbers of refugees, and intensified political and economic pressure on MNCs operating in and from conflict zones (political, economic, social and military). These dynamics at the global, regional, national and firm levels create new opportunities for research but at the same time present formidable challenges for data collection. It calls for new ways to capture HRM issues stemming from severe uncertainties and adversities to make sense of how uncertainties are perceived by the workforce from different backgrounds, how organisations respond to these uncertainties and adversities, and how these responses translate into HRM practices that may be firm-, sectoral- or national-specific. In this afterword, we provide three methods-related suggestions that may be helpful for future research of HRM to understand the paradox and complexity in high uncertainty contexts.

1. From phenomenon to theorisation: What is happening

A growing number of scholars have called for phenomenon-based research to make business and management research more relevant to the real world. In the high uncertainty context, this would require researchers to first identify scenarios in uncertainty and crisis, in other words, particularly interesting, if challenging, research contexts. Since what is happening/has happened may be alien to the researcher and people's perceptions of what happened are underpinned by their personal conditions, language used, societal values and so on, a qualitative approach would be helpful for the researcher to develop an understanding of the issue at hand from the perspective of those experiencing it. This should not be confined to the traditional qualitative methods of interviews, ethnographic studies, focus groups, and on-site observations might be difficult. In high uncertainty situation, there may be multiple sources of secondary data including government official statements, news coverage, media reports, social chatrooms, etc. This body of data may be large, unverified and, for some, unreliable. While the ability to process and select usable data is not per se a new skill required for HRM research, it does, however, present new challenges in high-uncertainty situations. The world presently faces a number of great challenges which transcend the weight of existing human experience, and, indeed, in some instances, past ones, obvious examples being runaway global heating and world pandemics (Phan and Wood, 2020). Not all theories will fit the new realities, and, as with the many crises of the early twentieth century, this opens up new many opportunities for novelty in theory building; such theory may have relevance to particular times and places, but may also provide the basis for the emergence of new theoretical traditions.

2. From traditional methods to new methods: How

Qualitative research presumes that meaning is subjectively endowed and constructed in the process of human interactions with the world. However, in high uncertainty and adversity situations, interactions between the researcher and the research targets may be rendered difficult or impossible. While software such as Zoom and Microsoft Teams may be able to provide some degrees of connectivity and interactions, this is highly contingent upon the availability of such technologies for both parties. Further, the collection of data in high-uncertainty and adversity environments may be time-bound/sensitive and linguistically challenging to non-native speakers. Collaborating with local researchers would be a productive way to overcome these constraints.

It is worth reflecting that within many rapidly growing emerging economies, there is a high degree of respect for intellectuals, in contrast to, say the United States and the United Kingdom, where they are frequently in the subject of vilification by right-wing populist politicians and their allies in the media. This affords scholars in the former a real advantage, and, of course, being open to new ideas and the findings of rigorous research may help explain why such economies are doing so well in the first place. This is a real opportunity for researchers and will greatly facilitate the geographical expansion of the knowledge base. This is especially so as there is an increasing consensus among referees in leading journals that at least 30 in-depth interviews are necessary for a study based on such methods. This consensus is something of a pity, as, whilst research depth is an important criterion, the rigour of the interviews, their length, and whether and how many follow-up interviews are conducted are also important.

In terms of quantitative methods, for the reasons alluded to above, it is also often much easier to secure high survey response rates for work in many emerging markets, affording advantages to researchers conducting work in such settings. However, this advantage is diminished, by again, a growing body of opinion that cross-sectional data is unacceptable owing to the possibility of common method variance bias. Again, this is an area where we would make the case for pragmatism. On the one hand, tests for common method variance bias such as Harman do have limitations (e.g., it is unlikely that a sole factor would emerge in any dataset, even if flawed). On the other hand, governments and commercial organisations often rely on single survey evidence to make important decisions, without always being led in the wrong directions. Moreover, there are many other methodological issues, including sampling procedures and representivity, which are at least as important, if not more so, but are often simply ignored by scholars. We would argue that the overall data and methods should stand the weight of scrutiny for rigour, rather than focusing on a single proxy. What constitutes robust survey evidence is not the only area where an over-focus on one issue may result in the neglect of a more holistic view of methodological rigour; for example, the over-fetishisation of p-values is a well-known phenomenon (see Concato and Hartigan, 2016).

3. From one study to more studies: Building blocks of the knowledge base

Increasingly, the analysis of text-rich qualitative sources of data needs to draw on not only intellectual skills but also methodological techniques including machine learning and other digital means for text mining and analysis. This requires the researcher to develop new skills such as data analytics. What is beneficial about these digital methods of data collection and analysis is that large de-sensitised data sets could be developed simultaneously in different parts of the world and to create knowledge base. Findings and insights generated from these qualitative data might be used to develop new theories and new research instruments, thus forming a virtuous circle.

The temporal and spatial dimensions of the phenomenon under investigation may offer insightful lenses through which theorisation can be carried out based on qualitative studies (e.g. Cooke, Wang and Wang, 2016). For example, during the highly contagious period of COVID-19, leading companies in developing countries like Indonesia have provided company transport to assist employees commuting to and from work to reduce their chance of being infected while taking public transport. Some companies have also provided temporary accommodations, food, doctors and nurses to Covid-positive employees as they were not able to access hospitals and other resources that should be provided through public institutions. Such provisions to some extent reflect a collectivist and paternalistic cultural tradition in which employers are expected to look after their employees like a parent and provide care and support when needed in return for the employees' hard work, obedience and loyalty. Similarly, polymerase chain reaction (PCR) tests were often carried out at the organisation. Employees and organisations have provided drinks, food, clothes and other daily supplies to support the medical staff who worked extremely long hours to complete the tests for a large number of people in a tight race against time. By contrast, organisations in western societies such as Australia have been focusing more on employees' psychological wellbeing. Offering employees counselling and other wellness interventions are typical HRM services to support employees through trying times, leaving material support to public institutions or commercial provisions sourced by the individuals. These diverse HRM practices reflect the legal and cultural traditions and institutional arrangements of the nations, as well as the risk management approach of the organisation (Cooke, Dickmann and Parry, 2022). It also brought to the fore that firms in developing countries may have a different understanding and felt obligation in assisting their employees and local communities during crises than their western counterparts. As such, the former may introduce organisational practices that redraw the notion of organisational time and space, pointing to new avenues of theorisation.

In short, developing a grounded understanding of how firms manage during times of high uncertainty and adversity necessitates a new methodological and epistemological approach. In particular, inductive theorisation based on qualitative data may easily lend itself to theory building than the hypothesised deductive logic based on quantitative data (even if the latter may facilitate theory testing and extension), and can help expand the epistemological framework of HRM research. Such an approach is valuable in generating new insights from high-uncertainty contexts which remain insufficiently understood and theorised. Thus, we encourage researchers to embrace an open, bottom-up and pluralistic approach to investigating how nations and firms perceive risks and uncertainties; how they measure them; how they prevent and manage them; what organisations expect from the employees; and what employees expect from their employers. Calling for theory building is one thing, building good theory is another. Here, we note that a fertile avenue would be the identification of potentially salient theories in other fields that might lend themselves to transposition and adaption, and, indeed, the possibilities for developing new theories based on indigenous knowledge.

References

Concato, J. and Hartigan, J.A. (2016). P values: from suggestion to superstition. *Journal of Investigative Medicine*, 64(7), 1166–1171.

Cooke, F. L., Dickmann, M. and Parry, E. (2022). Building sustainable societies through human-centred human resource management: emerging issues and research opportunities. *International Journal of Human Resource Management*, 33(1), 1–15.

Cooke, F. L., Wang, D. and Wang, J. (2018). State capitalism in construction: staffing practices and labor relations in Chinese construction firms in Africa. *Journal of Industrial Relations*, 60(1), 77–100.

Phan, P. H. and Wood, G. (2020). Doomsday scenarios (or the black swan excuse for unprepardeness). *Academy of Management Perspectives*, 34(4), 425–433.

Index

Note: Page numbers in **bold** refer to tables and those in *italics* refer to figures.

Academy of Management (AOM) 103–4
accelerated decision-making team 167–8
Adams, K. 15
adapting compensation packages 165–6
'adversity advantages' 35
Aezami Nejad, M. 158
Agar, M. H. 104
Aggarwal, R. 147
Ahammad, M. 9
Ahmadi, S. B. 159
Akhtar, P. 9
Akhtar, S. 11
Allen, N. J. 190
Ali, A. J. 158
Amable, B. 95
Anderson, N. R. 132
Andresen, M. 38
Anglo-Saxon countries 144
A-players 171
Asian Development Bank (ADB) 69
associational societal trust 129–30
associational trust 132, **140**
attitudinal employee outcomes 193
Audretsch, D. B. 95
average variances extracted (AVE) 193
Azerbaijan and Kyrgyzstan 93–4

Bacouel-Jentjens, S. 61, 84
Bae, J. 61, 84
Bakkevig Dagsland, Å. H. 98
Balali, M. 159
Bardoel, E. A. 9
Bartram, T. 10
behavioral employee outcomes 193
Bergdolt, F. 38
Biazzo, S. 63
Bititci, U. S. 63
Björkman, I. 49
Blum, T. C. 11
bolster/undermine wider societal trust 129
boundary conditions function 183
Bourne, M. 63
Boxall, P. 92

BP Statistical Review of World Energy
    (2018) 154–5
Branicki, L. 7, 10
Brewster, C. 13, 19
Brookes, M. 13
Bryant, S. 63
Buck, T. 83
Budhwar, P. S. 19
business strategy 139–41, **140**
Business Systems theory 12
Buyruk, L. 106

Calamai, R. 13
Cantwell, J. 114
capabilities 154
career i-deals 182
case selections 160–1
case study design 102–3
Central and Eastern Europe (CEE) 92
centrality of context sensitivity 61
Chahine, S. 19
Chan, A. 11
Chiva, R. 129
Chung, Y. 75
clerical and manual employees 139
CME vocational training system 109
co-deterministic employment relationship
    adjustment mechanisms 135, 142–4, **143**
Cogin, J. A. 15, 16
'commitment-paternalist HRM system' 83
communication 133
competitive labor markets 186
confirmatory factor analysis (CFA) 193
context-specific understanding of
    uncertainty 35–7
convenience sampling 160
Cooke, F. L.10
Cooper, B. 10
coordinated market economies (CMEs) 91
core self-evaluations (CSE) 186
Costa, A. C. 132
cost reduction strategy 157
Coutu, D. L. 8

The Cranet questionnaire 135
crisis-fostering environments 32
culture, institutions and HR practices 10–14
Cunha, R. 13

data analysis 43, 106–7, 162–3
Data Availability Statement *170*
data collection 41–3, 103–4, 161–2
Davies, S. E. 7
Debrah, Y. A. 15
De Cieri, H. 9
deep recession 187
degree of decision-making centralisation 36
Demina, N. 83
descriptive statistics **138**
Dibben, P. 13
Djankov, S. 135, 142, 144
Dodgson, M. 133
domicile practice, propositions 100–1
Dore, R. 95
Dorrenbacher, C. 100
Dunning, J. H. 114
Dweck, C. S. 33, 37
dynamic capability perspective 159–60
dynamic capability scholars 154

Edwards, P. 63
Eftekhar, N. 19, 158
Einarsen, S. 98
Ellis, F. Y. 15
Elyasi, G. M. 19
emerging markets (EMNCs) 35
emotional stability 186
employee dissatisfaction 157
employee organizational commitment 184
employee outcomes relationship *192*
employee resourcing 107–9
employees' bargaining power 154
employees' compensation packages 172
employer and employee psychological contract
    fulfillment 184
environmental uncertainties/state
    uncertainty 2
Essens, P. 7
estimated OLS regressions test 139
Eurozone central directives 185

Farhangi, A. 159
Feiz, D. 158
field observations 70
Fields, D. 11
Filatotchev, I. 83
financial crises 187
financial i-deals 182
financial information 134
Finnegan, R. 107
firm characteristics **72**
First Kyrgyz Revolution 69
flexibility i-deals 182

flexible cost management, HR
    operations 164–5
flexible training and development
    processes 164–5
Floyd, S. W. 102
Fong, C. P. 13
food processing 181
formalised communication systems 133
frequent and transparent communication with
    employees 166
Froese, F. J. 7
Fulmer, C. A. 132
function, HRM 91–2
further robustness checks 144

Garengo, P. 63
George, G. 7
Geppert, M. 100
Gholipor, A. 158
Goergen, M. 19
goldbricking 135
Golshahi, B. 158
Goodell, J. W. 147
government policy uncertainties 2
The Greek context 185
Greller, M. M. 199
Gronow, A. 44
Guest, D. E. 189
Guinot, J. 129

Harden, E. E. 75
"headcount resource" approach 76
heterogeneity of cases 160
high institutional uncertainty 73–4
Hofstede, G. 11, 94
home commodities production 181
Horak, S. 61, 84
hotel industry context 98
HR departments 172
Hudson, M. 63
Hui, C. 201
human resource (HR) departments 154
Hutchings, K. 79
Hyun, S. S. 158

i-deals: career, organizational commitment
    and psychological contract 189–90;
    content 192; employers and employees 184;
    ex-ante 187; ex-post 187; negotiation 181;
    timing 192; timing of negotiation and
    career 186–8
Ilhan, I. 106
impersonal management and tight job
    control 74–5
informal institutions 66
institutional theories 129
institutions and firm practice 96–7
internal organisational practice 94–6
internal recruitment 109

international human resource management (IHRM) research 33, 49–52, 92
interviewed MNCs **161**
interviewees 161, **161**, 162
intra-company IBM employee surveys 95
investment in workers 76–7, 79–81
Islamic Republic of Iran (IRI) 154–6

Jalalkamali, M. 158
Javadin, S. R. S. 159
Jaw, B.-S. 160
Joint Comprehensive Plan of Action (JCPOA) 155
Julio, B. 157

Katou, A. A. 19
Keefer, P. 131–2
Khan, Z. 9, 157
Knack, S. 128, 131–2
knowledge, skills and abilities (KSAs) 186–7
Krippendorff, K. 106
Kumaraswamy, A. 52
Kusluvan, S. 106
Kusluvan, Z. 106
Kyrgyzstan's uncertain environment 68–9

Laaser, K. 18
La Porta, R. 135, 136, 142, 144
Latifi, F. 158
Lawrence, P. R. 4
Lazonick, W. 16
Lee, C. 201
Lepak, D. P. 75
less competitive labor markets 182
'liabilities of emergingness' 35
Liao, H. 75
liberal market economies (LMEs) 96
Liesch, P. W. 52
local responsiveness 171
location i-deals 182
locus of control 186
long-term-oriented team 167–8
Lopez-de-Silanes, F. 135, 136, 142, 144
Lorsch, J. W. 4
Lundan, S. M. 114

macroeconomic uncertainties 2
Magnani, G. 33
Makhmadshoev, D. 18
Malik, A. 132
managerial implications 200
Manalsuren, S. 17
Marlow, S. 63
MAXQDA12 software 162–3
McCarthy, D. 157
McGaughey, S. L. 52
McMillan, L. 9
The measurement model 193–5
Mei, H. 10
Metwally, E. K. 13

Meyer, J. P. 190
Michailova, S. 83
Michalski, M. 17
Middle East and North Africa (MENA) 154–5
middle managers 70
Miller, D. 2
Minbaeva, D. B. 79, 83, 114
'mindset' concept: behavioural rationales and predispositions 37; defined 37; growth 37; people management practices 38; sociocultural, economic and political circumstances 37
Ministry of Economy and national business associations 70
MNC managers 157
Mongolia: banking sector and anti-money laundering reforms 34; biased conclusions and generalisations 34; elements of 43–5; highly uncertain institutional environment 34; influence of 45–8
The Mongolian business environment 39
Morgan, G. 100
Morley, M. J. 83
Morris, S. S. 13
Mplus 193
multilevel model (MLM) 193
multilevel structural equation modeling (MSEM) 193
multinational companies (MNCs) 133, 153, 154
multinational enterprises (MNEs) 14–17, 33, 91
Muratbekova-Touron, M. 114
Murphy, M. C. 33
Mykletun, R. J. 98

natural uncertainties 2
Nguyen, T. 63
Nikbin, D. 158
norm of reciprocity 184
North, D. C. 66
NVivo software 43
Nyuur, R. B. 15

office property landlords 3
organisational culture 7
organisations briefing employees: business strategy 139–41; financial performance **141**, 141–2
organizational citizenship behavior (OCB) 181
organizational commitment 190–1
orthodox rational choice approach 147
over-fetishisation of *p*-values 210

Pagano, M. 131
'parental' style of leadership 47
participants' profile **42**
Patel, C. 19
paternalism 83
paternalistic socialism 67

path-breaking market reforms 67–8
path-dependency 66–7
Patton, D. 63
performance management systems (PMS) 63,
    99, 111–12; egalitarian pay and collective
    bonuses 78–9; and incentive system 75–6
Perlmutter, H. V. 99, 115
personalized management and
    paternalism 77–8
Pettit, T. M. 9
political uncertainties 2
polymerase chain reaction (PCR) tests 210–11
'predatory value extraction' 16
Prouska, R. 83
Psychogios, A. 83
psychological contracts (PCs) 181, 183,
    184, 193
published reports 70
Puffer, S. 157

Ram, M. 63
Rao-Nicholson, R. 9
Redding, G. 11
relational contracts 189
research design 160
research participants, demographics 104–6
research questions 64
resilience 8–9, 158
resource-based view (RBV) 159
retaining 'star' 171
reward 110–11
rights based societal trust 129
'rights-based trust' 128–9
Rodgers, P. 157
Rousseau, D. M. 181, 199
Rowley, C. 61, 84

sample distribution **137**
sampling 40–1
Second Kyrgyz Revolution (2010) 69
Segal, S. 155
'selective deposit' biasing elements 107
'selective survival' biasing elements 107
self-efficacy 186
self-esteem 186
self-worth 184
semi-structured in-depth qualitative
    interviews 70
Serafini, G. O. 18
Shantz, A. 132
Shen, J. 61, 83, 84
Shenkar, O. 95
Shin, J. S. 16
Shleifer, A. 135, 136, 142, 144
shop-floor workers 70
Śliwa, M. 17
small and medium-sized enterprises
    (SMEs) 18, 185; challenges 62–3;
    garment industry of Kyrgyzstan 60; HRM
    systems 64–6; informal institutions and

path-dependency 66–8; jobs and economic
    growth 60; research method 69–71; research
    questions 64
Smart, A. 63
social exchange theory (SET) 184
social uncertainties 2
societal trust-based antecedents 129
socio-cultural and institutional contexts 33
Soltani, E. 159
staff development and training 46
Steyer, V. 7
Stoermer, S. 7
Stokes, P. 157
The structural model 195–6
subsidiaries' HR departments 168
Sullivan-Taylor, B. 7
Szamosi, L. T. 18, 99

talented employees 158
talent retention 166–7, 171
Tantoush, T. 13
Tarba, S. 9, 157
Tasavori, M. 19
task i-deals 181–2
Tayeb, M. 158
team-based team 167–8
Teece, D. J. 159
thematic analysis 162
Thompson, P. 65
Thomson, S. B. 79
Trading Economics (2019) 154–5
traditional structuralist sociology 12
transactional contracts 189
transcribed interviews 71
transitional peripheral economies (TPEs) 91
transition economies **68**
trust and HRM practice 132–5
trust levels 136
trust relations 129–30
Tsai, C. H.-C. 160
Tulip Revolution 69

unbalanced panel regressions 136
uncertainties on employees 163–4
uncertainties/shocks 4
undertaking business, uncertain
    environments 156–8

valuable, rare, inimitable, and non-
    substitutable (VRIN) resources 159
van der Vegt, G. S. 7
variety of capitalism (VoC) 92, 96
Vishny, R. W. 135, 136, 142, 144
Volpin, P. 131
Vorley, T. 9

Wahlström, M. 7
Wang, C. Y. -P. 160
Wang, J. 10, 132
Warner, M. 61, 84

Webster, E. 13
western high-performance work
    systems 10
The White House 155
Whitley, R. 45, 106
Wilkinson, A. 63, 159
Williamson, I. O. 15, 16
Wong, G. Y. Y. 11
Wood, G. 13, 19, 99
Wooldridge, B. 102
work engagement 181
worker's ability 134–5
workplace trust 132

World Values Survey (WVS) waves 135, 136
Wright, M. 83
Wyer, R. S. Jr. 13

Yook, Y. 157

Zaefarian, R. 19
Zak, P. J. 128
Zhang, M. 61, 83, 84, 94
Zhu, C. J. 61, 83, 84
Zoogah, D. B. 13
Zoom and Microsoft Teams 209
Zucchella, A. 33